In God We Trust

TOUR GUIDE

In God We Trust

TOUR GUIDE

FEATURING

America's Landmarks of Liberty

★

STEPHEN McDOWELL
MARK BELI·LES

Providence
Foundation
Charlottesville, Virginia

In God We Trust: Tour Guide
© 1998, Stephen McDowell
Second edition, first printing, 1998

Cover design: Jeremiah Pent

ISBN 1-887456-07-4

Printed in the United States of America

Table of Contents

For our children

Philip, Andrew, John, and Caroline

and
Benjamin, Emily, and Grace

Preface

🔔 Symbol indicating item to view

When you see this bell symbol in the book, it indicates an historic site, monument, building, memorial, statue, painting, room, plaque, or something to see. However, not all items to view are indicated by a bell, though they will be under a heading that does have a bell. For example, in the U.S. Capitol Building the Rotunda is indicated by a bell but the paintings listed under the section on the Rotunda are not. Various statues in the Capitol are also mentioned but not indicated by a bell. In these cases the text will clearly indicate that these are items to view.

Introduction

In the 1960's a young Christian from Indonesia was planning a trip to the United States of America. He had never been to America and knew little about this country, but he had seen some American money and was particularly excited about the phrase, "In God We Trust." He thought that this must be a great Christian nation because America even acknowledged her reliance upon God on millions and millions of pieces of her currency and coin. As a persecuted Christian in a non-christian nation, he was looking forward to visiting a nation that honored the God that had changed his life.

Americans are quite familiar with the phrase, "In God We Trust," inscribed on our money. Few Americans probably realize, however, that this is our official national motto and is by law placed on all our money. This phrase is also found in the fourth verse of our national anthem, "The Star-Spangled Banner." [See Appendix]

As we tour many historic sites in America, we will see these words and many other indications that America was a nation birthed by men who had a firm reliance upon Almighty God and His Son Jesus Christ. Inscribed upon our buildings, monuments, and national symbols is our nation's faith in God. Contained therein is the declaration that the source of our birth, liberty, and greatness is God.

When the Indonesian Christian arrived in the United States he was shocked at much ungodliness he witnessed in many places. He saw a nation that in some ways still externally declared a trust in God, yet internally had lost much of her faith.

As we take a Christian tour of various historic sites we will see an external expression of the faith of the American people of the past. This heart for God still exists among millions of Americans, but due to the ineffectiveness of the Church in recent generations to disciple the nation, leaders have risen to power in government, education, and the media who no longer hold to the faith of our fathers. Consequently, God is usually ignored in our schools, in our government, in the media, and in official tours of our nation's historic sites. However, through this tour we will see that the United States of America was birthed by God and that without Christianity there would be no America as we know it.

Washington, D.C. The United States Capital

The Library of Congress

The Library of Congress is the world's largest library with a collection of over 100 million items. This number is increasing at a rate of 10 items a minute or over 5 million per year. The services of the Library of Congress are utilized by government agencies and scholars and researchers from throughout the United States and world.

This mammoth library began with $5000 worth of books around 1800 during the presidency of John Adams as a resource library for Congress. It was housed in the Capitol Building until 1814, when British troops invaded and burnt the Capitol, destroying the small library.

Thomas Jefferson offered his personal library as a replacement and so in 1815 Congress appropriated $23,950 to buy his library of 6487 books. This was the foundation of what is now the world's largest library.

There are three buildings on Capitol Hill in the Library of Congress complex. The Thomas Jefferson Building is the oldest, completed in 1897. It is elaborately decorated with sculpture, murals, mosaics, and stained glass portraying themes relating to learning and knowledge. We will mention some of these later. Just east of the Jefferson Building is the John Adams Building which was opened in 1939. South of the Jefferson Building across Independence Avenue is the James Madison Memorial Building. When it was opened in 1980 it doubled the space of the Library of Congress on Capitol Hill.

Collections of the Library of Congress include:

- Over 100 million items of every subject and format from papyrus to microform
- 532 miles of shelves
- 20 million books and pamphlets in about 60 languages
- More than 35 million manuscripts
- Approximately 4 million maps and atlases dating back to the mid-1300's
- A 6 million-piece music collection including many rare instruments
- 10 million prints and photographs
- 1200 newspapers on permanent collections; some newspapers dating back to the 1600's

The Library of Congress offers a wide range of services. It is the research and reference arm of the United States Congress with 850 people on the Congressional Research Service staff. Yet it is not for Congress only, as scholars and any interested individual can use the facilities to study. Copyright protection is provided through the Copyright Office in the Library. In addition, the Library provides cultural programs, offers services to other libraries, and has books on braille and tapes.

Revealing our Faith in God

The Library of Congress contains a voluminous amount of Christian books, magazines, music, and art. The Rare Book and Special Collections Division has a Bible Collection with 1470 bibles dating from the beginning of printing. The division holds thousands of printed sermons and tens of thousands of broadsides that give information about denominational activities. The Continental Congress Broadsides collection has numerous documents revealing the government's numerous Christian actions.

🔔 Gutenberg Bible and Giant Bible of Mainz

In the corridor from the Great Hall to the Main Reading Room of the Thomas Jefferson Building two rare Bibles are kept on permanent display in two climate controlled cases. The Gutenberg Bible is one of only three surviving examples printed on vellum. It dates from the mid fifteenth century. Across from this Bible is the Giant Bible of Mainz, a hand-copied manuscript of the same time period as the Gutenberg.

It is only fitting for these Bibles to be displayed in this public building because the Bible is the foundation of the United States of America. The religious, social, educational, and political life of America was primarily shaped by the Bible. As President Andrew Jackson said on June 8, 1845 in reference to the Bible: "That book, Sir, is the Rock upon which our republic rests."[1]

Our states were colonized by people who desired to freely worship the God of the Bible, our schools were begun so that everyone would be able to read and understand the Bible for themselves, our universities were founded to train ministers who were knowledgeable of the Scriptures, our laws and constitutions were written based on Biblical ideas, and our founding fathers overwhelmingly had a Biblical worldview. Thomas Jefferson reflected the view of early Americans when he stated: "The Bible is the cornerstone of liberty. A student's perusal of the sacred volume will make him a better citizen, a better father, a better husband."[2]

Many today recognize our Biblical foundations. Newsweek Magazine stated in its December 26, 1982 issue that, "the Bible even more than the Constitution is our founding document." America's growth, greatness, and prosperity is a result of our being founded on

Christian principles by men and women who relied upon the God of the Bible. In recent generations America has been shifting from Biblical foundations to operate more on humanistic ideas where there is no God other than man. As a result we have experienced a loss of liberty and prosperity.

Noah Webster stated:

The moral principles and precepts contained in the Scriptures ought to form the basis of all our civil constitutions and laws. All the miseries and evils which men suffer from vice, crime, ambition, injustice, oppression, slavery, and war, proceed from their despising or neglecting the precepts contained in the Bible.[3]

On the walls and ceiling of the Library of Congress are many Biblical inscriptions. These include:

The light shineth in darkness, and the darkness comprehendeth it not. (John 1:5)

Wisdom is the principal thing therefore get wisdom and withall thy getting, get understanding. (Proverbs 4:7)

♫ The Main Reading Room

The Main Reading Room of the Library of Congress can be viewed from the Visitor's Gallery. Within this room, whose height from floor to dome is 160 feet, are statues of famous historical figures, each representing a field of knowledge. Religion is represented by two statues, that of Moses and the Apostle Paul. Science is represented by a statue of the Christian, Isaac Newton.

Above the pillar representing **Religion**, the following scripture is written:

What doth the Lord require of thee, but to do justly, and to love mercy and to walk humbly with thy God. (Micah 6:8)

Science bears the verse:

The heavens declare the glory of God; and the firmament showeth His handywork. (Psalm 19:1)

History is represented by the inscription:

One God, one law, one element, and one far-off divine event, to which the whole creation moves. (Alfred, Lord Tennyson)

☖ *The Supreme Court Building*

The present Supreme Court Building was opened in 1935. From 1800 to 1935 the Supreme Court met in seven different locations, spending most of their time in the Capitol Building. In its early years the Court was not as prominent or as busy as it is today; but as our National Government has ballooned in growth and much of our legal system has embraced the idea of Judicial Supremacy (as opposed to Constitutional Supremacy), the Supreme Court has extended both its volume of work and the extent of its rulings.

Thomas Jefferson expressed his concern for a Supreme Court that legislates through its decisions and is unbounded in its actions. He stated:

It has long, however, been my opinion. . . that the germ of dissolution of our Federal Government is in the Constitution of the Federal Judiciary. . . working like gravity by night and by day, gaining a little today and little tomorrow, and advancing its noiseless step like a thief, over the field of jurisdiction, until all shall be usurped from the States, and the government of all be consolidated into one. To this I am opposed, because when all government shall be drawn to Washington as the centre of all power, it will render powerless the checks provided. . . and will become as venal and oppressive as the government (of George III) from which we separated.[4]

The east pediment on the outside of the Supreme Court Building contains a marble relief entitled ''Justice, the Guardian of Liberty.''

The central figure in this pediment is Moses holding a tablet in each hand containing the Laws of God.

The foyer of the Supreme Court Building contains marble busts of previous Chief Justices. Many of these men were Christians, not only in their hearts but also in their approach to their public office. As an example, our first Chief Justice (from 1789-1795), John Jay, once stated: "Providence has given to our people the choice of their rulers, and it is the duty, as well as the privilege and interest, of our Christian nation to select and prefer Christians for their rulers."[5]

John Marshall, Chief Justice from 1801-1835, wrote: "The American population is entirely Christian, & with us, Christianity & Religion are identified. It would be strange, indeed, if with such a people, our institutions did not presuppose Christianity, & did not often refer to it, & exhibit relations with it."[6]

Judges today are primarily lawyers who have been trained at secular law schools. In contrast, lawyers for the first 200 years of American history never went to a law school, only to a seminary where they studied Theology before reading for the bar.

To enter the Court Chamber from the foyer one passes through two large oak doors. Engraved upon the lower half of each door are the Roman numerals I through X, representing the Ten Commandments of God.

At the beginning of each day that the Court is in session a crier raises his voice to announce the formal opening by calling:

> *Oyez, Oyez, Oyez! All persons having business before the Honorable, the Supreme Court of the United States, are admonished to draw near and give their attention, for the court is now sitting. God save the United States and this Honorable court.*

In the courtroom above the heads of the Supreme Court Justices is a carved marble relief, whereupon, the two central figures represent *The Power of Government* and *The Majesty of the Law*. A large stone tablet containing Roman numerals I through X, representing the Ten Commandments, is prominently placed between these two allegorical figures, with *The Power of Government* resting his arm upon the tablet. This serves as a reminder that the foundation of our law in America is the Bible.

Above the main entrance to the Supreme Court Building these words are engraved: *Equal Justice Under Law*. This is a Biblical idea. It was first seen in the system of government given by God through Moses to the children of Israel. Since the time of Christ, the more a nation has applied Biblical principles in its affairs the more its citizens have experienced *equal justice under law*.

△ *Union Station*

In years past a majority of persons visiting Washington would arrive by train at the Union Station. This building was considered the gateway to the nation's capital. In front of the Station, in the Columbus Fountain, is a 15-foot tall statue of the discoverer of the new world, Christopher Columbus. His name meant the "Christ-bearer," and as we will see in the Capitol, Columbus felt he was doing just that as he set out on his historic journey.

Six 18-foot tall granite statues are located on the front facade of Union Station. Beneath each statue is a theme inscription. The statue of "Fire and Electricity" has the words from Psalm 8 below it:

Thou hast put all things under his feet.

Under the statue "Freedom and Imagination" are Jesus' words from John 8:32:

The truth shall make you free. (John 8:32)

Beneath "Agriculture and Mechanics" is:

The desert shall rejoice and blossom like the rose. (Isaiah 35:1)

ᗗ *The Capitol Building*

The Capitol is a symbol of our nation's life and growth. Here laws are enacted, Presidents are inaugurated, and Congressmen work. President Washington laid the cornerstone of this building in September, 1793 and its first section was occupied in 1800. It has been enlarged a number of times since then. In 1851 new Senate and House wings were begun. Daniel Webster, then Secretary of State, gave an address and deposited it in the cornerstone. He concluded with these words:

If, therefore, it shall hereafter be the will of God that this structure should fall from the base, that its foundations be upturned, and this deposit brought to the eyes of men, be it then known, that, on this day the Union of the United States of America stands firm, that their constitution still exists unimpaired, and with all of its original usefulness and glory; growing every day stronger and stronger in the affection of the great body of the American people, and attracting more and more the admiration of the world. And all here assembled, whether belonging to public life or, to private life, with hearts devotedly thankful to Almighty God for the preservation of the liberty and happiness of the country, unite in sincere and fervent prayers that this deposit, and the walls and arches, the domes and towers, the columns and the entablatures, now to be erected over it, may endure forever.

God save The United States of America – Daniel Webster, Secretary of State of United States.

From the beginning of our nation we have prayed and relied upon God. Columbus lead his men in prayer; John Smith and the Jamestown settlers erected a cross and gave thanks to God when they first came ashore; the Pilgrims immersed their action in prayer; all the colonies participated in public and private prayer.

Every session of the House of Representatives and the Senate begins with prayer. The first Continental Congress met in September 1774. One of the first acts of the first session of this Congress was to appoint Rev. Duché to open Congress the next day in prayer. In 1789 the first Congress under the Constitution took office. One of their first acts was to appoint Chaplains of the House and Senate. When Congress moved to the newly erected Capitol Building in 1800, chaplains were there opening the sessions in prayer. This has continued through today.

The first colony-wide day of prayer and fasting occurred on July 20, 1775. Congress officially summoned all the people "to confess ... our many sins; and offer ... supplications to the all-wise, omnipotent, and merciful Disposer of all events..."[8] Twice that day Congress attended church where they prayed and heard sermons. It is estimated that about 2 million of the nearly 3 million people in the 13 colonies observed that day of fasting and prayer.

Structure

As you face the East Front of the Capitol, the House of Representatives is on the left wing and the Senate is on the right. An American flag flies over the wings of the Senate and House when they are in session. If either chamber is meeting at night, a lantern in the Capitol dome is lighted.

The Capitol divides Washington, D.C. into 4 quadrants (Northwest, Northeast, Southwest, Southeast). Atop the dome of the Capitol is the 19 1/2 foot tall Statue of Freedom. This 7 1/2 ton symbol of freedom was erected in 1863. Following are some dimensions of the Capitol:

- Capitol Height — 287 feet 5 1/2 inches from the East Front base to the top of the Statue of Freedom
- Capitol Width — 350 feet
- Capitol Length — greater than 751 feet
- Floor area — 16 1/2 acres
- Number of rooms in the Capitol — 540

Inaugurals

On January 20 every fourth year a presidential inauguration takes place. From the time of Andrew Jackson until Ronald Reagan the East Front steps of the Capitol had been the traditional scene of these ceremonies. In 1980 President Reagan was inaugurated on the West steps.

From George Washington to Ronald Reagan all Presidents have placed their left hand on a Bible, raised their right hand, and repeated the oath contained in the United States Constitution:

I do solemnly swear (or affirm) that I will faithfully execute the office of President of the United States and will to the best of my ability, preserve, protect, and defend the Constitution of the United States.

Washington added "so help me God" and all have followed his example. In 1862 this phrase became a part of the oath by law.

On the ceiling of the first floor corridor of the House wing is a painting of George Washington taking the oath of office with his hand on the Bible. Afterwards he gave his first inaugural address saying:

No people can be bound to acknowledge and adore the invisible hand which conducts the affairs of men more than the people of the United States. Every step by which they have advanced to the character of an independent nation seems to have been distinguished by some token of providential agency;...

We ought to be no less persuaded that the propitious smiles of Heaven can never be expected on a nation that disregards the eternal rules of order and right which Heaven itself has ordained;[9]

In the same corridor is a painting of Andrew Jackson being inaugurated in 1829 on the East Front steps of the Capitol. He also has his hand on the Bible.

As you enter the Capitol from the east steps you pass through the large Columbus Doors, which contain scenes from the life of Christopher Columbus. These doors were hung in recognition of the perilous journey Columbus made in 1492 when he discovered the new world and paved the way for the founding of America.

🔔 The Rotunda

As you stand in the Capitol Rotunda you immediately recognize its large size. This room is 100 feet across and 180 feet high. It is so high that the Statue of Liberty could fit within it without her torch touching the dome roof. The dome is made of iron and weighs 4455 tons. It has expanded and contracted as much as 4 inches on days of extreme change of temperature.

Inside the Rotunda are 8 large paintings. Each of these 12 by 18 foot paintings reveal the hand of God in the founding of the United States of America. In fact, two of them show prayer meetings and one a baptism.

The four paintings on the east side of the Rotunda depict two discoveries and two settlements. The two discoveries — "De Soto's Discovery of the Mississippi" (1541) and "The Landing of Columbus" (1492) — occurred about a century before the two settlements — Jamestown (1607) and Plymouth (1620). During the intervening period a very important event took place in Europe — the Protestant Reformation. The Reformation especially effected England, who became the chief colonizer of America. Therefore, the Jamestown and Plymouth colonies were Protestant even though De Soto and Columbus were Catholic. Catholic explorers, reflecting the governmental philosophy of Catholic nations, tended to operate in an authoritarian and often oppressive manner. However, De Soto and Columbus were God-fearing men. De Soto brought priests with him to America to lead natives to Christ. Columbus was an unusually bible-centered Catholic.

"The Landing of Columbus"

The painting of the "Landing of Columbus" reveals Columbus on the small island in the Bahamas where he first landed in 1492.

After coming ashore, he knelt, kissed the ground and gave thanks to God for his success. His men knelt around him. He then arose, drew his sword and took possession of the island for Spain christening it "San Salvador" meaning Holy Savior.

Columbus had risked his life and fortune to make this discovery. What motivated him to do this? Was he seeking wealth, fame, or adventure, as is often said of him today? Columbus reveals the answer in a book he wrote after his third voyage, entitled *Book of Prophecies*:

> *It was the Lord who put into my mind – I could feel His hand upon me – the fact that it would be possible to sail from here to the Indies... All who heard of my project rejected it with laughter, ridiculing me... There is no question that the inspiration was from the Holy Spirit, because He Comforted me with rays of marvelous illumination from the Holy Scriptures... For the execution of the journey to the Indies, I did not make use of intelligence, mathematics, or maps. It is simply the fulfillment of what Isaiah had prophesied... No one should fear to undertake any task in the name of our Savior, If it is just and if the intention is purely for His Holy service... the fact that the Gospel must still be preached to so many lands in such a short time – this is what convinces me.*[10]

"The Baptism of Pocahontas"

Jamestown was the first permanent English settlement in America. One of the first acts of the settlers after they landed in Virginia in April of 1607 was to erect a wooden cross on the shore at Cape Henry. It was at the foot of this cross that Reverend Robert Hunt led the 149 men of the Virginia company in prayer, thanking God for their safe journey and recommitting themselves to God's plan and purpose for this New World. The Virginia Charter of 1606 reveals that part of their reason for coming to America was to propagate the "Christian Religion to such People, as yet live in Darkness and miserable Ignorance of the true knowledge and worship of God."[11]

Pocahontas was an Indian Princess who providentially saved John Smith's life (the carved relief above the west door shows this incident) and helped preserve Jamestown as a settlement. She was later brought into the knowledge of the saving grace of Jesus Christ by the ministry of Rev. Alexander Whitaker. This painting records her baptism and reminds us of one primary reason why many individuals originally came to America.

"Departure of the Pilgrims"

Next to the "Baptism of Pocahontas" is a painting of the departure of the Pilgrims from Holland to America. Before leaving Holland, the Pilgrims set aside a day of fasting and prayer to cry out to God. This painting shows Pastor Robinson, Governor Carver, William Bradford, Miles Standish, and others in prayer. In the center of the painting, Elder William Brewster has an open Bible on his lap upon which are written the words: "The New Testament of our Lord and Savior Jesus Christ." This is the Geneva Bible. It was produced in 1560 by English reformers who had fled to Geneva to escape persecution in their home country. It was of great importance because it was the first English Bible divided into chapter and verse, it was relatively portable and affordable, and it contained many marginal notes addressing relevant topics, including governmental tyranny.

On the sail of the small ship can be seen the phrase, "God With Us." This marks well the entire lifestyle of these men and women who have been called the "Parents of our Republic."

From their earliest years in England through the establishment of the Plymouth Colony, their words and actions reveal their entire life was centered around God and doing His will. William Bradford, governor of Plymouth Colony for 33 years, relates how in their early years in Scrooby, England these people's lives "became enlightened by the Word of God and had their ignorance and sins discovered unto them, and began by His grace to reform their lives..." But this enlightening brought much persecution from the religious system of England and after some years of enduring evil, the Pilgrims "shook off this yoke of antichristian bondage, and as the Lord's free people joined themselves (by a covenant of the Lord) into a church estate, in the fellowship of the gospel, to walk in all His ways... whatsoever it should cost them, the Lord assisting them.''[12]

This desire to worship God freely was costly. They were exiled to Holland where they encountered persecutions, poverty, and much hard work, but by God's grace and their Christian character they were able to overcome the difficulties.

After 12 years in Holland they decided to sail to the new land of America. Their decision was prompted by a desire to find a home where they could more freely worship God and that was more conducive to raising godly children. They were also motivated, in the words of Bradford, by ''a great hope and inward zeal... of laying some good foundation, or at least to make some way thereunto, for the propagating and advancing the gospel of the kingdom of Christ in those remote parts of the world; yea, though they should be but even as stepping stones unto others for the performing of so great a work.''[13]

When the Mayflower set sail in 1620, it bore more than just 102 Pilgrims and strangers. The Pilgrims carried with them Bible-based principles that were to become the seeds of the greatest and freest nation the world has ever known.

After 66 days at sea the Mayflower reached America. The Pilgrims intended to settle just north of the Virginia Colony but were providentially blown off course to a region that was outside the jurisdiction of the Virginia Land Company. Being unable to sail southward due to the weather, they put ashore at Cape Cod. Had they arrived here some years earlier they would have been met by the Patuxet Indians and would have found no place to settle. These Indians had murdered many white men who landed on their shores, but in 1617 a plague had mysteriously wiped them out and now neighboring tribes were afraid to come near the place for fear that some great supernatural spirit had destroyed them.

Being out from under the authority of the Virginia Company caused some of the non-separatists to talk mutinously of abusing their liberty once they went shore, so before leaving the ship the Pilgrims drew up their own governmental compact which states:

> *. . . Having undertaken for the Glory of God and advancement of the Christian Faith, and the Honour of our King and Country, a Voyage to plant the First Colony in the Northern Parts of Virginia, do by these presents solemnly and mutually in the presence of God and one of another, Covenant and Combine ourselves together into a Civil Body Politic. . .*[14]

This document, the Mayflower Compact, placed the Pilgrim's civil government on a firm Christian base and was the beginning of American constitutional government.

Upon arriving on shore the Pilgrims fell to their knees and blessed and thanked God and confirmed their reliance upon Him. That first winter one half of their number died. The next spring when the Mayflower returned to Europe, however, not one went back. They had not come for personal convenience or reward but that they might walk in liberty with their God and be even as stepping stones for others to do the same.

Carved Relief of Penn's Treay with the Indians

Before examining the four paintings on the west side of the Rotunda, which focus on the American Revolution, we can see another founder of an American colony on a carved relief above the door which leads from the Rotunda to the Senate wing. This shows the founder of Pennsylvania, William Penn, making a treaty with the Indians. When Quaker minister William Penn was given the land between New York and Maryland in 1681 he said that "my God that has given it to me...will, I believe, bless and make it the seed of a nation."[15]

In 1682 the *Great Law of Pennsylvania* was enacted revealing the desire of Penn and the inhabitants of the colony to establish "...laws as shall best preserve true Christian and civil liberty, in opposition to all unchristian, licentious, and unjust practices, (whereby God may have his due, Caesar his due, and the people their due)..."[16]

Thomas Jefferson called Penn ''the greatest law-giver the world has produced.'' Penn, whose wisdom was ''derived from that book of gospel statutes,'' recognized Christian character as the basis of good government. He states in *Frame of Government of Pennsylvania*:

> *Governments like clocks, go from the motion men give them; and as governments are made and moved by men, so by them they are ruined too. Wherefore governments rather depend upon men, than men upon governments... Let men be good, and the government cannot be bad; if it be ill, they will cure it ...*[17]

At a later time William Penn told the Russian Czar, Peter the Great, that ''if thou wouldst rule well, thou must rule for God, and to do that, thou must be ruled by Him.''[18]

''The Signing of the Declaration of Independence''

In 1776 the colonists declared their independence. This painting shows the representatives from the 13 colonies signing that document that forms the foundational covenant of America. In the *Declaration* we see their belief that man's laws and rights should come from God. Britain's denial of these rights caused the colonists to declare:

> *We hold these truths to be self-evident, that all men are created equal, that they are endowed by their Creator with certain inalienable rights, that among these are life, liberty and the pursuit of happiness...*

The Declaration ends with the Congressional Representatives ''appealing to the Supreme Judge of the World'' and acknowledging ''a firm reliance on the protection of Divine Providence.'' We will see more of the Christian ideas contained within this document under the section on the National Archives.

Of the 56 men who signed the Declaration, all but 2 or 3 were orthodox Christians. Franklin was one who was unorthodox, but he was by no means anti-Christian — he acknowledged that ''God governs in the affairs of men.'' Some put Jefferson in this catagory, but at this time in his life there is nothing to indicate that he was anything but orthodox in his beliefs. Seven months after Jefferson drafted the *Declaration,* he started and financially supported the Calvanistical Reformed Church in Charlottesville, Virginia, that was pastored by an Evangelical minister, Charles Clay. Later, in 1803, he wrote "I am a Christian." (See section 11 for more on Jefferson.)

The men who signed that document did so only after much thought and consideration. After all, they had more to lose than any one in the colonies. They were the brightest minds, had the greatest talents, almost all were wealthy and many had large estates (some were the wealthiest in America), and most had families they loved dearly. In signing that document they did not see it as a avenue for fame, glory, or future advancement. They all knew they would be identified above all others by the British as the leaders of the "rebellion", and consequently, those most likely to suffer retribution. They knew that "history was strewn with the bones and blood of freedom fighters."[19] They were up against the greatest military power on earth, and so faced a very real chance of losing everything.

They all suffered in some way. Virtually all the men had greater wealth before taking up the cause of liberty than afterwards. One writer summarizes the price the Signers paid:

> *Nine Signers died of wounds or hardships during the Revolutionary War. Five were captured or imprisoned, in some cases with brutal treatment. The wives, sons, and daughters of others were killed, jailed, mistreated, persecuted, or left penniless. One was driven from his wife's deathbed and lost all his children. The houses of twelve Signers were burned to the ground. Seventeen lost everything they owned. Every Signer was proscribed as a traitor; every one was hunted. Most were driven into flight; most were at one time or another barred from their families or homes. Most were offered immunity, freedom, rewards, their property, or the lives and release of loved ones to break their pledged word or to take the King's protection. Their fortunes were forfeit, but their honor was not. No Signer defected, or changed his stand, throughout the darkest hours. Their honor, like the nation, remained intact.[20]*

These men have died and most have been forgotten by American's today. It is sad that we have forgotten these founders of America, but it is tragic that we have forgotten the high price they paid for liberty — that liberty which we possess today, but may lose if we forget its great cost.

"The Surrender of General Burgoyne"

On October 17, 1777 British General Burgoyne was defeated by Colonial forces at Saratoga. This was a much needed victory and an answer to prayer. General Washington had experienced many defeats at the hands of the British, such as the Battle of Brandywine the month before where 1200 Americans lost their lives. In great need, Washington prayed fervently for a "signal stroke of Providence."[21]

Others recognized the precarious position of the American cause. One Sunday in Sharon, Connecticut Rev. Smith proclaimed that though a long night of disaster had been occurring, God would soon bring a signal victory for the American army. Before the service ended, a messenger arrived with news that British General Burgoyne had surrendered at Saratoga!

The Providence of God was evident in this victory. Earlier, General Howe was supposed to have marched north to join Burgoyne's 11,000 men at Saratoga. However, in his haste to leave London for a holiday, Lord North forgot to sign the dispatch to General Howe. The dispatch was pigeon-holed and not found until years later in the archives of the British army. This inadvertence, plus the fact that contrary winds kept British reinforcements delayed at sea for three months, totally altered the outcome at Saratoga in favor of America.

In response to the victory, the Continental Congress proclaimed a day of thanksgiving and praise to God. In part, they stated, "Forasmuch as it is the indispensable duty of all men to adore the superintending providence of Almighty God,...and it having pleased Him in His abundant mercy ... to crown our arms with most signal success...: it is therefore recommended... to set apart Thursday, the 18th day of December, for solemn thanksgiving and praise..." They recommended for everyone to confess their sins and humbly ask God, "through the merits of Jesus Christ, mercifully to forgive and blot them out of remembrance" and thus He then would be able to pour out His blessings upon every aspect of the nation.[22]

"Surrender of Cornwallis"

In October of 1781, British General Cornwallis had his troops stationed at Yorktown, Virginia. While Cornwallis waited for reinforcements, Washington marched his troops from New York to Yorktown. Unknown to Washington or Cornwallis, a French fleet under Admiral De Grasse arrived just in time to defeat the British fleet sent to relieve General Cornwallis at Yorktown.

Without reinforcements, Cornwallis was barely holding out against the siege of the American and French forces. As a last resort he decided to attempt a retreat across the York River. At 10 o'clock on the night of October 17th, sixteen large boats were loaded with troops and embarked for Gloucester. After the first few boats had landed a great turn of events occurred. In the official dispatch to his superior, Cornwallis wrote: "...But at this critical moment, the weather, from being moderate and calm, changed to a violent storm of wind and rain, and drove all the boats, some of which had troops on board, down the river." Due to this miraculous weather change, Cornwallis was unable to complete his intended retreat and found his force divided when Washington's batteries opened at daybreak. When the boats finally returned, he ordered them to bring back the troops that had passed during the night. Later that day he surrendered his forces to General Washington. This essentially marked the end of the war.

General Washington and our Congress recognized the Providence of God in the battle of Yorktown. The Journals of the Continental Congress record this entry:

Resolved, that Congress will, at two o'clock this day, go in procession to the Dutch Lutheran Church, and return thanks to Almighty God, for crowning the allied arms of the United States

and France, with success, by the surrender of the Earl of Corn-
wallis.'[23]

And in his congratulatory order to the allied army on the day after
the surrender, General Washington concluded:

> *The General congratulates the army upon the glorious event*
> *of yesterday...Divine service is to be performed tomorrow in the*
> *several brigades and divisions. The commander-in-chief recom-*
> *mends that the troops not on duty should universally attend with*
> *that seriousness of deportment and gratitude of heart which the*
> *recognition of such reiterated and astonishing interpositions of*
> *Providence demand of us.*[24]

"General Washington Resigning His Commission"

This painting depicts General George Washington resigning his
commission to Congress as Commander in Chief of the army. This
event, which took place at Annapolis, Maryland on December 23,
1783, assured that America's revolution would end with the civilian
sector in control of the military. Most revolutions, before and after,
have ended with the military governing. Washington's example set
the standard for America, which has always experienced peaceful
transition of power.

A few months prior to this event, on June 8, Washington wrote a
letter to the Governors of all the States giving his advice on what
needed to be done to assure the success of the newly formed nation.
He wrote:

> *I now make it my earnest prayer, that God would have you,*
> *and the State over which you preside, in his holy protection...*
> *that he would most graciously be pleased to dispose us all to do*
> *justice, to love mercy, and to demean ourselves with that char-*
> *ity, humility, and pacific temper of mind, which were the charac-*
> *teristics of the Divine Author of our blessed religion, and*
> *without an humble imitation of whose example in these things,*
> *we can never hope to be a happy nation.*[25]

His advice to the Governors was to imitate Jesus Christ and His
character.

A few of the other paintings in the Capitol which reflect our faith in God include "Scene at the Signing of the Constitution," located on the East Stairway of the House wing, "Washington at Valley Forge, 1778", found on the south wall of the Senate Appropriations room, and "First Reading of the Emancipation Proclamation," on the West Staircase of the Senate wing.

Carved Relief, Frieze, and Replica of the Magna Charta

We have mentioned two of the carved reliefs above the doors in the Rotunda. The other two include scenes of the Landing of the Pilgrims and Conflict of Daniel Boone and the Indians.

The Rotunda Frieze is a painting that looks like sculpture. It contains scenes of significant events in the history of the United States from the Landing of Columbus to the flight of the Wright Brothers. The 300 foot circumference frieze is nine feet high, but does not look its height due to being 75 feet above the floor.

A replica of the Magna Charta is displayed in recognition of this "Charter of Liberty" as a fundamental source of civil freedom for Englishmen and Americans. (See the section on the Archives for more on the Magna Charta.)

Statues

Many statues of ministers and Christians are found within the Capitol. Some include George Washington, James Garfield, Samuel Adams, Rev. Peter Muhlenberg, Rev. Roger Williams (founder of Rhode Island), Rev. Marcus Whitman (founder of Washington State), Daniel Webster, Robert E. Lee, Lew Wallace, Rev. Jason Lee (founder of Oregon), John Winthrop, Rev. Jonathan Trumbull, Missionary Joseph Ward, Roger Sherman, William Jennings Bryan, and Christian Reformer Frances Willard.

On the ground floor near the gift shop is a statue presented by the state of Georgia to honor Crawford W. Long, M.D. These words are carved in the base of the statue:

Discoverer of the use of sulphuric ether as an anaesthetic in surgery on March 30, 1842 at Jefferson, Jackson County, Georgia U.S.A. "My profession is to me a ministry from God."

The statue of President James Garfield can be seen in the Rotunda.

James Garfield

In 1881 James A. Garfield was inaugurated the 20th President of the United States. About six months after taking office he was assassinated. Were it not for God's Providence, he would have died many years earlier in his youth.

As a boy Garfield worked on a canal. He was unable to swim which almost proved fatal one day when he fell into the water. While gasping for breath and trying to keep above water, he grabbed hold of a tow rope that had accidentally fallen into the water. As he was sinking he somehow managed to throw the rope, which wrapped around a fixture on the barge and he then pulled himself to safety. After recovering, Garfield attempted for three hours to throw the same rope around the same fixture and have it attach, but he was unable to duplicate the feat.

Garfield concluded that God had providentially saved his life. He went on to attend seminary and became a minister for the Disciples of Christ denomination. He led hundreds to Christ, publically debated evolutionists, and influenced the public sector in many different ways. He was elected to Congress and eventually became President.

In 1876, at the Centennial of our Declaration of Independence, Garfield wrote these words, which must be understood by Americans today:

Now, more then ever before, the people are responsible for the character of their Congress. If that body be ignorant, reckless, and corrupt, it is because the people tolerate ignorance, recklessness, and corruption. If it be intelligent, brave, and pure, it is because the people demand these high qualities to represent them in national legislature... Congress must always be the exponent of the political character and culture of the people; and if the next centennial does not find us a great nation, with a great and worthy Congress, it will be because those who represent the enterprise, the culture, and the morality of the nation do not aid in controlling the political forces which are employed to select the men who shall occupy the great places of trust and power.[26]

Rev. Peter Muhlenburg

In the South Small Rotunda which connects the Capitol rotunda with Statuary Hall we see a statue honoring a Revolutionary Minister, Peter Muhlenberg. Historian Benson Lossing writes of Muhlenberg:

When the war for independence was kindling, he was a clergyman in Virginia, and at the close of 1775, he concluded a sermon with the words of Scripture: 'There is a time for all things — a time to preach and a time to pray;' but those times, he said, had passed away; and then, in a voice that sounded like a trumpet-blast through the church, he exclaimed: 'There is a time to fight, and that time has now come.' Then laying aside his sacerdotal gown, he stood before his flock in the full uniform of a Virginia colonel. He ordered the drums to be beaten at the church door for recruits; and almost the entire male audience, capable of bearing arms, joined his standard. Nearly three hundred men enlisted under his banner that day.[27]

This statue shows Rev. Muhlenberg laying aside his gown with his military uniform exposed underneath.

Muhlenberg was one of numerous ministers who joined the cause of American independence, either as chaplains or fighting directly. The British called them the "Black Regiment." These men saw it as their divine duty to be involved in public affairs.

When one of Muhlenberg's relatives complained that he had abandoned the church for the army, he said:

I am a clergyman, it is true, but I am a member of society as well as the poorest layman, and my liberty is as dear to me as to any man. Shall I then sit still and enjoy myself at home when the best blood of the continent is spilling?... Do you think if America should be conquered I should be safe? Far from it. And would you not sooner fight like a man than die like a dog?[28]

Muhlenberg became a major-general and distinguished himself in many battles. After the war he served in many positions of civil government including numerous terms as a member of the United States Congress.

♤ Statuary Hall — The Old House Chamber

South of the Rotunda is Statuary Hall. Today this room houses statues of famous men and women from various states in the Union. Initially, two statues from each state were to be placed here, but the weight was so great that many of the statues had to be distributed throughout the Capitol Building. Many of these state heroes (we mentioned some before) were Christians and some were ministers.

A few of the people honored with statues in the Hall include: Marcus Whitman, a medical missionary and founder of Washington state, seen in his buckskins carrying a Bible and medical bag; Jason Lee, a missionary and founder of Oregon; Lew Wallace, who became a Christian while writing the great Christian classic, *Ben Hur*; Junipero Serra, a Franciscan missionary and founder of California, seen holding a cross up in his hand; Frances E. Willard, a leader in the temperance movement and associated in the evangelist movement with D.L. Moody; and other Christians such as Robert E. Lee and Daniel Webster.

Church Services in the House Chamber

This section of the Capitol first opened in 1800 and served as the House of Representatives Chamber. It also was the meeting place for numerous church services. In December of 1800, one month after the Capitol Building was opened, the Congress approved having church services within the building. Senate Chaplain, Thomas Claggett (1783-1816), wrote a letter on February 18, 1801, describing "a course of Sermons which I have delivered on Sundays in the Capitol on the truth of the Divine System."[29] Church meetings actually began in the Capitol even while it was under construction.[30]

Ministers from all denominations preached in the House over the years, using the Speaker's chair as the pulpit. Money for various Christian projects was raised during these church services, including funds to build new church buildings.[31]

While President, Thomas Jefferson regularly attended church services held in the Capitol. One contemporary wrote that "Jefferson during his whole administration, was a most regular attendant. The seat he chose the first day sabbath, and the adjoining one, which his private secretary occupied, were ever afterwards by the courtesy of the congregation, left for him."[32] Minister and congressman from Massachusetts, Manasseh Cutler (1742-1823), recorded that Jefferson "constantly attended public worship in the Hall," once even riding through a storm to arrive on time.[33] The wife of a senator from New York, Catharine Mitchill, recorded in a letter on April 8, 1806, that at the end of a church service in the House, she stepped on the President's toes, and was "so prodigiously frighten'd that I could not stop to make an apology."[34] Examining the content of the numerous sermons preached at the Capitol services reveals that "the president and his fellow worshipers received a steady diet of high octane, New Testament Christianity."[35]

Over the years Presbyterians, Methodists, Congregationalists, Quakers, Baptists, Episcopalians, Roman Catholics, and others preached at the Capitol. Even women, on occasion, would preach. The first to do so was Dorothy Ripley (1767-1832) on January 12, 1806. With Jefferson and Vice President Aaron Burr in attendance, Ripley concluded her sermon by observing that "very few" in attendance had been born again, and then exhorting all that "Christ's Body was the Bread of Life and His Blood the drink of the righteous."[36] The next time a woman preached was 21 years later, when, in January, 1827, Harriet Livermore, whose father and grandfather had both been members of Congress, preached to a packed house. Attendants included President John Quincy Adams, who "sat on the steps leading up to her feet because he could not find a free chair."[37]

⌂ Hall of Columns

Located on the ground floor of the House side of the Capitol, the Hall of Columns contains many statues. One honors Father Damien, the priest who went as a missionary to Hawaii in 1864. From 1873 until his death in 1889 he ministered to the lepers on the island of Molokai. The "Martyr of Molokai" died of leprosy, contracted from those he came to serve.

Another statue honors the first Governor of the Puritans, John Winthrop. In the spring of 1630 some 1000 Puritans sailed to America under the leadership of this man whom historian John Fiske calls "the Moses of the great Puritan exodus." While at sea in passage to America, Winthrop wrote *A Model of Christian Charity* which contains their reasons for starting a new colony and the goals they wished to accomplish. Winthrop spoke of their desire to be "as a city upon a hill" that all the people of the earth could look upon and then say of their own land, "Lord make it like that of New England." Winthrop also gave a sound warning to the settlers, but which also applies equally well to us today: *"If we shall deal falsely with our God in this work we have undertaken and so cause Him to withdraw His present help form us, we shall be made a story and a byword through the world."*[38]

The corridor that intersects with the Hall of Columns contains paintings of Washington and Jackson taking the oath of office with their right hands on the Bible.

⌂ The Prayer Room

In 1954 the eighty-third Congress set aside a room in the Capitol Building to be used exclusively for prayer by members of the Senate and House of Representatives. This room is located just off the west hallway that is connected to the Rotunda.

The room contains an open Bible sitting on an altar in front of a stained glass window. George Washington kneeling in earnest prayer is the focal point of the window. Behind Washington a prayer from the first verse of Psalm 16 is etched: "Preserve me, O God, for in Thee do I put my trust."

Both sides of the Great Seal of the United States are also within the window, as well as two open Bibles and a candle, signifying the light of God's word. Near the top of the window, across the center, are the words, "This Nation Under God." (See Appendix for more on the Great Seal.)

Samuel F.B. Morse Plaque

On May 24, 1844 Samuel F.B. Morse sent the first telegraph message in history from the Supreme Court Chamber, which was then in the Capitol, to Baltimore. Today, a metal plaque is fastened on the wall in the Capitol outside the old Supreme Court Chamber which contains the historic message that Morse first sent:

"What hath God Wrought!"

Concerning these words, Morse wrote: "I need only add that no words could have been selected more expressive of the disposition of my own mind at that time, to ascribe all the honor to Him to whom it truly belongs."[39]

The Old Supreme Court Chamber

From 1800 to 1935 the Supreme Court met in seven different locations in the capital. This room was their home for many of those years, from 1810 to 1860. Both Manasseh Cutler and John Quincy Adams describe church services that were conducted in the Supreme Court chamber. Adams records in his diary of February 2, 1806, that Presbyterian pastor, James Laurie, was preaching in the "Court-House" in the Capitol, and that it "was so crowded that I could not get within the room."[40] It is not surprising that then Chief Justice John Marshall would have approved such meetings, for he had shown in the past his approval of government support for Christianity. He would later serve as vice-president of the American Bible Society.[41]

During those early years of the Court, the Judges' opinions reflected the Biblical worldview of the people of America. Since our founding, the Supreme Court has ruled a number of times that we are a Christian nation and people. For example, in a ruling in 1892 the court reviewed numerous governmental and historical documents supporting the fact that America "is a Christian nation," and then they stated:

> *There is no dissonance in these declarations. There is a universal language pervading them all, having one meaning; they affirm and reaffirm that this is a religious nation. These are not individual sayings, declarations of private persons: they are organic utterances; they speak the voice of the entire people. . . . These, and many other matters which might be noticed, add a volume of unofficial declarations to the mass of organic utterances that this is a Christian nation.*[42]

☖ The House Chamber

The chamber of the House of Representatives is the largest legislative chamber in the world measuring 139 feet by 52 feet. Here 435 elected officials gather to make laws to secure the God-given rights of all American citizens. These public servants are constantly reminded of the basis for good government and good governing officials by our national motto, "In God We Trust," which is inscribed in letters of gold behind the Speaker's rostrum. This became the United States' official motto in 1955 and a House resolution in 1962 provided for the placing of the National Motto on the panel (see Appendix).

In 1857 new Senate and House wings were opened to house the growing number of congressmen. The first public function held in the Chamber that year, even before a legislative meeting, was a church service. Holding church services in government buildings was not only in keeping with precedence in the national congress, but was also common occurrence on the state and local levels.

Between 1865 and 1868, the House permitted the First Congregational Church of Washington to meet in the Chambers. This was at the same time that Congress passed the Fourteenth Amendment, which some modern jurists have argued prohibits religious activities on public property.[43] The pastor of the newly organized First Congregational Church, Charles Boynton, was also the chaplain of the House. The church was meeting in the "Hall of Representatives" while they raised money for their own building. "Nearly 2000 assembled every Sabbath," making this congregation that met in the House "the largest Protestant Sabbath audience then in the United States."[44]

Twenty-three marble relief portraits of noted "Lawgivers" are found over the Gallery doors of the House Chamber. As the greatest lawgiver of all, Moses is in the center (opposite the Speaker's chair) and is the only full-face portrait. The other lawgivers are seen in profile and include many Christians, such as Hugo Grotius, William Blackstone, and George Mason.

The first speaker of the House, Frederick A.C. Muhlenberg, was a minister, and was the brother of Peter Muhlenberg. This involvement in public affairs by the Colonial Clergy was not uncommon, for they believed this type of action was a natural part of being God's ambassador on the earth. This minister presided over the Congress that approved the First Amendment, that is interpreted by some today to mean we should not mix Christianity and governmental affairs.

The Senate Chamber

Two Senators from each state, who are elected for six-year terms, meet in this room to decide on various legislative issues. As in the House Chamber, our national motto appears in the Senate Chamber over the door that is opposite the chair of the President of the Senate, who is the Vice-president of the United States. The three Latin phrases found on our National Seal are also found above other doors in the Senate Chamber. (See Appendix for more on the Seal.) These phrases are:

Annuit Coeptis — "He (God) has blessed our undertakings"

Novus Ordo Seclorum — "A New Order of the Ages"

E Pluribus Unum — "One out of the many"

🔔 *The Washington Monument*

The most prominent feature of the skyline of Washington, D.C. is the 555 foot 5 1/8 inch Washington Monument. This marble obelisk, believed to be the tallest masonry structure in the world, was built between 1848 and 1884 to honor George Washington for his achievements and unselfish devotion to Christian principle and to this country.

The monument's width at the base is 55 feet 1 1/2 inches and its walls are 15 feet thick. At the top of the shaft the width is 34 feet 5 1/2 inches, with 18 inch thick walls. The capstone of the monument is topped with a solid aluminum tip, upon which are inscribed the Latin words, *Laus Deo*, which means "Praise be to God." President William Howard Taft said of the monument that ". . . with its stately simplicity and the high qualities of manhood it honors, it is fitting that the aluminum tip that caps it should bear the phrase 'Laus Deo.'"

When the monument opened in 1888, visitors could either walk up the 898 steps or ride a steam-driven elevator which took 10 minutes to reach the top. (Actually, only men could ride the elevator because it was not considered safe — women and children had to walk for their safety.) Today, the elevator ascent takes 60 seconds. Due to vandalism of the memorial stones in recent years, only those who take a specially guided tour are allowed to walk down the stairs. Along the stairway within the monument are set 190 carved tribute blocks that were donated by states, cities, individuals, societies, and foreign powers. Many of these contain scriptures and references to God. Following are a few of these inscriptions:

Holiness to the Lord

Exodus 28:36;39:30; Zechariah 14:20

Search the Scriptures

John 5:39; Acts 17:11

The Memory of the just is blessed

Proverbs 10:7

May Heaven to this union continue its beneficence

In God We Trust

Train up a child in the way he should go, and when he is old, he will not depart from it. Proverbs 22:6

☖ *The Smithsonian Institution*

Seven Smithsonian Museums are located on the Mall between the Capitol and the Washington Monument. The most visited of these is the **National Air and Space Museum.** Here, you can see the original Kitty Hawk Flyer, Charles Lindbergh's Spirit of St. Louis, samples of moonrock, the Apollo 11 command module Columbia, and much more. The movies that regularly show on the museum's five stories high and seven stories wide screen are well worth the time and small admission fee.

The National Gallery of Art contains many paintings by Christians as well as many paintings of Christian themes. Some of the most famous painters whose works are in the museum are Leonardo da Vinci, Raphael, Rembrandt, Vermeer, and Renoir. Paintings include da Vinci's portrait of *Ginevra de Benci, Daniel in the Lion's Den* by Rubens, 1615, and *The Adoration of the Magi* by Fra Angelico and Fra Filippo, early fifteenth century.

To get a feel for everyday life in the American past you should visit **The National Museum of American History.** Here you can see replicas of ancient American homes and rooms, early cars and locomotives, the American flag that flew over Ft. McHenry and inspired Francis Scott Key to write The Star-Spangled Banner, and a Foucault Pendulum. Unfortunately, the role of Christianity in America's history is barely mentioned.

Each of these museums reflect the advancement of society (and in particular American society) in various ways. Historically, to the degree that a nation or society applies Biblical truths to all of life is the degree to which that nation has advanced and made improvements in all areas. Our technological, scientific, governmental, artistic, educational, and economic advancements are due to a Biblical philosophy of life.

The National Museum of Natural History is an excellent place to visit to learn of the wonders of God's creation. The museum contains the largest African elephant ever bagged by a hunter in our time (13 feet high), a room full of precious gems including the legendary Hope diamond, a 92-foot-long model of a blue whale, as well as a host of other fascinating displays.

The National Archives

The National Archives preserves and makes available for reference and research the valuable records of the United States government. The *Declaration of Independence* and the *United States Constitution* are the best known and the most important. In addition to these the Archives keeps:

- Billions of pages of textual documents
- 2 million cartographic items
- 12 million still photographs
- 9 million aerial photographs
- 118,000 reels of motion picture film
- 200,000 video and sound recordings

These items have all been created by federal government agencies since the beginning of the nation. While this is an extremely large number, the Archives today only keeps about 2-3% of Federal records generated each year.

The National Archives operates 15 records centers, 13 regional archives, and 9 Presidential libraries in 17 states. The National Archives Building on Constitution Avenue in Washington, D.C. is the best known records center and is where the *Declaration of Independence* and the *U.S. Constitution* are housed.

The spot where this building is located was originally designed by Charles L'Enfant, who laid out the plan for Washington, D.C., to be the site of a National Cathedral. It was at another location in 1907 that the cornerstone was laid for The National Cathedral. It was only recently completed. It is located in the northwest part of Washington, near the intersection of Massachusetts and Wisconsin Avenues.

Structure

Construction on this building began in 1932 and was completed in 1937. It's exterior structure contains 72 columns weighing 95 tons apiece. Within the building are 21 levels of steel and concrete stack areas to house records.

Two massive bronze doors slide shut to close the building's main entrance on Constitution Avenue. Each of these doors weighs 6 1/2 tons, is 38 feet 7 inches high, and is nearly 10 feet wide and 11 inches thick.

As you enter the building you will walk over a large, circular, bronze design on the floor which contains four allegorical winged figures. These represent *Legislation, Justice, History,* and *War and Defense*. The Ten Commandments of God stand out on this design with *Senate* and *Justice* to the right of them, which symbolizes that our legal system has its origins in the Ten Commandments.

The Rotunda

The Rotunda or Exhibition Hall of the Archives constantly displays a number of important documents including original copies of the *Declaration of Independence* and the *U.S. Constitution* with the *Bill of Rights*. The top of the dome of the Rotunda is 75 feet above the floor. On the walls of the Rotunda are two large painted murals 13 feet 10 inches high and 34 feet 10 inches long. The mural on the left as you enter the rotunda is "The Declaration of Independence." It represents Thomas Jefferson presenting a draft of the Declaration to John Hancock, the president of the Continental Congress. On the right is "The Constitution." This painting shows James Madison submitting the Constitution to George Washington and the Constitutional Convention.

The Magna Charta

Also on display in the Rotunda is a copy of the Magna Charta dating from the thirteenth century. In 1621 Sir Edward Coke called the Magna Charta "the Charter of Liberty because it maketh freemen." The seeds of liberty contained in this civil document were a result of Biblical ideas springing up in the hearts of Englishmen who were descended from Anglo-Saxons and Normans.

In twelfth century England, the Norman system of government removed the rights of the people. The kings abused all the people, the barons as well as commoners. Things worsened to the point under King John that the English barons drew up a contract that addressed the abuses and guaranteed the barons certain rights and privileges as contained in Biblical law. King John, needing the help of the barons to raise money, reluctantly signed the Magna Charta in 1215. A clergyman, Stephen Langton, is likely the chief architect of the document.

The Magna Charta embodied the principle that both sovereign and people are beneath the law and subject to it. Later, both Englishmen and American colonists cited the Magna Charta as a source of their freedom.

🔔 The Declaration and Constitution

The Declaration and Constitution are kept in helium-filled bronze cases that lower into a vault 20 feet below the floor to protect the documents at night or in case of emergency. The vault is made of reinforced concrete and steel and weighs 50 tons. Why are such extreme measures taken to preserve these few pieces of paper? It is not as much for their historical value as it is the fact that the ideas inscribed thereon have changed the course of world history.

Christian Nature of the Declaration of Independence

The *Declaration of Independence* is a Christian civil document. This is seen in a number of ways. One, it is based on Biblical ideas of man and government. These ideas can be summed up by the following four points:

1. All men are equal.

"We hold these Truths to be self-evident, that all Men are created equal..."

2. Man, being created in the Divine image, has independent value.

"...that they are endowed by their Creator with certain unalienable Rights, that among these are Life, Liberty, and the Pursuit of Happiness..."

3. Man is superior to the state.

"That to secure these rights, governments are instituted among Men."

4. The state exists for man.

"...deriving their just Powers from the consent of the governed"

"...whenever any form of government becomes destructive of these ends, it is the right of the People to alter or to abolish it, and to institute new Government..."

The Declaration also directly refers to God four times:

1. "...the Laws of Nature and of Nature's God..."

2. "..Men are created equal...[and] endowed by their Creator..."

3. "...appealing to the Supreme Judge of the World..."

4. "And for the support of this Declaration, with a firm Reliance on the Protection of divine Providence, we mutually pledge to each other our Lives, our Fortunes and our sacred Honor."

Jefferson's original draft did not contain reference 2, 3, or 4. The Committee added reference 2, while the whole Congress added 3 and 4. These were the only major additions to Jefferson's original draft. Through these additions the Congress wanted all the world to know their trust and reliance was upon God.

Finally, the Declaration was primarily the product of Christian men in a Christian society. Even those who were not orthodox Christians, such as Jefferson and Franklin, still had a Biblical world-view.

On July 4, 1776 the Declaration of Independence was approved by the Continental Congress and signed by the President and Secretary of the Congress (John Hancock and Charles Thomson respectively). Beginning on August 2 all the members of the Congress signed an engrossed copy of the document. In so doing they were placing themselves in a very dangerous position because they were openly declaring to the King of England that they were leading this "rebellion" (as it was in the mind of the King).

After signing the Declaration, John Hancock said with a smile, "His Majesty can now read my name without glasses. And he can also double the price on my head."[45] Then he went on to say at this tense moment, "We must be unanimous; there must be no pulling different ways; we must all hang together."

Benjamin Franklin responded in his characteristic wit, "Yes, we must indeed all hang together, or most assuredly we shall all hang separately!"[46]

Concerning independence, Samuel Adams, the Father of the American Revolution, declared:

"We have this day restored the Sovereign, to whom alone men ought to be obedient. He reigns in heaven, and . . . [f]rom the rising to the setting sun, may His Kingdom come."[47]

The men who helped give birth to America understood what was taking place. They saw in the establishment of America the first truly Christian republic in history.

United States Constitution

The United States Constitution was signed by the delegates in convention on September 17, 1787 and then sent to the states for ratification. Our new government officially began in March of 1789. All but two or three of the men who signed the Constitution were of the Christian faith and three of them were clergymen. Those who were not orthodox believers still thought and acted like Christians. One of these men, Benjamin Franklin, called the Constitutional Convention to prayer when it was on the verge of breaking up in the summer of 1787. In his address to the President of the Convention, George Washington, he said:

In the beginning of the contest with Britain, when we were sensible of danger, we had daily prayers in this room for Divine protection. Our prayers, Sir, were heard and they were graciously answered. All of us who were engaged in the struggle must have observed frequent instances of a superintending Providence in our favor... Have we now forgotten this powerful Friend? Or do we imagine we no longer need His assistance?

I have lived, Sir, a long time, and the longer I live, the more convincing proofs I see of this truth: that God governs in the affairs of man. And if a sparrow cannot fall to the ground without His notice, is it probable that an empire can rise without His aid? We have been assured, Sir, in the Sacred Writings that except the Lord build the house, they labor in vain that build it. I firmly believe this...

I therefore beg leave to move that, henceforth, prayers imploring the assistance of Heaven and its blessing on our deliberation be held in this assembly every morning.' [48]

During the celebration of the Centennial of the Constitution, President Grover Cleveland said:

As we look down the past century to the origin of our Constitution, as we contemplate its trials and its triumphs, as we realize how completely the principles upon which it is based have met every National peril and every National need, how devoutly should we confess, with Franklin, "God governs in the affairs of men."

Christian Power and Form

It has been said that America's Constitution, next to the Holy Bible, is the most important document ever written for the benefit of mankind. A statement made in 1867 by the prestigious literary journal, the North American Review, reveals why this is true:

The American government and Constitution is the most precious possession which the world holds, or which the future can inherent. This is true — true because the American system is the political expression of Christian ideas. [49]

Both the spirit and the form of our Constitution are Christian. Some of the Christian ideas (or spirit) of the Constitution include:

1. The Reign of Law — "This Constitution... shall be the supreme law of the land." (Art. VI, Sec. 2)

America's civil government is a government of laws, not of rulers. Throughout most of history people have been governed by laws imposed by their rulers. In this they had no choice.

In America, for the first time ever, the people formed their own Constitution and consented to it. They had established a government of people's law, not of ruler's law. The law they established was based on Biblical truth. This is essential for protecting the individual's right to life, liberty, and property. Citizens must not only be protected from harmful acts of other citizens but also from abuses by their own government. Since the law is supreme and not the rulers, the people will be protected from ruler's tyranny.

2. Trial by Jury of Peers under Law — "The right of trial by jury shall be preserved." (Amendment 7)

In a nation under law, any violation of the law requires a judge. Wrongdoers must be punished and required to make restitution to deter crime, yet, there must be an orderly process of justice where the guilty and innocent are distinguished.

The Bible requires judges "to be honest, to refuse bribes, and not to show favoritism (Ex. 23:1-8). A person was presumed innocent unless at least two witnesses testified against him (Deut. 17:6), and the penalty for perjury was severe (Deut. 19:16-21)."[50]

The United States Constitution provides numerous protections for persons accused of crimes. Many of these rights are contained in Amendments 4, 5, 6, and 7 of the Constitution. These rights are derived from the idea that since man is created in the image of God, his life has great value and should be guarded with care.

3. Creator Endowed Rights, not Government Granted — "To ... secure the blessings of liberty." (Preamble)

Since man is created in the image of God, man has an inherent value and dignity. God has endowed certain rights to His valuable creation, that He expects all peoples and governments to recognize. The commands of Scripture reveal God has given man the right to life, liberty, and property:

- "You shall not murder." (Exodus 20:13) – right to life
- "He who kidnaps a man . . .shall surely be put to death." (Exodus 21:16) – right to liberty
- "You shall not steal" (Exodus 20:15) – right to property

According to the Declaration of Independence, men's rights are "endowed by their Creator. . . That to secure, these rights, Governments are instituted among men."

4. Christian Self-government – "We, the people" (Preamble)

For a nation to be free from the tyranny of centralized government, each individual citizen must be self-governing. The Bible and history reveal that if men do not govern themselves under God, then others will rule over them, and those rulers will eventually become tyrants. William Penn said, "men must be governed by God or they will be ruled by tyrants."

Robert C. Winthrop, speaker of the U.S. House of Representatives from 1847-1849, recognized the necessity of individual self-government for the functioning of the American Republic. He said:

All societies of men must be governed in some way or other. The less they may have of stringent State Government, the more they must have of individual self-government. The less they rely on public law or physical force, the more they must rely on private moral restraint. Men, in a word, must necessarily be controlled either by a power within them, or by a power without them; either by the Word of God, or by the strong arm of man; either by the Bible or the bayonet.[51]

As Americans have become less self-governed, our civil government has grown larger and larger and become more centralized. The more centralized a civil government becomes, the more loss of individual liberty will occur.

5. Religious Freedom – "Congress shall make no law. . . prohibiting the free exercise [of religion]" (Amendment 1)

The First Amendment guarantees the right of citizens to freely worship God without fear of the national government interfering or forcing people to adhere to a certain religious belief. While this keeps the state out of the church, it in no way removes God from government. It is impossible to remove God from government; every civil government operates on some religion. America was founded on the Christian religion but in recent years has been shifting to a man-centered, humanistic religion. If this continues to occur, we will lose more and more of our freedom and prosperity.

6. Private Property Rights – ". . .nor be deprived of. . . property, without due process of law" (Amendment 5)

Private property rights are a basic necessity for any society that desires to be free and prosperous. The founders of America acknowledged this truth and the Constitution protects property rights of individuals.

Noah Webster wrote:

Let the people have property and they will have power – a power that will forever be exerted to prevent a restriction of the press, and abolition of trial by jury, or the abridgement of any other privilege.[52]

The private property rights found in Amendment 5 and other places in the Constitution flowed out of the understanding by our Founders of the internal aspect of private property rights. James Madison, the chief architect of the Constitution, wrote:

Property. . .In the former sense, a man's land, or merchandise, or money, is called his property. In the latter sense, a man has a property in his opinions and the free communication of them. He has a property of peculiar value in his religious opinions, and in the profession and practice dictated by them... He has an equal property in the free use of his faculties, and free choice of the objects on which to employ them. In a word, as a man is said to have a right to his property, he may be equally said to have a property in his rights.[53]

God has created everything, including us, and given us the right to possess property, both internal (opinions, ideas, talents, etc.) and external (land, merchandise, money, etc.). *The Declaration of Independence* acknowledges this right is endowed by God; the *Constitution* secures this God-given right.

7. Union and Covenant — "... in order to form a more perfect Union" (Preamble)

The United States of America is an example of a Christian Union. The original external union among the states was the result of an internal unity of ideas and principles in the hearts of the people. This voluntary working together or covenanting together is the basis of Christian union. America's motto, *E Pluribus Unum* ("from many, one"), expresses this unity with union.

While the United States reveals a Christian union, the former Soviet Union was an example of an nonbiblical union. External force and fear was used to hold all the people groups together. It was an involuntary union and, hence, did not last. In America, unity brings union; in the USSR, the union attempted to force unity.

Stronger internal bonds will produce a stronger union and action. If the original colonies had never formed a union, they would have never individually made the positive impact upon the world that corporately the United States has been able to make. In fact, they might not ever have survived.

8. Defense — "the right of the people to keep and bear arms, shall not be infringed." (Amendment 2)

The American people established the Constitution to "provide for the common defense." Congress was given specific powers to accomplish this function of civil government. The Second Amendment to the Constitution recognizes "a well-regulated militia" is "necessary to the security of a free state," and therefore secures "the right of the people to keep and bear arms." This right of defense comes from the Biblical idea of man.

Since we are God's property and He requires us to be good stewards, we have a responsibility to preserve our lives. It follows that we have a right to defend our persons and families against those who may try to harm us. We establish police forces to help defend our life, liberty, and property from evildoers within our nation. State and national armies are established to defend citizens from aggressive nations.

Our Founders understood that a nation can only have liberty and peace through strength. Consider some of their remarks:

[I]f we desire to secure peace. . . it must be known that we are at all times ready for war.[54] – George Washington

To be prepared for war is one of the most effectual means of preserving peace.[55] – George Washington

It is absurd, the pretending to be lovers of liberty while they grudge paying for the defense of it.[56] – Benjamin Franklin

There is much truth in the Italian saying, ''Make yourselves sheep, and the wolves will eat you.''[57] – Benjamin Franklin

Aspects of the form of America's government that are Christian include:

1. Representation — ''Representatives shall be. . .chosen. . . by the people'' (Art. 1, Sec. 2)

The United States Constitution secures for each state a republican form of government (Art. 4, Sec 4). One characteristic of a republic is that the people choose representatives to stand in their place in the seat of government.

The principle of self-government reveals to us the right of each individual to participate in government. The people, under God, are the source of power for governments. Therefore, a Biblical civil government will be democratic in nature. A true democracy, however, has a number of shortcomings. In a democracy just over 50% of the people rule. If they desire to abuse the individual rights of the minority they can. Hence, a democracy tends to majority tyranny.

A democracy also requires direct participation by citizens in all government matters, which is impractical. Individuals choosing their representatives allows participation in government in every situation.

Representative government had its origin in the Hebrew nation. Moses told the people to ''choose wise and discerning and experienced men ['able men who fear God, men of truth, those who hate dishonest gain'] and I will appoint them as... heads over you, leaders of thousands, and of hundreds, of fifties and of tens, and officers for your tribes." (Deuteronomy 1:13-17; Exodus 18:21-27)

Noah Webster revealed the importance of being involved in choosing your representatives:

> *When you become entitled to exercise the right of voting for public officers, let it be impressed on your mind that God commands you to choose for rulers, "just men who will rule in the fear of God." The preservation of a republican government depends on the faithful discharge of this duty; if the citizens neglect their duty and place unprincipled men in office, the government will soon be corrupted; laws will be made, not for the public good, so much as for selfish or local purposes; corrupt or incompetent men will be appointed to execute the laws; the public revenues will be squandered on unworthy men; and the rights of the citizens will be violated or disregarded. If a republican government fails to secure public prosperity and happiness, it must be because the citizens neglect the divine commands, and elect bad men to make and administer the laws.*[58]

2. Separation of Powers – "All legislative powers herein granted shall be vested in a Congress" (Art. 1, Sec. 1); "The Executive power shall be vested in a President" (Art. 2, Sec. 1); "The judicial power of the United States, shall be vested in one Supreme Court" (Art. 3, Sec. 1).

America's national government is divided into three branches with an intricate system of checks and balances. This division is based upon the Biblical idea that mankind is sinful and in a fallen state. While man is capable of some civic virtue, he also is self-centered and must be limited and checked in the power he exercises. If rulers are given too much power, they will abuse it for their gain and their subjects' harm.

James Madison stated in *The Federalist* No. 51:

But what is government itself, but the greatest of all reflections on human nature? If men were angels, no government would be necessary. If angels were to govern men, neither external nor internal controls on government would be necessary. In framing a government which is to be administered by men over men, the great difficulty lies in this: you must first enable the government to control the governed; and in the next place oblige it to control itself.[59]

A balance of power between the governed and the governing must therefore be established.

Every government has three basic functions:

1. Legislative – making laws

2. Executive – enforcing laws

3. Judicial – interpreting laws

The Bible speaks of these three governmental functions in the Godhead (Isaiah 33:22). God, being perfect, can administer all three; with man it should be otherwise.

In 1748, in his book *Spirit of Laws*, Montesquieu said that these three functions of government must be separated to prevent tyranny. The founders of America studied his writings and agreed with his assessment. Madison wrote:

The accumulation of all powers, legislative, executive, and judiciary, in the same hands, whether of one, a few, or many. . . may justly be pronounced the very definition of tyranny.[60]

This is why they separated the powers of government into three branches and set up checks and balances between the branches.

3. Dual Form or Federalism — ". . .every State in this Union" (Art. 4, Sec. 4)

The tenth amendment to the Constitution states the idea of federalism: "The powers not delegated to the United States by the Constitution, nor prohibited by it to the States, are reserved to the States respectively, or to the people." The basic idea was to get government as close to the people as possible. The more remote it is from the people, the more dangerous it becomes.

Jefferson said:

> *The way to have good and safe government is not to trust it all to one, but to divide it among the many;. . . it is by dividing and subdividing these republics, from the great national one down. . . that all will be done for the best.*[61]

James Madison explained:

> *The powers delegated by the. . .Constitution to the federal government are few and defined. Those which are to remain in the State governments are numerous and indefinite.*[62]

In the federal republic established by the Constitution, most powers rested with the state and local governments. In recent years the national government has ballooned in growth, disrupting the balance of powers between the national and state and local governments. Greater centralization of power has come as individuals have failed to govern themselves on a local level. However, much power still rests with the local communities, and it is here that we must begin to get involved socially, politically, educationally, and economically if we hope to re-establish our nation on Godly foundations.

⌂ *The White House*

The first building constructed in the nation's capital was the White House. The cornerstone was laid in 1792 during George Washington's presidency and was completed during the term of our second president. John and Abigail Adams were the first occupants.

An inscription that John Adams authored is cut into the marble facing of the State Dining Room fireplace. It reads:

> *I pray Heaven to Bestow the Best of Blessings on THIS HOUSE and on All that shall hereafter Inhabit it. May none but Honest and Wise Men ever rule under this Roof.*

Each of our 42 Presidents, from Washington to Clinton, have attended church and associated with the Christian religion, taken the oath of office with their hand on a Bible, and referred to God in their inaugural addresses. Most of these have also declared National Days of Prayer and Thanksgiving.

An excerpt from Washington's Inaugural Address was given earlier. Following are excerpts acknowledging God from Inaugural Addresses of a few more of our Presidents:

John Adams, March 4, 1797

And may that Being who is supreme over all, the Patron of Order, the Fountain of Justice, and the Protector in all ages of the world of virtuous liberty, continue His blessing upon this nation and its Government and give it all possible success and duration consistent with the ends of His providence.

James Monroe, March 4, 1817

. . . I enter on the trust to which I have been called by the suffrages of my fellow-citizens with my fervent prayers to the Almighty that He will be graciously pleased to continue to us that protection which He has already so conspicuously displayed in our favor.

John Quincy Adams, March 4, 1825

. . . and knowing that "except the Lord keep the city the watchmen waketh but in vain," with fervent supplications for His favor, to His overruling providence I commit with humble but fearless confidence my own fate and future destinies of my country.

William Henry Harrison, March 4, 1841

I deem the present occasion sufficiently important and solemn to justify me in expressing to my fellow-citizens a profound reverence for the Christian religion and a thorough conviction that sound morals, religious liberty, and a just sense of religious responsibility are essentially connected with all true and lasting happiness.

Franklin Pierce, March 4, 1853

. . . It must be felt that there is no national security but in the nation's humble, acknowledged dependence upon God and His overruling providence.

Stephen Grover Cleveland, March 4, 1893

. . . Above all, I know there is a Supreme Being who rules the affairs of men and whose goodness and mercy have always followed the American people, and I know He will not turn from us now if we humbly and reverently seek His powerful aid.

William McKinley, March 4, 1897

. . . I assume the arduous and responsible duties of President of the United States, relying upon the support of my countrymen and invoking the guidance of Almighty God. Our faith teaches that there is no safer reliance than upon the God of our fathers, who has so singularly favored the American people in every national trial, and who will not forsake us so long as we obey His commandments and walk humbly in His footsteps.

Warren G. Harding, March 4, 1921

I have taken the solemn oath of office on that passage of Holy Writ where in it is asked: "What doth the Lord require of thee but to do justly, and to love mercy, and to walk humbly with thy God?" This I plight to God and country.

Calvin Coolidge, March 4, 1925

America seeks no earthly empire built on blood and force. No ambition, no temptation, lures her to thought of foreign dominions. The legions which she sends forth are armed, not with the sword, but with the cross. The higher state to which she seeks the allegiance of all mankind is not of human, but of divine origin. She cherishes no purpose save to merit the favor of Almighty God.

♨ *St. John's Church*

Located north of the White House across Lafayette Park, St. John's Episcopal Church is know as the "Church of the Presidents" because more Presidents have woshipped here than in any other church in the capital. St. John's was the first building constructed on Lafayette Square after the White House. Every President since James Madison has worshipped here at some time. This attendance has caused St. John's to designate Pew 54 as the traditional seat of worship for the First Family. Presidents who made this church their home include Madison, James Monroe, John Quincy Adams, Martin Van Buren, William Henry Harrison, Tyler, Taylor, Fillmore, and Arthur.

Other historic churches in the D.C. area include: New York Avenue Presbyterian Church, attended by President Lincoln, and pastored by Senate Chaplain Peter Marshall from 1937-1949; the National Presbyterian Church, home to many Presidents; and Christ Church in Alexandria, Virginia, parish church for Washington.

♨ *Thomas Jefferson Memorial*

Dedicated in 1943, the Jefferson Memorial was designed as a circular colonnaded structure because Jefferson greatly admired this architectural style and is credited with having introduced it into this country, as seen in his designs for the rotunda at the University of Virginia and his home, Monticello. Within the center of the 152 foot diameter memorial is a 19 foot bronze statue of Thomas Jefferson. Jefferson was a brilliant man who contributed greatly to the founding of America.

Jefferson, though unorthodox in some of his views, claimed to be a Christian, went to church, and, most importantly, held to a Biblical worldview. Jefferson even started a church in 1777 and invited an evangelical minister to be the pastor. (See Section 11 for more on Jefferson's life and faith.)

Four inscriptions are engraved on the interior walls of the memorial room which describe Jefferson's beliefs and religious convictions. One contains excerpts from the *Declaration of Independence*.

A second inscription is from his *Virginia Statute for Religious Freedom*. It states:

> *Almighty God hath created the mind free. All attempts to influence it by temporal punishments or burthens. . .are a departure from the plan of the Holy Author of our religion. . .No man shall be compelled to frequent or support any religious worship or ministry or shall otherwise suffer on account of his religious opinions or belief, but all men shall be free to profess and by argument to maintain, their opinions in matters of religion. I know but one code of morality for men whether acting singly or collectively.*

A third inscription states in part:

> *God who gave us life gave us liberty. Can the liberties of a nation be secure when we have removed a conviction that these liberties are the gift of God? Indeed I tremble for my country when I reflect that God is just, that his justice cannot sleep forever.*

Senator Byrd of West Virginia (in a speech to members of the Senate in shocked response to the Supreme Court ruling State written prayer in the schools unconstitutional in 1962) cited these words of Jefferson as "a forceful and explicit warning that to remove God from this country will destroy it."

♤ *The Lincoln Memorial*

At the dedication of the Lincoln Memorial in 1922, Supreme Court Justice Taft called the monument "a sacred religious refuge in which those who love country and love God can find inspiration and repose."[63] This is a fitting description for a Memorial that honors the 16th President of the United States, Abraham Lincoln, for he was an example of one who unselfishly served his country and honored God.

The retaining wall of the Memorial is 14 feet high, 257 feet long, and 187 feet wide. The structure sitting upon this has a motif that symbolizes the Union. The 36 marble Doric columns surrounding the walls represent the 36 states in the Union at the time of Lincoln's death. The names of the states are engraved on the frieze above the row of columns. The names of the 48 states in the Union in 1922 are inscribed on the attic walls above the frieze. Within the Central Chamber of the 99 foot high Memorial is a 19 by 19 foot seated statue of Lincoln.

Excerpts from addresses by Abraham Lincoln, all of which reveal his Christian thought and character, are inscribed within the Memorial. Carved on the south wall is *The Gettysburg Address*. It ends exclaiming "that this nation, under God, shall have a new birth of freedom – and that government of the people, by the people, and for the people, shall not perish from the earth."

On the wall of the north chamber are inscribed excerpts from Lincoln's second inaugural address:

> *. . . Both read the same Bible and pray to the same God, and each invokes His aid against the other. It may seem strange that any men should dare to ask a just God's assistance in wringing their bread from the sweat of other men's faces, but let us judge not, that we be not judged. The prayers of both could not be answered. That of neither has been answered fully. The Almighty has His own purposes. 'Woe unto the world because of offenses; for it must needs be that offenses come, but woe to that man by whom the offense cometh' (Matthew 18:7).*

Following are a few instances in the life of Abraham Lincoln which reveal his Christian character: (taken from *Abraham Lincoln the Christian* by William J. Johnson)

1. As the Civil War began, Lincoln relied totally upon Almighty God for strength and wisdom in fulfilling his duty as President in preserving the Union and abolishing slavery.

> *One day during the war a minister said in Lincoln's presence that he hoped "the Lord" was "on our side," to which Mr. Lincoln*

replied, *"I am not at all concerned about that, for I know that the Lord is always on the side of the right; but it is my constant anxiety and prayer that I and this nation should be on the Lord's side."*

From the day of his election the President was animated by a profound conviction: *"If we do right, God will be with us; and if God is with us, we cannot fail."*[64]

2. General James F. Rusling, of Trenton, New Jersey, relates a significant conversation which he heard on Sunday, July 5, 1863, in the room in Washington where General Sickles lay wounded, just after the great victory at Gettysburg. In reply to a question from General Sickles whether or not the President was anxious about the battle at Gettysburg, Lincoln gravely said, *"No, I was not; some of my Cabinet and many others in Washington were, but I had no fears."* General Sickles inquired how this was, and seemed curious about it. Mr. Lincoln hesitated, but finally replied: *"Well, I will tell you how it was. In the pinch of your campaign up there, when everybody seemed panic-stricken, and nobody could tell what was going to happen, oppressed by the gravity of our affairs, I went to my room one day, and I locked the door, and got down on my knees before Almighty God, and prayed to Him mightily for victory at Gettysburg. I told Him that this was His war, and our cause His cause, but we couldn't stand another Fredericksburg or Chancellorsville. And I then and there made a solemn vow to Almighty God, that if He would stand by our boys at Gettysburg, I would stand by Him. And He did stand by you boys, and I will stand by Him. And after that (I don't know how it was, and I can't explain it), soon a sweet comfort crept into my soul that God Almighty had taken the whole business into his own hands and that things would go all right at Gettysburg. And that is why I had no fears about you."* Asked concerning Vicksburg, the news of which victory had not yet reached him, he said, *"I have been praying for Vicksburg also, and believe our Heavenly Father is going to give us victory there, too."* General Rusling says that Mr. Lincoln spoke *"solemnly and pathetically, as if from the depth of his heart,"* and that his manner was deeply touching.[65]

3. A Negro clergyman writes of a visit to the servants at the White House, in which he says: "In the year 1865, while a chaplain at Freedmen's Village, on Arlington Heights, after the assassination, but three weeks before Mrs. Lincoln left the White House, I dined with the servants employed at the house, some of whom had been engaged in personal attendance upon Mr. Lincoln. My object was really to know more about him whose memory is still dear to me. I asked the servants how Mr. Lincoln treated them. I was told that frequently, late at night, Mr. Lincoln came down stairs to teach them to read, and often took such occasions to draw their thoughts toward the Saviour of all mankind. He also prayed with them."[66]

4. On the day of the receipt of the news of the capitulation of Lee, as we learn from a friend intimate with the late President Lincoln, the cabinet meeting was held an hour earlier than usual. Neither the President nor any member was able, for a time, to give utterance to his feelings. At the suggestion of Mr. Lincoln all dropped on their knees, and offered, in silence and in tears, their humble and heartfelt acknowledgments to the Almighty for the triumph He had granted to the national cause.[67]

5. Shortly before his death an Illinois clergyman asked Lincoln, "Do you love Jesus?" Mr. Lincoln solemnly replied: "When I left Springfield I asked the people to pray for me. I was not a Christian. When I buried my son, the severest trial of my life, I was not a Christian. But when I went to Gettysburg and saw the graves of thousands of our soldiers, I then and there consecrated myself to Christ. Yes, I do love Jesus."[68]

Arlington National Cemetery

This 617-acre shrine is located upon a portion of the area known as the Arlington estate. The land for this estate was first purchased in 1778 by George Washington's stepson, John Parke Custis. Before building a home here he died in the Revolutionary War. His son, George Washington Parke Custis (who had been raised by his grandparents, George and Martha Washington) began construction on his home in 1802 and completed it in 1820. His only surviving child, Mary Ann, married Lt. Robert E. Lee in 1831, after which they lived in Arlington House for 30 years until the War between the States. The Federal Government confiscated the house and land in 1864 when Mrs. Lee failed to appear in person and pay her property tax. The government set aside a 200-acre section as a military cemetery. This was the beginning of today's Arlington National Cemetery.

In 1882 the Supreme Court restored the property to Lee's heirs, who then sold it back to the Government for $150,000. Over the past century Arlington National Cemetery has become a national shrine where those serving in the military, Medal of Honor recipients, high-level government officials and their dependents are buried. Among the more than 200,000 persons that are buried here are Presidents William Howard Taft and John F. Kennedy, Astronauts Virgil Grissom and Roger Chaffee, U.S. Supreme Court Justices Oliver Wendell Holmes, Jr. and William O. Douglas, Explorer Richard E. Byrd, General Omar Bradley, and World Heavyweight Boxing Champion Joe Lewis.

🔔 Tomb of the Unknown Soldier

This famous monument in Arlington Cemetery was carved from a single rectangular block of marble to honor unknown soldiers who gave their life for the cause of liberty. Entombed here are the unknown soldier of World War I and the Unknown Servicemen of World War II, Korea and Vietnam. The rear panel of the Tomb bears the inscription:

**HERE RESTS IN HONORED GLORY AN AMERI-
CAN SOLDIER KNOWN BUT TO GOD**

🔔 Arlington House — Robert E. Lee Memorial

The home that George Washington Parke Custis built in the early 1800's and in which Robert and Mary Ann Lee lived for thirty years was restored this century and serves as a Memorial to Robert E. Lee.

General Lee's leadership and Christian character gained him respect in both the North and the South.

Robert E. Lee's "correspondence reveals him as a man who lived in the presence of God; who looked to God continually for guidance and strength; whose mind and heart were saturated with faith and trust in God."[69]

Historian William Johnson said:

> *After years of study of the life and character of Robert Edward Lee, I fail to find, in his whole career, from the cradle to the grave, a flaw in his relations to his family, his friends, his associates, or his enemies; in his conduct at home, in school, in the field, in the college, or in the church; and in his moral, social, and religious character.*[70]

The following two incidents reveal something of the character of this Christian man: (from *Robert E. Lee, the Christian* by William J. Johnson)

> *1. Long after the war a Northern Grand Army man told of meeting Lee in the field at Gettysburg under circumstances which revealed to him the true heart of the Southern commander:*
>
> *"I had been a most bitter anti-South man, and fought and cursed the Confederates desperately. I could see nothing good in any of them. The last day of the fight I was badly wounded. A ball shattered my left leg. I lay on the ground not far from Cemetery Ridge, and as General Lee ordered his retreat, he and his officers rode near me.*
>
> *"As they came along I recognized him, and, though faint from exposure and loss of blood, I raised my hands, and looked Lee in the face, and shouted as loud as I could — 'Hurrah for the Union!'*
>
> *"The General heard me, looked, stopped his horse, dismounted, and came toward me. I confess I at first thought he meant to kill me. But, as he came up, he looked down at me with such a sad expression upon his face that all fear left me, and I*

wondered what he was about. He extended his hand to me, grasping mine firmly, and looking right into my eyes, said:

    " 'My son, I hope you will soon be well.'

    "If I live a thousand years, I shall never forget the expression on General Lee's face. There he was, defeated, retiring from a field that had cost him and his cause almost their last hope, and yet he stopped to say words like these to a wounded soldier of the opposition who had taunted him as he passed by! As soon as the General had left me, I cried myself to sleep there on the bloody ground."[71]

    2. General Lee often issued orders for his troops to observe days of fasting and prayer, and attend services. In one such order on Thursday, August 13, 1863, Lee told his army to cry out to God for forgiveness of their sins and humble before Him. He asked God to save their enemies as well as their own troops, and declared that "God is our only refuge and our strength."[72]

    Chaplain Jones relates the effect this order had:

    I can never forget the effect produced by the reading of this order at the solemn services of that memorable fast-day. A revival was already in progress in many of the commands – the day was almost universally observed – the attendance upon preaching and other services was very large. The solemn attention and starting tear attested the deep interest felt, and the work of grace among the troops widened and deepened and went gloriously on until over fifteen thousand of the soldiers of Lee's army professed repentance toward God and faith in Jesus Christ as a personal Saviour. How far these results were due to this fast-day, or the quiet influence and fervent prayers of the commanding general, eternity alone shall reveal.[73]

    Lee did much to promote revival in his army and saw every soldier as a soul to be saved. So concerned was Lee for the spiritual welfare of his soldiers that one of his biographers says, "One almost feels as if he cared more for winning souls than battles, and for supplying his army with Bibles than with bullets and powder."[74]

Section 2

Washington and Mount Vernon

☖ *Mount Vernon*

George Washington had an immense love for his estate of Mount Vernon. As President he stated:

I can truly say I had rather be at Mount Vernon with a friend or two about me, than to be attended at the seat of Government by the Officers of State and the Representatives of every Power in Europe.

Washington spent one third of his life in service to his country. He was motivated not by personal glory or gain, but from a heart to serve and a love of his country and of liberty. He received no pay for the 8 years he was commanding the American forces during the Revolution, he attended the Constitutional Convention only at the insistence of others (he was overcoming a bad illness), and served as President only because he felt his country needed him. During his many years of public service, he not only missed being at the home he loved so much, where his happiest hours were spent, but his estate also suffered.

Location

Mount Vernon is located 16 miles south of Washington, D.C. on the Virginia side of the Potomac River. It can be reached from downtown Washington by taking the George Washington Memorial Parkway which runs directly to the estate.

History

George Washington was born to Augustine and Mary Washington on February 22, 1732, in Westmoreland County, Virginia. At the age of three he moved with his family to Little Hunting Creek. In 1743 his father died and the estate was deeded to Lawrence, George's elder half-brother. Lawrence changed the name to Mount Vernon, in honor of Admiral Edward Vernon, whom he admired and served under in the British Navy.

The original part of the now familiar house was built by Augustine in about 1735. It was a small one and 1/2 story farmhouse. After Lawrence died in 1752, George leased Mount Vernon from Lawrence's widow. When she died a few years later, the estate legally became his.

In 1759 George married a widow, Martha Custis (who had two children), and they moved into Mount Vernon. Martha was a virtuous woman who read the Bible and prayed daily. Her original, autographed Bible was on display at the museum on the grounds until recently.

Over the years the house was gradually extended until it reached its present size with 17 rooms. It is constructed of "rusticated boards" which are wooden panels, painted with sand firmly secured upon them. It resembles stone or cement, yet it is only wood.

The original estate was 8000 acres with 5 independently managed farms. Products included tobacco (until the 1760's),and wheat and cereals which were ground and processed on the farm. There was also a fishing industry at Mount Vernon. Washington Irving writes in his *Life of Washington* that before the Revolutionary War, the products of his estate "became so noted for faithfulness, as to quality and quantity, with which they were put up, that it is said any barrel of flour that bore the brand of George Washington, Mount Vernon, was exempted from the customary inspection in the West India ports."

Mount Vernon is beautifully situated overlooking the Potomac River. Washington said of his home: "No estate in United America is more pleasantly situated than this."[1]

During the eight years of the American Revolution (1775-1783), Washington visited Mount Vernon only twice. After his resignation from the army he returned home, but in 1787 he was called to serve as the President of the Constitutional Convention, and in 1789 he was elected as President of the United States of America. After eight years of service in this capacity, he returned to his beloved Mount Vernon where he lived the last two years of his life. In 1799 he was stricken with a sudden illness and died.

♤ Washington's Tomb

Washington was buried at Mount Vernon. Martha joined him when she died a few years later in 1802. Some years later the remains of George and Martha Washington were moved to a nearby tomb which stands today at the foot of Mount Vernon. On the rear wall of the tomb are the words of Jesus:

> *I am the Resurrection and the Life; sayeth the Lord. He that believeth in Me, though he were dead yet shall he live. And whosoever liveth and believeth in Me shall never die. (John 11:25-26)*

After their deaths, Mount Vernon gradually fell into disrepair. In the mid-1800's, an invalid, Pamela Bird Cunningham of South Carolina "made up her mind that the home which George Washington loved should not be allowed to fall down in ruins from neglect."[2] She founded The Mount Vernon Ladies' Association in 1853 with a desire to preserve the home and memory of this great man. The Association purchased two hundred acres of the original estate and restored the house to its condition when Washington lived there.

Articles at Mount Vernon

A few items of interest that can be seen today at Mount Vernon include:

1. Washington's family Bible with his record of birth in it.

2. The *Book of Common Prayer* bearing Martha Washington's signature.

3. A 1792 Commentary on the Book of Psalms, with Martha's signature.

4. A concordance of the Bible that is thought to have been a gift from George to his sister, Betty.

5. Martha Washington's Bible had been on display in the museum until recently, being removed for it needed a "rest."

George Washington, A Man Prepared and Used by God

George Washington rightly deserves the title, "the father of this country." Every American youth would do well to make Washington their role model and be closely acquainted with him.

Following the death of Washington, Henry Lee told Congress that Washington was "first in peace, first in war, and first in the hearts of his countrymen."[3] Nobody has been as well loved and admired in the history of America as George Washington. He has been the hero and role model of many people in many countries, not only since his death, but even while he was living. The people so admired Washington during his life that John Adams expressed the sincere fear that the people were making a god of him.

One man, in particular, had Washington as his hero. This man grew up on the frontier and had only a few books – the *Bible*, Bunyan's *Pilgrim's Progress, Aesop's Fables*, and Parson Weem's *Life of Washington*. These few books he devoured, which helped implant a desire within him to be like Washington. Washington made a lasting impression on him for all his life. The man who emulated Washington was Abraham Lincoln.

For generations the example of Washington was put before young Americans to inspire them to greatness of moral character, forthright honesty, quiet modesty, thoughtful consideration for others, thoroughness, kindness, and generosity.

Many historians and leaders throughout the world have acknowledged that *"Washington was without an equal, was unquestionably the greatest man that the world has produced in the last one thousand years."*[4]

Abraham Lincoln wrote:

Washington is the mightiest name on earth – long since mightiest in the cause of civil liberty, still mightiest in moral reformation. On that name no eulogy is expected. It can not be. To add brightness to the sun, or glory to the name of Washington is alike impossible. Let none attempt it.

In solemn awe we pronounce the name and in its naked splendor leave it shining on.[5]

An Example of Christian Character

George Washington provides us with an excellent example of Christian character. Character has been defined as a convictional belief that results in consistent behavior, which is readily seen in Washington's life. The winter at Valley Forge provides a good example.

The winter of 1777-1778 was one of the most important in our nation's history, for that winter was the turning point of the American Revolution. During that winter the American Army faced as great an ordeal as any army in history.

Before the American Army moved into Valley Forge in December of 1777, it consisted of undisciplined men who had obtained few victories in their war with Britain, but the next spring they marched out as a well-disciplined band, committed more than ever to their General and the cause of liberty. They were now prepared to see victory through their efforts.

What was the ordeal this Army faced? How did such a change occur during the stay at Valley Forge? What was the cause behind this change?

As the American Army, under the command of George Washington, moved toward their wintering spot at Valley Forge, army troops had no clothes to cover their nakedness, nor blankets to lie on, nor tents to sleep under. Washington stated: "For the want of shoes their marches through frost and snow might be traced by the blood from their feet, and they were almost as often without provisions as with them."[6]

Their situation even worsened after their arrival at Valley Forge on December 19th. Lack of food and provisions for his men was central to Washington's appeals to Congress. In a letter to Congress dated December 23, 1777 Washington wrote, "Men are confined to hospitals, or in farmers' houses for want of shoes. We have this day no less than two thousand eight hundred and ninety-nine men in camp unfit for duty, because they are barefoot and otherwise naked..."[7]

About one third of all his troops were unfit for service, and this number increased as winter progressed. "The unfortunate soldiers were in want of everything. They had neither coats, hats, shirts, nor shoes," wrote Lafayette. "The men," said Baron Von Steuben, "were literally naked, some of them in the fullest extent of the word."[8]

Hunger was even a greater danger. "The army frequently remained whole days without provisions," said Lafayette. "One soldier's meal on a Thanksgiving Day declared by Congress was a 'half a gill of rice and a tablespoonful of vinegar!' In mid-February there was more than a week when the men received no provisions at all."[9]

Dr. Waldo gives this description:

There comes a soldier, his bare feet are seen through his worn out shoes, his legs nearly naked from the tattered remains of an only pair of stockings; his breeches are not sufficient to cover his nakedness, his shirt hanging in strings, his hair dishevelled, his face meagre. His whole appearance pictures a person forsaken and discouraged. He comes and cries with an air of wretchedness and despair, "I am sick, my feet lame, my legs are sore, my body covered with this tormenting itch". . . . [10]

Due to this lack of food and clothing, hundreds of the troops fell sick. Many men's "feet and legs froze till they became black, and it was often necessary to amputate them."[11] During most of January and February there were "constantly more than 4,000 soldiers who were incapacitated as a result of exposure, disease, and undernourishment."[12]

And in the midst of all of this they persevered! Beyond this, the patient attitude with which they endured this misery was no less than supernatural. Washington wrote April 21, 1778 to a congressional delegate:

. . . *For, without arrogance or the smallest deviation from the truth, it may be said that no history now extant can furnish an instance of an army's suffering such uncommon hardships as ours has done, and bearing them with the same patience and fortitude. Their submitting without a murmur is a proof of patience and obedience which in my opinion can scarce be paralleled.* [13]

What could possibly have held this army together through this ordeal? Baron Von Steuben said no European army could have held together in such circumstances. How then could an inexperienced American Army stick together? Was it due to good discipline? "With regard to military discipline," Von Steuben states, "no such thing existed."[14]

Could it have been the financial reward they would receive? Not hardly, for their meager pay was already four to five months past due, and complete payment would never come. What was it then?

Most historians agree that the reason for their perseverance at Valley Forge can be attributed to their love of liberty and to their General George Washington, and his amazing quality of leadership. George Bancroft states that "love of country and attachment to their General sustained them under their unparalleled hardships; with any other leader, the army would have dissolved and vanished."[15]

His character and encouragement inspired the army to follow his example. From the beginning he tirelessly traveled throughout the camp, his very presence bringing strength to the men. His heart was for his men as well as for his country. As Washington observed his naked and distressed soldiers, he said: "I feel superabundantly for them, and from my soul I pity those miseries which it is neither in my power to relieve or prevent."[16]

Washington knew that the cause for which they fought was well worth any price — even the suffering at Valley Forge — for they purchased liberty, not only for them, but for the generations to come. While at Valley Forge, blood was not shed in battle, yet the American Army shed much blood.

The blood that stained this ground," writes Henry Brown, *"did not rush forth in the joyous frenzy of the fight; it fell drop by drop from the heart of a suffering people. They who once encamped here in the snow fought not for conquest, not for power, not for glory, not for their country only, not for themselves alone. They served here for Posterity; they suffered here for the Human Race; they bore here the cross of all the peoples; they died here that freedom might be the heritage of all.*[17]

It was Washington's character that helped sustain the army, but what sustained Washington? This question could easily be answered by Washington's troops or officers, for they knew his trust was completely in God. The army had frequently seen Washington order his men to attend church and to observe days of prayer and fasting and days of Thanksgiving.

Washington was also very instrumental in securing chaplains for the army. Rev. Henry Muhlenberg relates how General Washington "rode around among his army... and admonished each and every one to fear God, to put away the wickedness that has set in and become so general, and to practice the Christian virtues."[18]

It was said of Washington, in a sketch written by an American gentleman in London in 1779 that "he regularly attends divine service in his tent every morning and evening, and seems very fervent in his prayers."[19] General Knox was one among many who gave testimony of Washington frequently visiting secluded groves to lay the cause of his bleeding country at the throne of grace.

A number of people have recorded the story of how a Tory Quaker, Isaac Potts, came upon Washington while he was on his knees in prayer in the woods. Benson J. Lossing relates that Potts later made the following remarks to his wife:

If there is anyone on this earth whom the Lord will listen to, it is George Washington; and I feel a presentiment that under such a commander there can be no doubt of our eventually establishing our independence, and that God in his providence has willed it so.[20]

On May 6, 1982, President Reagan remarked on this event in his National Day of Prayer Proclamation:

The most sublime picture in American history is of George Washington on his knees in the snow at Valley Forge. That image personifies a people who know that it is not enough to depend on our own courage and goodness; we must also seek help from God, our Father and Preserver.

In this most difficult of times, General Washington constantly relied upon God and trusted in Him for success. God was faithful to answer his prayers, and through Washington He eventually established our independence and secured the beginning of the most free and prosperous nation the world has ever seen.

How did God answer Washington's prayer? One miracle occurred that winter which helped eliminate their near-starving situation. Bruce Lancaster relates the event as follows:

*One foggy morning the soldiers noticed the Schuylkill River
seemed to be boiling. The disturbance was caused by thousands
and thousands of shad which were making their way upstream
in an unusually early migration. With pitchforks and shovels, the
men plunged into the water, throwing the fish onto the banks.
Lee's dragoons rode their horses into the stream to keep the
shad from swimming on out of reach. Suddenly and wonderfully,
there was plenty of food for the army.*[21]

God's providence can again be seen as Baron Von Steuben, a
veteran Prussian soldier, came to Valley Forge on February 23 and
offered his services to the American Army. No one could have been
more valuable at the time, for he trained the men to move together as
a well-disciplined army.

His rigorous drilling and training of the troops gave them confidence in themselves as soldiers, even as Washington had given them
confidence as men. Not only had godly character and strength been
forged and tempered within the army, but military skill had also been
imparted to them at last.

Another providential event occurred that winter when France
became an ally to America. This meant much needed French money
and troops would begin to pour into the new nation. The Continental
Congress acknowledged this as the hand of God as they declared a
National Day of Thanksgiving on May 7.

In Washington's orders issued at Valley Forge, May 5, 1778, he
proclaimed:

*It having pleased the Almighty Ruler of the Universe propi-
tiously to defend the cause of the United American States, and finally by raising up a powerful friend among the Princes of the
earth, to establish our Liberty and Independence upon a lasting
foundation; it becomes us to set apart a day for gratefully acknowledging the Divine Goodness, and celebrating the event,
which we owe to His benign interposition.*[22]

The troops' survival, the molding of a disciplined army, Washington's amazing leadership, and all the miraculous occurrences

during the winter at Valley Forge can only be attributed to Almighty God. George Washington said following all this: "The hand of Providence has been so conspicuous in all this, that he must be worse than an infidel, and more than wicked, that has not gratitude enough to acknowledge his obligation."[23]

The Power of Christian Character

Washington was not very loud or talkative but he was very commanding in his words and presence. It has been said that the value and force of words depends upon who stands behind them; that is, upon the character of him who utters them. The following incident recorded by William Johnson reveals this to be true in Washington's life:

So far back as 1756 we find him endeavoring to impress upon the soldiers under his command a profound reverence for the name and the majesty of God, and repeatedly, in his public orders during the Revolution, the inexcusable offense of profaneness was rebuked.

On a certain occasion he had invited a number of officers to dine with him. While at table one of them uttered an oath. General Washington dropped his knife and fork in a moment, and in his deep undertone, and characteristic dignity and deliberation, said, 'I thought that we all supposed ourselves gentlemen.' He then resumed his knife and fork and went on as before. The remark struck like an electric shock, and, as was intended, did execution, as his observations in such cases were apt to do. No person swore at the table after that. When dinner was over, the officer referred to said to a companion that if the General had given him a blow over the head with his sword, he could have borne it, but that the home thrust which he received was too much — it was too much for a gentleman![24]

"King George"

As the Revolutionary War was coming to a close, a number of officers and soldiers began to grumble due to the many problems that existed in the new nation, including their lack of pay. As a solution to the problems that Congress seemed unable to resolve, many officers wanted to set up a monarchy making George Washington king. Col. Lewis Nicola proposed the idea to him in a letter in the Spring of 1782. It is possible that Washington could have become king, for the army and the people would have supported him. Washington's response reveals well the heart of this great man. In a letter to Colonel Lewis Nicola dated May 22, 1782, he wrote:

> *Sir, With a mixture of great surprise and astonishment, I have read with attention the sentiments you have submitted to my perusal. Be assured, Sir, no occurrence in the course of the war has given me more painful sensations, than your information of their being such ideas existing in the army, as you have expressed, and I must view with abhorrence and reprehend with severity. . .*
>
> *I am much at a loss to conceive what part of my conduct could have given encouragement to an address, which to me seems big with the greatest mischiefs, that can befall my country. If I am not deceived in the knowledge of my self, you could not have found a person to whom your schemes are more disagreeable. At the same time, in justice to my own feelings, I must add, that no man possesses a more sincere wish to see ample justice done to the army than I do; and as far as my powers and influence, in a constitutional way, extend, they shall be employed to the utmost of my abilities to effect it, should there be any occasion. Let me conjure you, then, if you have any regard for your country, concern for yourself or posterity, or respect for me, to banish these thoughts from your mind, and never communicate, as from yourself or any one else, a sentiment of like nature. I am, Sir, your most obedient servant.*[25]

Washington's response to the proposition of his being declared king was first, to rebuke the officer who suggested the idea, and then to look within himself to see if his heart or actions were in anyway in agreement with the idea, because he said as far as he knew, he was more against the idea than anyone.

Military Coup Averted

Many people have declared that George Washington was the American Revolution because without his leadership we would have probably not won our struggle for independence. He also thwarted an attempt to set up a monarchy as seen above. Shortly after the attempt to make him King, Washington was instrumental in stopping a military coup.

Ten months after Washington wrote to Nicola urging him to consider a constitutional means of resolving the problems facing them, a circular letter began appearing among the army calling for a military revolt. To avert national turmoil, Washington met with his officers on March 15, 1783, to hear their grievances and help them. He let them know, however, that he strongly opposed any civil discord. After talking at length, the officers were still sullen and silent. His plea had failed to persuade them. Finally, he reached into his pocket and pulled out a letter. He said there were Congressman anxious to help and he wanted to read a letter describing what was being planned. He held up the letter and tried to read it (the writing was small due to a paper shortage). Flexner writes:

> *The officers stirred impatiently in their seats, and then suddenly every heart missed a beat. Something was the matter with His Excellency. He seemed unable to read the paper. He paused in bewilderment. He fumbled in his waistcoat pocket. And then he pulled out something that only his intimates had seen him wear. A pair of glasses. He explained, "Gentlemen, you will permit me to put on my spectacles, for I have not only grown gray but almost blind in the service of my country."*
>
> *This simple statement achieved what all Washington's rhetoric and all his arguments had been unable to achieve. The officers were instantly in tears, and from behind the shining drops,*

their eyes looked with love at the commander who had led them all so far and long.

Washington quietly finished reading the congressman's letter, walked out of the hall, mounted his horse, and disappeared from the view of those who were staring from the window.[26]

All voted to support Washington for a peaceful, constructive approach to solve their problems (with one abstention). Historians point to this speech as pivotal. Jefferson wrote of Washington a year later:

The moderation and virtue of a single character have probably prevented this revolution from being closed, as most others have been, by a subversion of that liberty it was intended to establish.[27]

In addition to his influence mentioned above in the birth of the United States of America, Washington was also instrumental in the establishment of our new Republic under the Constitution. His role as President of the Constitutional Convention provided the stability necessary for the delegates to agree on a new constitution. After he was elected President of the convention he stated: ". . . Let us raise a standard to which the wise and the honest can repair; the event is in the hand of God."[28]

Commenting on Washington's immense influence in the convention, James Monroe wrote to Jefferson on July 12, 1788: "Be assured General Washington's influence carried this government." He also assured it's initial success by serving as the first President of the United States of America under the U.S. Constitution.

God's Preparation Principle

Washington's Christian character was evident throughout his life. As a young colonel in his early twenties, he commanded the Frontier Forces of Virginia during the French and Indian War. At the end of the war his officers wrote to him praising him and giving him much tribute (most of the officers were older than Washington). They ended the letter:

> *In you we place the most implicit confidence. Your presence is all that is needed to cause a steady firmness and vigor to actuate in every breast, despising the greatest dangers and thinking light of toils and hardships; while led on by the man we know and love.*

Christian strength and character were already manifest in his life while yet a young man. Washington gives us a good example of how God will prepare us so we may be able to accomplish His plans and fulfill the destiny He has for us. From his youth, George's parents taught him Christian qualities and helped develop Godly character within him. A few examples follow from William Wilbur's *The Making of George Washington:*

Obey Cheerfully

> *Father August was just as interested in obedience as Mother Mary was. He implemented his instruction by introducing George, at a very early age, to a few of the rules of conduct which he had learned at Appleby Grammar School in England.*

> *August was careful to differentiate between the Ten Commandments and the Appleby rules. ''The Ten Commandments'', he told the children, ''cover the major moral issues of life; there is nothing that equals them in definiteness or general application to our greatest problems. However, there are many every-day matters of lesser importance which the Ten Commandments do not cover.*

> *''At Appleby Grammar School in England, where I went to school as a very small boy, they had an excellent set of rules. These rules give us a very good guide to many minor aspects of our conduct.*

> *''Take the basic idea of obedience,''; he continued, ''it is not sufficient just to obey, you must learn to obey cheerfully.*

> *''That isn't always easy. For example, if your Mother corrects you, or I do — or you or told to do something over again, you may*

not like it. Then simple obedience is not enough; the way in which you except the correction becomes even more important than the obedience.

"One of the Appleby rules was designed to guide us in such a situation. It was, 'accept corrections thankfully.' It is an excellent rule, but one that isn't always easy to carry out. Spend some time thinking about it." Then Augustine stated the rule again, "Accept corrections thankfully."[29]

Think before You Speak

In teaching his children August had a quiet way of employing a simple practical illustration to explain his meaning and to drive home the lesson. For example, one day George lost his temper and blurted out an unwarranted, extreme remark because his sister Betty did not understand something he was trying to teach her. The quiet, kindly little girl was hurt, and started to cry.

By the time that Father August had grasped the situation George was very sorry for what he had done.

With some deliberateness August cut two branches from a bush, then said, "Here are two branches that I have cut from this bush. I want each of you to take a branch and break it into two separate sticks."

In a moment each child had two halves, each one frayed at the point where it had been broken.

"George," August then said, "can you put your two pieces back together, just as they were before you broke them?"

George put the frayed ends of his sticks together, but realized at once, the hopelessness of the task.

"Betty, can you put your stick back together, make it as good as new?"

The little girl put the ends together and then ruefully shook her head. "No, Father," she said, "I can't."

"You both agree," said August, "that you can't put them together. I can't either. No human being can. No matter how much we may wish to do so, we can never put the pieces back together. We cannot undo what we have done."

Then he went on. "These sticks illustrate a very important lesson. Just before I asked you to break them, George lost his temper and said something for which he is now very sorry.

"He wishes, oh so deeply, that he could somehow bring back those words, and unsay them. But no matter how sorry you may be George, you cannot recall those harsh, unwarranted terms. The words are something like the stick. It is broken into two parts and the two parts can never be put back together.

"One of the rules that I learned at Appleby Grammar School fits our problem very well. It was a simple one, 'Think before you speak.'

"Another Appleby rule also applies. It was 'Speak no injurious words, either in jest or in earnest.' "

August didn't need to say more.[30]

George's Size

George's size and strength were often commented on by well-meaning friends and neighbors. When such a thing happened Father August made comment like, "George, we are all very pleased that you are big and strong. But while you also, can be pleased, you should realize that you have no reason to preen yourself about it. My father was a big man. He passed on to me an unusually fine, powerful body. The Lord has seen fit to pass it on to you. You have not achieved it by your own thinking or working. It is entirely a gift from others.

"The same would be true," Father went on, "if someone should tell you, or your sister Betty, that you are handsome, have beautiful hair, or fine eyes, or a nice mouth. You have no cause to assume credit for any of these things. They are all a gift from your parents and your grandparents.

"But if someone should say, 'George is a very well-behaved boy!', 'How obedient and thoughtful George is!', or 'How considerate Betty is!' 'How helpful both George and Betty are!' If someone made comments like these, then the situation would be very different. Then you could be proud and somewhat satisfied because you, yourself, had created a situation that brought deserved praise.''

As a result of this kind of early training George acquired both modesty and humility, qualities which he displayed throughout his life.[31]

God not only prepared George through the training of his parents, but also used his experiences in life to assure that he was well equipped to fulfill his destiny. At the age of 16, George traveled to the western wilderness of Virginia to survey land for Lord Fairfax. While here he gained a personal knowledge of the country and a spirit of self-reliance which helped fit him for his later duties as a commander. At the age of 22 he delivered a message for the Governor of Virginia to the French forces that occupied forts on the frontier of the colonies. His experiences during this winter trek not only reveal the preparation of God, but also the protection of God. He was almost killed by an Indian, nearly drowned, and could have easily frozen to death, but was miraculously preserved.

Another incident of God's providential care occurred during the French and Indian War. Washington was second in command to British General Braddock as the British and Colonial troops marched out into the wilderness to drive the French off of British territory. Washington tried to warn Braddock that European military tactics would not work in the American frontier, but the General wouldn't listen and they were soundly defeated. Only Washington's fearlessness and leadership saved the day.

During this battle Gen. Braddock was slain. Washington had three bullets pass through his coat, one bullet through his hat, and two horses shot from under him, yet he escaped unhurt, ''although,'' as he later wrote, ''death was leveling my companions on every side of me.''[32]

Washington was fired upon numerous times from near point-blank range and remained unharmed. An Indian who took part in the battle later stated, "Washington was not born to be killed by a bullet! For I had seventeen fair fires at him, and after all could not bring him to the ground."

The chief and several of his Indians had singled out Washington to kill him, and when they couldn't they "concluded that he was under the protection of the Great Spirit, had a charmed life, and could not be slain in battle."[33]

In a letter to his brother, Washington wrote: "But by the all-powerful dispensations of Providence, I have been protected beyond all human probability or expectation."[34]

Fifteen years later Washington met an Indian Chief who was at this battle and had given orders to his men to kill Washington. Upon witnessing "a power mightier far than we," who "shielded him from harm," the chief said: "The Great Spirit protects that man, and guides his destinies—he will become the chief of nations, and a people yet unborn will hail him as the founder of a mighty empire."[35]

Rev. Samuel Davies preached a sermon on August 17, 1755, wherein he cites the preservation of young Washington. He spoke of "that heroic youth, Colonel Washington, whom I cannot but hope Providence has hitherto preserved in so signal a manner for some important service to his country."[36]

As commander of the Virginia Forces from age 23 to 26, he learned struggles of securing men, money, goods, etc. which is exactly what he faced during the Revolutionary War. Irving writes:

In the hand of Heaven he stood, to be shaped and trained for its great purpose; and every trial and vicissitude of his early life but fitted him to cope with one or other of the varied and multifarious duties of his future destiny.

After General Lee said that Washington was "first in war, first in peace, first in the hearts of his countrymen," he went on to observe: "The finger of an overruling Providence, pointing at Washington as the man designed by Heaven to lead us in war and in peace, was not mistaken. He laid the foundations of our policy in the unerring principles of morality based on religion."[37] God's providential preparation of Washington was instrumental in bringing liberty to America and the world.

Section 3

William Penn and the City of Brotherly Love

The Beginning of Pennsylvania

Pennsylvania was established in 1681 when Quaker William Penn was given a tract of land between New York and Maryland by the King of England in payment for a debt the Crown owed to William's father, Admiral William Penn. Having experienced much persecution for his Christian beliefs, Penn asked for the land desiring to plant a colony *"which should open its doors to every kindred"* and be a refuge for men of all creeds. He wanted it to be a model state — *"a holy experiment"* — in which his ideals could be realized; an example of toleration and liberty on a grand scale.

After Penn received the charter for Pennsylvania he wrote that *"...my God that has given it me through many difficultys, will, I believe bless and make it the seed of a nation."*[1]

William suggested the name Sylvania (meaning *woods*) for the colony but King Charles added Penn in honor of William's father. Concerning receiving the charter for Pennsylvania, William wrote:

> For my country, I eyed the Lord in the obtaining of it, and more was I drawn inward to look to him and to owe it to his hand and power, than to any other way. I have so obtained it, and desire that I may not be unworthy of his love, but do that which may answer his kind providence, and serve his truth and people; that an example may be set up to the nations; there may be room there, though not here, for such an holy experiment.[2]

Penn and his colony did set an example for the nations and proved to be a great blessing to many. Pennsylvania played a great part in bringing liberty to America and the world. As he desired, he built "a free colony for all mankind."

There are numerous statues and memorials in Philadelphia and Pennsylvania that honor William Penn. The most famous is Calder's bronze statue atop the City Hall in Penn Square, Philadelphia.

The Life of William Penn

In December, 1668, William Penn was thrown in jail for expressing his religious views. While imprisoned for over eight months he wrote the book, *No Cross, No Crown*, in which he states that *"Christ's Cross is Christ's way to Christ's Crown."* Penn's life is a great example of one who bore the cross and, therefore, did bear the crown. He brought the crown to millions more as well.

William was born on October 24, 1644, in London England, the son of Sir William Penn, a wealthy Admiral in the King's navy. William had a good moral upbringing and education and was instilled with Puritan convictions. His father had high hopes that his namesake would follow in his footsteps, benefiting from the wealth and prestige and noble friends he had obtained. When William began associating as a young man with the new religious sect called Quakers, it was more than the Admiral could bear. These people, whom the Admiral regarded as simple and ignorant Puritan fanatics, were leading his son William astray.

Penn first heard Quaker Thomas Loe speak as a teenager living with his parents in Ireland. Penn forgot Loe's message as he pursued his education, first at Christ Church College in Oxford, and then in France, and then more study of law back home in London. In 1665 a plague drove him to his father's country estate in Ireland. One day while he was there he happened to hear Thomas Loe preach at a Quaker meeting. *"On this crucial day the old man preached from the text: 'There is a faith that overcometh the world, and there is faith that is overcome by the world.' He made the greatest convert of his career, for the young gentleman doubted no longer. On that day William Penn definitely and finally became a Quaker.'*[3]

Penn's Cross

From the beginning Penn had many crosses to bear. Shortly after his conversion, Penn was at a Friends gathering where a soldier burst into the room to stop the meeting. Unlike most Quakers, Penn was not the passive type, so he grabbed the soldier and started to toss him down the stairs. Other Friends had to stop him and remind him that Quakers did not use violence. Penn reluctantly released the soldier.

Everyone was arrested and thrown in jail. Penn did not suffer in silence like hundreds of Quakers who had been jailed before him. He dashed off letters to his father's friend, a leader in the province, reminding him their only "crime" was choosing their own religion. As a result they were released, but Penn's father was notified of his son's actions and associates, and he asked William to return to London.

In England Penn openly and actively identified with the Friends by writing and speaking on their behalf. When William met with his father, the Admiral tried everything to get William to give up his Friends and his new found religion, and to continue on a good career and follow in his father's steps. At one point in their lively discussion, the Admiral said he was going to get down on his knees and pray that William would not be a Quaker. Upon hearing this William ran to the window and threatened to jump out if he prayed such a thing. William's mother was helpless in calming them down. She was thankful that a friend came by to visit at this moment which stopped the hysterical scene.

After William kept speaking at Friends meetings, his father kicked him out of the house and said he would leave his money and large holdings to someone else. This did not change William's mind.

In 1668 Thomas Loe died. On his death bed Loe spoke to William Penn:

> *Bear thy cross, and stand faithful to God; then He will give thee an everlasting crown of glory, that shall not be taken from thee. There is no other way which shall prosper, than that which the holy men of old have walked in. God hath brought immortality to light, and life immortal is felt. Glory, Glory to Him! for He is worthy of it. His love overcomes my heart, nay, my cup runs over: glory be to His name forever.[4]*

In this same year, Penn published *"The Sandy Foundation Shaken,"* and in December he went to the tower on account of it. About his imprisonment in the Tower, Penn wrote:

> *I was committed the beginning of December, and was not discharged till the Fall of the Leaf following; wanting about fourteen days of nine months.*

> *As I saw very few, so I saw them but seldom, except my own Father and Dr. Stillingfleet, the present Bishop of Worcester. The one came as my relation, the other at the Kings command to endeavour my change of judgment. But as I told him, and he told the King that the Tower was the worst argument in the world to convince me; for whoever was in the wrong, those who used force for Religion could never be in the right...[5]*

Penn later wrote Lord Arlington that this action might make hypocrites but not converts.[6]

The Bishop told Penn he must take back what he had written or stay in prison. Penn's response was: *"My prison shall be my grave before I will budge a jot; for I owe my conscience to no mortal man."*[7]

It was during this imprisonment that Penn wrote *No Cross, No Crown*, probably his most famous work.

Penn was released from the Tower in August of 1669. In September he went to Cork, Ireland, to his father's estate. He found the Friends "under general persecution and those of the city of Cork almost all in prison."[8] He immediately took up their cause and labored to get them out of prison, and succeeded in getting an order-in-council on June 4, 1670, for the release of Quaker prisoners in Ireland.

His father had become ill, so soon after this Penn returned to England to be with him. On August 14, 1670, Penn and fellow Friend, William Mead, went to a Quaker meeting in Gracechurch Street, London. The meeting house had been padlocked by the authorities, so Penn preached in the street to the group that remained. Penn and Mead were arrested for this, and after two weeks in that "noisome and stinking" prison, they went to trial on September 1. Later, William would publish a complete report on the trial.[9]

Penn and Meade were charged with unlawful assembly by force of arms, disturbing the peace, conspiring to preach, and terrorizing the people. After pleading "not guilty," the prisoners were put aside and forced to wait the rest of the day while other cases were heard. Court was then adjourned until the third.

Upon entering the court, well-meaning police, wishing to avert problems for the defendants and knowing that Quakers were conscientiously opposed to doing so themselves, took off Penn's and Meade's hats so that they would comply with court policy. Upon approaching the bench, orders were given to have their hats put on, and then a fine of forty marks was laid to each man for contempt of court. William said that since the bench was responsible for their hats being on, the bench should be fined.

During proceedings, William explained to the jury that they were guilty of nothing but worshiping God and asked the bench to let the jury and himself know upon what law he was prosecuted. The bench replied that it was upon the common law. William then asked, *"Where is that common law?"* The answer being it was too difficult to produce, William responded: *"If it be common, it should not be so hard to produce."*

In defense of common rights and individual liberties, Penn quoted Lord Coke's *Institutes*, which he had studied in school, even mentioning page numbers. This infuriated the judges, mayor, and recorder, who shouted to a guard to take William away and throw him into the bale-dock, which was a small pen partitioned off in the courtroom.

As he was being hauled away, Penn exclaimed: *"I plead for the fundamental laws of England. . . . If the ancient fundamental laws which relate to liberty and property. . . are not. . . maintained and observed. . . our liberties are openly to be invaded, our wives to be ravished, our children slaved, our families ruined, and our estates led away."*

Meade then began to defend himself with the same insightfulness as Penn, which caused the bench's rage to increase to the point where one judge bitterly remarked to Meade: *"You deserve to have your tongue cut out."*

Meade was also ordered to the bale-dock. Then the recorder began giving the charge to the jury, pointing out how the defendants were surely guilty. As this was occurring, Penn climbed to the top of the bale-dock wall and shouted to the court and jury that the proceedings of the court were *"void of all law, on offering to give the jury their charge in the absence of the prisoners. I say it is directly opposite to and destructive of the undoubted right of every English prisoner,"* and he quoted Coke's *Institutes.*

The Recorder screamed: *"Pull that fellow down! Pull him down!"*

He then ordered them to be thrown into "the Hole," a stinking place of confinement in Newgate Prison.

After some hours of deliberations, the jury reached a verdict. The only thing the defendants were guilty of was speaking in Gracechurch Street. This infuriated the judges who began to menace the jury. One observer said the mayor and recorder *"exceeded the bounds of all reason and civility."* The bench ordered the jury to be *"locked up without meat, drink, fire, and tobacco"* until *"we have a verdict that the court will accept."*

As the jury was being removed to their chambers, William cried out to them: *"You are Englishmen, mind your privilege, give not away your right."*

After spending the night without food or drink or proper accommodation, the jury brought back the same defiant verdict. The bench would not accept it and began threatening the jury. William declared: *"It is intolerable that my jury should be menaced. What hope is there of ever having justice done, when juries are threatened and their verdicts rejected?"*

The Mayor roared: *"Stop his mouth! Jailer, bring fetters and stake him to the ground."*

The jury was forced to spend another night without food, fire, or other accommodations until they brought back the *right* verdict. The next morning, their resolve had not weakened, but had grown stronger. Their verdict: not guilty of anything. The approval of the spectators in the courtroom was matched by the disapproval of the judges, who fined the jury forty marks each, and ordered their imprisonment until it was paid.

William Penn bore the cross in many other ways as he determined to stand for truth and follow the leading of God. He went on many missionary trips, often preached at Quaker meetings, and worked unceasingly to get Quakers and religious dissenters out of jail. He faced more imprisonments, persecution, and ostracism, but gladly endured them all. Since he gladly bore the cross, he also received a crown.

Penn's Crown

Reconciliation with Father

After the above mentioned trial, Penn was placed in jail, not to be released until his fine was paid. To this he refused, but some unknown friend paid it for him and he was released on September 7. His father was quite sick and so William was glad to be able to go and see him. The Admiral died nine days later. During this time he and his son were completely reconciled. He came to admire the convictions of his son. Shortly before his death, the Admiral told William: *"Son, William, let nothing in this world tempt you to wrong your conscience."*[10]

The Admiral not only left William most of his large estate, but also obtained assurances from his friends, King Charles II and the Duke of York (who would become King James II), that they would watch out for his son. This would prove to be of great help, not only for William, but also for the multitude of those who benefited from Penn's colony and work.

Precedent Trial

The September trial was reviewed by higher authorities and became a precedent in English history for the rights of juries. There is a William Penn Memorial Tablet in the Sessions House on the site of Old Bailey, London, England commemorating the trial and courage of Penn, Mead, and the jury. The engraving concludes with these words: ''The case of these Jurymen was reviewed on a Writ of Habeas Corpus and Chief Justice Vaughan delivered the opinion of the Court which established 'The Right of Juries' to give their Verdict according to their convictions.''[11]

Religious Freedom

One historian wrote: *''The sufferings and the death under persecution of the Quakers marked the end of grand-scale persecution for conscience sake in the English-speaking world.''*[12]

William Penn was instrumental in the fight to secure liberty of conscience for all men. The principles he advocated were victorious in the Act of Toleration Parliament passed in 1689.

♧ Welcome Park

Located across 2nd Street from the City Tavern is Welcome Park, which was the site of William Penn's house in Philadelphia. Displays trace much of the early history of Penn and Philadelphia.

Establishment of Pennsylvania

It has been mentioned that Penn set up an example of toleration and liberty on a grand scale in his colony of Pennsylvania. In addition, Penn worked to establish a government in the colony where the power rested in the people under God. After obtaining a charter from King Charles II, where Penn was made Governor and Proprietor of Pennsylvania, he revealed his designs in a letter to the scattered Swedish, Dutch, and English settlers already in the colony:

> *My Friends, I wish you all happiness, here and hereafter. I have to let you know that it hath pleased God in His Providence to cast you within my lot and care. It is a business that, though I never undertook before, yet God has given me an understanding of my duty, and an honest mind to do it uprightly.... [Y]ou are now fixt, at the mercy of no Governour that comes to make his fortune great; you shall be governed by laws of your own making, and live a free, and, if you will, a sober and industrious people. I shall not usurp the right of any, or oppress his person; God has furnished me with a better resolution, and has given me his grace to keep it.... And so I beseech God to direct you in the way of righteousness, and therein prosper you and your children after you. April 8, 1681, London.*[13]

Penn worked more than a year on formulating a constitution or *Frame of Government* for Pennsylvania, which was adopted in England on April 25, 1682. The preface to the *Frame of Government* contains Penn's best expression of his ideas of government, and all people would profit by knowing them. Following is an excerpt:

> *Governments like clocks, go from the motion men give them; and as governments are made and moved by men, so by them they are ruined too. Wherefore governments rather depend upon men, than men upon governments. Let men be good, and the government cannot be bad; if it will be ill, they will cure it. . .*

> *Some say, let us have good laws, and no matter for the men who execute them: but let them consider, that though good laws do well, good men do better: for good laws may want good men, and be abolished or evaded by ill men; but good men will never want good laws, nor suffer ill ones. It is true, good laws have some awe upon ill ministers, but that is where they have not power to escape or abolish them, and the people are generally wise and good: but a loose and depraved people love laws and an administration like themselves. That, therefore, which makes*

a good constitution, must keep it, viz: men of wisdom and virtue, qualities, that because they descend not with worldly inheritances, must be carefully propagated by a virtuous education of youth.[14]

From the beginning of his colony, and throughout his life, William Penn not only dealt justly with the Quakers and other Europeans who came to settle there, but also with the Indians who lived in the area. He had obtained the land from the King but paid the Indians for it as well. *"It would be an ill argument to convert to Christianity, to expel, instead of purchasing them out of, those countries,"*[15] William said. Fair trade, equal and just treatment, and freedom of movement and settlement were part of the treaty of friendship Penn entered into with the Indians at Shackamaxon. To the Indians, William declared:

> *We meet on the broad pathway of good faith and good will; no advantage shall be taken on either side, but all shall be openness and love. . . . We are the same as if one man's body was to be divided into two parts; we are all one flesh and blood.*[16]

The Indians replied:

> *We will live in love with Onas [Penn's Indian name] and his children as long as the creeks and rivers run and while the sun, moon, and stars endure.*[17]

This was the only treaty with the Indians "that was not ratified by an oath and that was never broken." Due to Penn's applying Christian virtues in his relations with the natives, "no drop of Quaker blood was ever shed by an Indian."[18]

A modest monument at Penn Treaty Park commemorates Penn's treaty with the Indians. Here was the site of the famous treaty elm, blown down in 1810. Benjamin West captured the scene of the treaty very vividly in his painting, *"Penn's Treaty with the Indians."* West's own replica of this painting can be seen in Old City Hall next to Independence Hall.

Penn's Death

William Penn died in England in 1718 at the age of 74. Many people came to his burial service and many others sent memorials. Numerous Friends in Pennsylvania sent a memorial testimony that ended with these words:

> ... *the love of God remained with him, and his sense thereof was frequently strong and evident, and, we doubt not, the blessing of the Almighty was his Omega. So that we have assured hope... immortality is given him by our Lord Jesus, and as he faithfully bore the cross, the crown, which was his hope, and long since is his eye, is his possession; and his soul received into that bliss prepared and appointed for the righteous.*[19]

The man who bore the cross throughout his life, now received the eternal crown.

Philadelphia, City of Brotherly Love

Philadelphia was founded in 1682 by William Penn. Due to the tolerant spirit of Penn and his followers, the city grew rapidly and attracted settlers from many countries and of many Christian sects and denominations (especially, in the first years, Quakers, Moravians, Mennonites, and Dunkers). Over 7000 emigrants arrived in Philadelphia in the first three years, most from Great Britain and the German provinces. The character and skill of these early settlers caused the city and state to flourish in commerce, industry, education, science, and civil and religious freedom.

Philadelphia and her citizens played a leading part in many of the great events of early America. During the struggle for independence the First and Second Continental Congress met here, plus she served as the seat of government throughout the war, except when the British occupied the city. The Declaration of Independence was written, signed, and adopted in Philadelphia; the Constitutional Convention met here in 1787 and drafted the U.S. Constitution; the national capital was located here from 1790 to 1800; Washington and Adams were inaugurated President of the United States in Philadelphia.

Benjamin Franklin is Philadelphia's most famous citizen. He helped establish in the city the first public library in the U.S. in 1731, the first hospital in the U.S. (1752), the first volunteer fire department in America (1737), the University of Pennsylvania, and much more. Other well known citizens include Robert Morris, the financier of the American Revolution, Betsy Ross, who sowed the first American flag, and astronomer and scientist David Rittenhouse.

Philadelphia is a "city of firsts." In addition to those mentioned above, the list includes: the first public protest in America against slavery was presented in 1688 in the Germantown Friends' Meeting House; the first Bible in America, in a European language (German), was printed in Germantown in 1743 (this was 40 years before an English Bible was printed in the colonies); the first daily newspaper in the U.S. has its home here, a lineal descendant of Franklin's weekly, founded in 1728; the first bank in North America, chartered in 1781; the first Law School in U.S., 1790; the first U.S. mint, 1792; the first magazine, 1741; and many, many more.

The five central squares of Philadelphia were the first public parks in America, being dedicated to the people in 1682. These include Penn Square (originally called Center Square), occupied by City Hall, and Washington, Franklin, Rittenhouse, and Logan Squares. Many other parks are found in Philadelphia including the largest landscaped city park in the world, Fairmont Park. The most famous park is Independence National Historic Park which contains Independence Hall and the Liberty Bell.

In a book celebrating the 150th anniversary of the signing of the Declaration of Independence, the authors wrote of Philadelphia:

> *Here still stands the halls in which were enunciated the principles of human rights that gave birth to free institutions. Here are the very houses where the patriotic men of old assembled and first framed the legislative foundations of free government. Here are the historic scenes where the Revolutionary leaders*

and soldiers fought and sacrificed for the principles and institutions at stake. Here are still visible mansions, sites, and relics that remind us that not brick and mortar but sentiment and character build a nation.[20]

☖ *Carpenters' Hall*

The First Continental Congress met in Carpenters' Hall on September 5, 1774. The Provincial Assembly of Pennsylvania was in session at the State House when representatives from all the colonies, except Georgia, gathered in Philadelphia, and so they were unable to meet there. When the Carpenters' Company offered the use of their fine guild hall, the Congress accepted.

This assembly marked the beginning of the Union of the States, as this was the first time representatives from most of the states met together (twelve states participated). After presenting their credentials and setting rules of conduct, the members passed the following resolve on Tuesday, September 6:

That the reverend Mr. Duché be desired to open the Congress tomorrow morning with prayers, at the Carpenter's Hall at nine o'clock.[21]

The Journal of Wednesday, September 7, 1774, has this entry:

Agreeable to the resolve of yesterday, the meeting was opened with prayers by the reverend Mr. Duché.

Voted, That the thanks of the Congress be given to Mr. Duché, by Mr. Cushing and Mr. Ward, for performing divine service, and for the excellent prayer, which he composed and delivered on the occasion.[22]

The effect of that excellent prayer was recorded by John Adams, a delegate from Massachusetts, in a letter he wrote to his wife on September 16:

When the Congress first met, Mr. Cushing made a Motion, that it should be opened with Prayer. It was opposed by Mr. Jay of N. York and Mr. Rutledge of South Carolina, because we were so divided in religious Sentiments, some Episcopalians, some Quakers, some Anabaptists, some Presbyterians and some Congregationalists, so that We could not join in the same Act of Worship. — Mr. S. Adams arose and said he was no Bigot, and could hear a Prayer from a Gentleman of Piety and Virtue, who was at the same Time a Friend to his Country. He was a Stranger in Phyladephia, but had heard that Mr. Duché (Dushay they pronounce it) deserved that Character, and therefore he moved that Mr. Duché, an episcopal Clergyman, might be desired, to read Prayers to the Congress, tomorrow Morning. The Motion was seconded and passed in the Affirmative. Mr. Randolph our President, waited on Mr. Duché, and received for Answer that if his Health would permit, he certainly would. Accordingly next Morning he appeared with his Clerk and in his Pontificallibus, and read several Prayers, in the established Form; and then read the Collect for the seventh day of September, which was the Thirty fifth Psalm. — You must remember this was the next Morning after we heard the horrible Rumour, of the Cannonade of Boston.— I never saw a greater Effect upon an Audience. It seemed as if Heaven had ordained that Psalm to be read on that Morning.

"After this Mr. Duché, unexpected to every Body struck out into an extemporary Prayer, which filled the Bosom of every Man present. I must confess I never heard a better Prayer or one, so well pronounced. Episcopalian as he is, Dr. Cooper himself never prayed with such fervour, such Ardor, such Earnestness and Pathos, and in Language so elegant and sublime—for America, for the Congress, for The Province of Massachusetts Bay, and especially the Town of Boston. It has had an excellent Effect upon every Body here.[23]

Silas Deane described this event in a letter to his wife on September 7:

The Congress met and opened with a prayer made by the Reverend Mr. Duché which it was worth riding one hundred miles to hear. He read the lessons of the day. . . [then] prayed without book about ten minutes so pertinently, with such fervency, purity, and sublimity of style and sentiment. . . [that] even Quakers shed tears.

An early painting of the *First Prayer in Congress* shows George Washington, Patrick Henry, Richard Henry Lee, John Jay, and many others kneeling in prayer, and by their side there stands, bowed in reverence, the Puritan Patriots of New England. (A depiction of this painting can be seen in the stained-glass Liberty Window at Christ Church, Philadelphia.)

During their two months of secret sessions they discussed their disagreements with the King's government; they adopted a Declaration of Rights, stating clearly how their rights had been violated by eleven different acts passed since the accession of George III; they framed memorials to the King and the English people; and they formed an association to put a stop to all trade with England until the tyrannical laws were repealed. Before adjourning they provided for the Continental Congress to meet again the next Spring.

🔔 *Independence Hall*

Independence Hall was built as the State House for the Commonwealth of Pennsylvania. The Legislature first met in this building in October, 1736. Ben Franklin served as the clerk for this assembly. The East Room, now known as the Declaration Chamber, was finished in 1743. It was here that George Washington accepted his appointment as General and Commander-in-Chief of the Continental Army, June 16, 1775; the Continental Congress adopted the Declaration of Independence, July 4, 1776, signing it August 2 and thereafter; the Congress adopted the American flag, June 14, 1777; the Articles of Confederation were drawn up and signed by the first eight States, July 9, 1778; the Constitutional Convention framed the *Constitution* between May and September in 1787 and then sent to the states for ratification.

Many speeches and orations have been given inside and outside of Independence Hall. From the steps of this "temple of freedom" John Nixon, on July 8, 1776, gave the first public reading of the Declaration of Independence to thousands who had gathered. From the same spot Samuel Adams pronounced an oration on the great event, in which he said:

> *Brethren and fellow-countrymen! If it was ever granted to mortals to trace the designs of Providence and to interpret its manifestations in favor of their cause, we may, with humility of soul, cry out, "Not unto us, not unto us, but to thy name be praise."[24]*

The Constitutional Convention

The two most significant events that occurred in Independence Hall were the adoption of the Declaration of Independence in 1776 and the Constitutional Convention of 1787.[25] In the summer of 1787, fifty-five representatives from 12 states met together in this building and constructed a new form of government for America. This United States Constitution is possibly, next to the Holy Bible, the most important document ever written for the benefit of mankind.

The delegates at the Constitutional Convention had to overcome many difficulties in framing this document, so much so, that they called it miraculous. Benjamin Franklin wrote:

> *Our General Convention. . . when it formed the new Federal Constitution, [was]. . . influenced, guided, and governed by that omnipotent and beneficent Ruler in whom all. . . live, and move, and have their being.[26]*

James Madison wrote:

> *It is impossible for the man of pious reflection not to perceive in it [the Constitutional Convention] a finger of that Almighty hand.[27]*

The "Rising Sun" Chair

On September 17 thirty-nine delegates signed the Constitution, sending it to the states for ratification. Skousen writes of this event:

It seems that James Madison, who had taken the most copious notes of the entire convention, wanted to watch the expressions on the face of each of the delegates as he signed the Constitution. Madison therefore placed his chair immediately adjacent to the table on which the famous document lay.

The most elderly member of the convention was 81-year-old Benjamin Franklin, who was suffering from a bladder stone larger than an egg, and this caused him excruciating pain whenever he tried to walk. Nevertheless, the old man shuffled slowly up to the table on which the Constitution was spread out awaiting his signature.

Ever since 1754, Benjamin Franklin had been pleading, petitioning, and struggling to get the thirteen little colonial republics to form into a brotherhood of perpetual union so they could someday grow into a mighty nation.

No doubt all of these years of struggle, frustration, and numerous failures must have crowded into the memory of Benjamin Franklin as he approached the table. For a moment he hesitated, and then the stoop-shouldered patriarch of the convention put his feathered quill to the sacred document. Slowly and carefully he wrote his name with a firm hand. As he did so, James Madison wrote in his notes, "The old man wept."

After this Franklin, referring to a picture of the sun on the back of Washington's chair, said: *"I have watched that sun on the president's chair and wondered if rising or setting — now I am happy to know it is a rising sun!"*[28]

The original "rising sun" chair and desk can be seen in the Declaration Chamber.

Concerning the completed work of the Constitutional Convention, historian John Fiske writes: *"Thus after four months of anxious*

toil, through the whole of a scorching Philadelphia summer, after
earnest but sometimes bitter discussion, in which more than once the
meeting had seemed on the point of breaking up, a colossal work had
at last been accomplished, the results of which were powerfully to
affect the whole future career of the human race.'[29]

♫ *Congress Hall*

In 1790 construction of Congress Hall was completed. From that
year until 1800 it served as the home of the United States Congress,
while the Capitol in Washington, D.C. was being built. The House
of Representatives met on the main floor and the Senate met upstairs.

Washington was inaugurated President for a second term in this
building in 1793. Here in 1797 John Adams took the oath as President
and Jefferson as Vice-President. Three states were admitted to the
Union during this time: Vermont (1791), Kentucky (1792), and
Tennessee (1796). In these chambers the Bill of Rights was added to
the Constitution, the Navy was established, the First Bank of the U.S.
was chartered, and the United States Mint was established.

♫ *The Liberty Bell*

The Liberty Bell was first cast in England in 1752 by order of the
Legislature of Pennsylvania in 1751 to commemorate the fiftieth
anniversary of the Charter of Privileges signed by William Penn in
1701. This charter insured the freedom of Pennsylvania citizens, and
so an appropriate scripture was selected to be placed on the bell —
Lev. 25:10.

The Bell was hung in the Hall Tower at the State House in
Philadelphia and cracked on its initial sounding in 1753. It was recast
twice by Pass and Stowe before it had a clear and pleasant sound. As
far as the Superintendents of the State House knew, this was the first
time a colonial foundry had ever attempted to cast a bell, especially

of this size. The bell weighed 2080 pounds, was twelve feet in circumference around the lip, seven and one-half feet around the crown, and three feet high.

The Liberty Bell contains the following inscription:

> *By order of the Assembly of the Province of Pennsylvania for the State House in Philadelphia, 1752.*

And underneath this:

> *Proclaim Liberty throughout all the land, unto all the inhabitants thereof. Lev. XXV X*

Watson, in his *Annals of Philadelphia*, says of the motto on the bell: *"That it was adopted from Scripture (Lev. 25, 10) may to many be still more impressive, as being also the voice of God — that great Arbiter, by whose signal providences we afterwards attained to that 'liberty' and self-government which bid fair to emancipate our whole continent, and in time to influence and meliorate the condition of the subjects of arbitrary government throughout the civilized world!'*[30]

This inscription on America's most venerated symbol reminds us that civil liberty is a result of biblical truth infused in the life of a nation. Noah Webster stated:

> *Almost all the civil liberty now enjoyed in the world owes its origin to the principles of the Christian religion. . . . The religion which has introduced civil liberty, is the religion of Christ and his apostles, which enjoins humility, piety, and benevolence; which acknowledges in every person a brother, or a sister, and a citizen with equal rights. This is genuine Christianity, and to this we owe our free constitutions of government.*[31]

The Liberty Bell was intended to be rung on public occasions, such as the meetings of the Assembly and courts. However, it was rung at numerous other times, especially for fires and church events, so much so that many people living nearby made complaints. On July 8, 1776, the Liberty Bell called together its most important meeting, the assembly of the citizens to hear the first public reading of the

Declaration of Independence, and then led the celebration by its ringing.

On September 18, 1777, the Liberty Bell was taken to Allentown, Pennsylvania to prevent the British from capturing it and melting it down for use as a cannon. It was hidden for almost a year in Zion Reformed Church.

For 82 years the Liberty Bell tolled important events in the beginning of America. On July 8, 1835, the Bell cracked while being rung in memory of Chief Justice John Marshall of Virginia who had died on July 6.

🔔 *Benjamin Franklin Museum*

The Benjamin Franklin Museum is located at the site of Franklin's third home. As was stated earlier, Benjamin Franklin helped to make Philadelphia a "city of firsts." He was certainly Philadelphia's first citizen and, next to Washington, was the most well-known American at the time of our independence. Franklin speaks of his humble beginnings in his *Autobiography*:

...Having emerged from the poverty and obscurity in which I was born and bred, to a state of affluence and some degree of reputation in the world, and having gone so far through life with a considerable share of felicity, the conducing means I made use of, which with the blessing of God so well succeeded, my posterity may like to know, as they may find some of them suitable to their own situations, and therefore to be imitated.

...I was the youngest son of the youngest son for five generations back.... Josiah, my father married young, and carried his wife with three children into New England, about 1682.... By the same wife he had four children more born there, and by a second wife ten more, in all seventeen; of which I remember thirteen sitting at one time at his table, who all grew up to be men and women, and married; I was the youngest son, and the youngest child but two, and was born in Boston...

Franklin's industry was evident from his youth. He wrote:

This library afforded me the means of improvement by constant study, for which I set apart an hour or two each day, and thus repair'd in some degree the loss of the learned education my father once intended for me. Reading was the only amusement I allow'd myself. I spent no time in taverns, games, or frolicks of any kind; and my industry in my business continu'd as indefatigable as it was necessary. I was indebted for my printing-house; I had a young family coming on to be educated, and I had to contend with for business, two printers who were established in the place before me. My circumstances, however, grew daily easier. My original habits of frugality continuing, and my father having, among his instructions to me when a boy, frequently repeated a proverb of Solomon: "Seest thou a man diligent in his calling, he shall stand before kings, he shall not stand before mean men," I from thence considered industry, as a means of obtaining wealth and distinction, which encourag'd me, tho' I did not think that I should ever literally stand before kings, which, however, has since happened; for I have stood before five, and even had the honor of sitting down with one, the king of Denmark, to dinner.[32]

Many people today reject the idea that America was founded as a Christian nation, citing that some of the founders were not Christians. They usually mention Benjamin Franklin and Thomas Jefferson. While Franklin was not an orthodox believer (not personally embracing the Deity of Christ), he was by no means an atheist or secularist or anti-Christian. A deist does not accurately describe Franklin either (where a deist is someone who believes in a god who is detached from His creation). He attended church, promoted Biblical standards of conduct, was friends with many pastors and Christian leaders, and generally had a Biblical worldview. He could be called a Biblical theist, in that he believed in one God (as described in the Bible), Who was actively involved in, and watched over, His creation. His words calling the Constitutional Convention to prayer in June 1787, reveal his understanding "that God governs in the affairs of man." He said that "if a sparrow cannot fall to the ground without

His notice, is it probable that an empire can rise without His aid? We have been assured, Sir, in the Sacred Writings that except the Lord build the house, they labor in vain that build it. I firmly believe this"[33]

In debating qualifications for congressmen in the Constitutional Convention, Franklin referenced the Bible. He said, "we should remember the character which the Scripture requires in Rulers, that they should be men hating covetousness."[34]

Franklin helped establish the first hospital in the United States, the Pennsylvania Hospital chartered in 1751. The cornerstone of the original building, erected in 1755, has this inscription by Franklin:

> *In the year of Christ MDCCLV, George the Second happily reigning (for he sought the happiness of his people) Philadelphia flourishing (for its inhabitants were publick spirited) this building, by the bounty of the government and of many private persons, was piously founded for the relief of the sick and miserable; may the God of Mercies bless the undertaking.*

Franklin also helped establish the University of Pennsylvania in 1751. It was one of the first colleges not started by a denomination, but its laws reflect its Christian character. Consider the first two *Laws, relating to the Moral Conduct, and Orderly Behaviour, of the Students and Scholars of the University of Pennsylvania* (from 1801):

> *1. None of the students or scholars, belonging to this seminary, shall make use of any indecent or immoral language: whether it consist in immodest expressions; in cursing and swearing; or in exclamations which introduce the name of GOD, without reverence, and without necessity.*

> *2. None of them shall, without a good and sufficient reason, be absent from school, or late in his attendance; more particularly at the time of prayers, and of the reading of the Holy Scriptures.*[35]

Toward the end of his life, Benjamin Franklin wrote a reply to Thomas Paine seeking to dissuade him from publishing a work of an irreligious tendency which spoke against Christian fundamentals. He told Paine that no good would come from his publishing his ideas, writing that *"He that spits against the wind, spits in his own face."* Franklin pointed out to Paine that *"perhaps you are indebted to. . . your religious education, for the habits of virtue upon which you now justly value yourself. . . . Among us it is not necessary, as among the Hottentots, that a youth, to be raised into the company of men, should prove his manhood by beating his mother."* Only evil would result if Paine's ideas succeeded, for, as Franklin wrote, *"If men are so wicked with religion, what would they be if without it."*[36]

Franklin may have not personally accepted all the tenets of Christianity, but he greatly approved of the effects of Christianity in America. Commenting on the impact of the preaching of George Whitefield during the First Great Awakening, around the year 1739, he wrote:

> *It was wonderful to see the change soon made in the manners of our inhabitants. From being thoughtless or indifferent about religion, it seem'd as if all the world were growing religious, so one could not walk thro' the town in an evening without hearing psalms sung in different families of every street.*[37]

⌂ *Old City Hall / Supreme Court*

This building was the home of the first United States Supreme Court, which met here from 1791-1800. **John Jay** presided as the first Chief Justice. Like many of the Founders, Jay lived a productive Christian life.

Jay, born in New York City on December 12, 1745, came from a wealthy family. He received two degrees from King's College (now Columbia), was admitted to the bar, and successfully practiced law for six years. He first began his quarter of a century of public service in 1774 when he was elected to the First Continental Congress. In 1777 he wrote New York state's first constitution, and shortly thereafter was elected its first chief justice. He returned to Congress in 1778 and was elected its president. The next year he was appointed minister to Spain, and in 1782 he joined Franklin and Adams on the peace commission in Paris to negotiate the treaty ending the Revolutionary War. Jay signed the Treaty of Peace in 1783. After returning to America he served for five years as secretary for foreign affairs. Experiencing first hand the short-comings of the government under the Articles of Confederation, Jay strongly supported the new United States Constitution, even writing some of the essays of the *Federalist Papers* in its support. After the new Constitution went into effect, Jay was appointed the first Supreme Court Chief Justice in 1789, where he served for five years. He then was appointed as a special minister to England, and upon his return in 1795 was elected governor of New York. After two terms in office, he retired in 1801 to live on his farm in New York, dying there in 1829.

Jay did much to promote the spread of Christianity. As Chief Justice his geographic responsibilities included the northern circuit. For court preparations he believed that "the custom in New England of a clergyman's attending, should in my opinion be observed and continued."[38] Jay served as President of the American Bible Society and a member of the American Board of Commissioners for Foreign Missions. Of the Bible he says:

> *The Bible is the best of all books, for it is the word of God and teaches us the way to be happy in this world and in the next. Continue therefore to read it and to regulate your life by its precepts.*[39]

The Bible and its Author were not only important for man's personal well-being, but also for the nation's well-being. Jay said:

> *I . . . recommend a general and public return of praise and thanksgiving to Him from whose goodness these blessings descend. The most effectual means of securing the continuance of our civil and religious liberties, is always to remember with reverence and gratitude the source from which they flow.*[40]

In his last will and testament John Jay continued to express his Christian faith:

Unto Him who is the author and giver of all good, I render sincere and humble thanks for His manifold and unmerited blessings, and especially for our redemption and salvation by his beloved Son. . . . Blessed be his holy name.[41]

🔔 *Graff House*

This reconstructed house is the site where Thomas Jefferson drafted the *Declaration of Independence* and submitted it for corrections to his committee, comprised of Benjamin Franklin, John Adams, Roger Sherman, and Robert Livingston. Jefferson rented two furnished rooms in Jacob Graff's home while he stayed in Philadelphia as a delegate to the Second Continental Congress from Virginia.

Churches and Meeting Houses

Quakers, or Friends, comprised a large number of the early settlers of Philadelphia. They organized societies, first met in homes, and then built meeting houses, yet due to the ideas of religious freedom of William Penn, many other churches organized in the area as well. Penn stated:

The first fundamental of the government in my province shall be that everyone shall have and enjoy free possession of his faith and exercise of worship in such way and manner as every such person shall in conscience believe most acceptable to God.[42]

🔔 Christ Church

Christ Church was founded in 1695 in accordance with the provisions of the charter given by King Charles II to William Penn. The present building was erected from 1727 to 1754. Christ Church is one of the most historic churches in America. In 1739 George Whitefield preached here and raised funds to help build a school, which subsequently became the University of Pennsylvania. Franklin occupied a pew in the church and was a member of the committee which built the spire, completed in 1754. Since the steeple was the highest point in Philadelphia, Franklin originally intended to try his electrical experiments from the spire.

The minister of Christ Church, Jacob Duché, was asked to open the First Continental Congress in prayer. In 1775, after the Continental Congress received word of the Battle of Lexington, the members all gathered at Christ Church to fast and pray.

It was at Christ Church in September, 1785, that representatives of the Episcopal Church in seven states gathered and resolved that the Protestant Episcopal Church of the United States should be organized.

George and Martha Washington occupied pew number 58 from 1790 to 1797. Also occupying the "President's Pew" was John Adams while he was President, and Lafayette on his second visit to America in 1826. Other worshipers at the church have included Robert Morris; Francis Hopkinson, signer of the Declaration of Independence, and his son, the author of *Hail Columbia*; James Wilson, signer of the Declaration, first Professor of Law in America, and Justice of the Supreme Court of the United States; and Henry Clay.

The graves of Benjamin Franklin and his wife, Deborah, can be found in Christ Church Burial Ground. More Colonial and Revolutionary War leaders are buried here than any other non-military cemetery in the U.S.

🔔 Free Quaker Meeting House

At the time of the American Revolution the majority of Quakers were pacifists, so when fighting began with the British most Quakers remained neutral. However, there was a group of unusual Quakers who responded to the call of taking up arms to defend their country and their liberty. This was not an easy decision for these "fighting" Quakers knew they would be disowned or "read out" of their meetings. This separation forced the Free Quakers of Philadelphia to build their own meeting house in 1783, called the Free Quaker Meeting House. After the war the differences diminished so that by 1834 there were only two Free Quakers left. Betsy Ross, who is thought to have sewed the first flag of Stars and Stripes under the direction of General Washington, was one. Services stopped around this time.

St. George's United Methodist

St. George's was dedicated in 1769 and is the oldest existing Methodist Church building in the world. In October, 1771, Francis Asbury was sent by Wesley from England to Philadelphia, and it was at St. George's that he preached his first sermon in America. He served as the pastor here before extending his duties as Bishop. It was in St. George's that the first American "love-feast" was held on Friday, March 23, 1770, and the first American "watch-night," on November 4, 1771, both traditions in the Methodist Church.

Gloria Dei (Old Swedes') Church

Gloria Dei is the oldest church building in Philadelphia, dedicated in 1700. It was built on the site where the early Swedes had met for church services since 1677. The church congregation was founded in 1643, almost 40 years before Penn arrived in Pennsylvania, by Swedish Lutherans who were the earliest settlers in the area.

Old Pine Street Church

The Pine Street Presbyterian Church, built in 1767, was the third of that denomination in Philadelphia. Rev. **George Duffield** was pastor of Pine Street Presbyterian Church from 1772 to 1790. He served as chaplain of the Continental Congress and of the Pennsylvania militia during the war. Duffield delivered many fiery, patriotic sermons to the many prominent men who attended his church. He inspired many to action, including John Adams, who was a member of his congregation while in Philadelphia.

In May 1776 John Adams listened to a sermon of Rev. Duffield that likened the way King George III treated the Americans to the way Pharaoh had treated the Israelites. Duffield concluded that God intended for the Americans to be liberated just as He intended the Israelites to be liberated. On May 17 Adams wrote to his wife:

Is it not a saying of Moses, Who am I that I should go in and out before this great people? When I consider the great events which are passed, and those greater which are rapidly advancing, and that I may have been instrumental in touching some springs, and turning some small wheels, which have had and will have such effects, I feel an awe upon my mind, which is not easily described. Great Britain has at last driven America to the last step, complete separation from her; a total, absolute independence. . . .[43]

J.T. Headley writes of the influence of Rev. Duffield:

The patriots of the first Congress flocked to his church, and John Adams and his compeers were often his hearers. . . . In a discourse delivered before several companies of the Pennsylvania militia and members of Congress, four months before the Declaration of Independence, he took bold and decided ground in favor of that step, and pleaded his cause with sublime eloquence, which afterwards made him so obnoxious to the British that they placed a reward of fifty pounds for his capture.[44]

Later on in that sermon, Duffield delivered a prophetic word we must heed today:

Whilst sun and moon endure, America shall remain a city of refuge for the whole earth, until she herself shall play the tyrant, forget her destiny, disgrace her freedom, and provoke her God.[45]

As chaplain of the Pennsylvania militia, **George Duffield**, was frequently in camp, where "his visits were always welcome, for the soldiers loved the eloquent, earnest, fearless patriot." Headley gives the following incident of the courageous Duffield:

When the enemy occupied Staten Island, and the American
forces were across the river on the Jersey shore, he repaired to
camp to spend the Sabbath. Assembling a portion of the troops
in an orchard, he climbed into the forks of a tree and com-
menced religious exercises. He gave out a hymn. . . . The British
on the island heard the sound of the singing, and immediately di-
rected some cannon to play on the orchard, from whence it pro-
ceeded. Soon the heavy shot came crashing through the
branches, and went singing overhead, arresting for a moment
the voices that were lifted in worship. Mr. Duffield. . . proposed
that they should adjourn behind an adjacent hillock. They did
so, and continued their worship, while the iron storm hurled
harmlessly overhead.[46]

One of the most prominent attendants of Duffield's church was
Benjamin Rush (1745-1813). Though many people today do not
know his name, Benjamin Rush was one of the most influential and
significant founding fathers. He was a signer of the Declaration of
Independence; a member of the Pennsylvania Constitutional Convention; a doctor and professor of medicine, making many contributions
in that field in practice and writing; surgeon general of the Continental army; a leader in societies for the abolition of slavery; president
of various Bible and medical societies; a principal founder of Dick-
enson College; treasurer of the Mint of the United States; and a leader
in education. Concerning education he wrote:

I proceed, in the next place, to enquire what mode of education
we shall adopt so as to secure to the state all the advantages that are
to be derived from the proper instruction of youth; and here I beg
leave to remark that the only foundation for a useful education in a
republic is to be laid in religion. Without this, there can be no virtue,
and without virtue there can be no liberty, and liberty is the object
and life of all republican governments.[47]

True religion to Rush, as to our founders, was Christianity. In
1806 he wrote:

In contemplating the political institutions of the United
States, I lament that we waste so much time and money in pun-

*ishing crimes and take so little pains to prevent them. We pro-
fess to be republicans, and yet we neglect the only means of establishing and perpetuating our republican forms of
government, that is, the universal education of our youth in the
principles of christianity by the means of the bible. For this Divine book, above all others, favors that equality among mankind, that respect for just laws, and those sober and frugal
virtues, which constitute the soul of republicanism.*[48]

To Rush, the liberty of America was a product of Christianity. He
wrote: *"Christianity is the only true and perfect religion, and that in
proportion as mankind adopt its principles and obeys its precepts,
they will be wise and happy.'*[49]

🔔 Todd House and Bishop White House

Two other sites of interest in historic downtown Philadelphia
include the Todd House, home of Dolley Payne Todd, who married
James Madison to become Dolley Madison (see Section 8), and the
Bishop White House, home of the first bishop of the Episcopal
Diocese of Pennsylvania.

* * * * * *

As William Penn was leaving Philadelphia in 1684, after his first
visit to his colony, he pronounced the following farewell benediction
as he sailed down the Delaware River:

*And thou, Philadelphia, the virgin settlement of this prov-
ince, named before thou wert born, what love, what care, what
service, and what travail has there been to bring thee forth and
preserve thee from such as would abuse and defile thee! My soul
prays to God for thee, that thou mayest stand in the day of trial,
that thy children may be blessed of the Lord, and thy people
saved by his power.*[50]

Jamestown: The First Permanent English Settlement

☖ Jamestown Historical Park

Jamestown was the first permanent English settlement in the New World. Previous colonies were attempted in what would become the original United States but none succeeded. Prior to the beginning of Jamestown in 1607, colonies were successfully planted in Canada and Central and South America, but in God's providence the primary settlers of the American colonies were Englishmen and other Europeans who were products of the Protestant Reformation and who had a firm belief in God and the Bible. Their desire to establish a land of civil and religious freedom and to propagate the Gospel was evident in their lives, their laws, and their words.

Richard Hakluyt and the Vision for Colonization

No man was more influential in the establishment of the American colonies than Richard Hakluyt. This minister, who from Biblical inspiration became the greatest English geographer of the Elizabethan epoch, compiled the records of numerous European explorations, voyages, and settlements with the view of encouraging England to establish colonies in the new world. True to the calling God had put into his heart, the spreading of the gospel and establishment of the Christian faith in new lands was at the forefront of his motives in undertaking this great task. Hakluyt also foresaw America as a land where persecuted Christians could find refuge.

Early attempts at colonization for purely economic reasons had failed. Hakluyt wrote that if past attempts *"had not been led with a preposterous desire of seeking rather gaine than God's glorie, I assure myself that our labours had taken farre better effecte. But wee forgotte, that Godliness is great riches, and that if we first seeke the kingdome of God, al other thinges will be given unto us, and that as the light accompanieth the Sunne and the heate the fire, so lasting riches do wait upon them that are jealous for the advancement of the Kingdome of Christ, and the enlargement of his glorious Gospell: as it is sayd, I will honour them that honour mee.''*[1]

In 1584 Hakluyt presented his *Discourse on Western Planting* to Queen Elizabeth where he set forth the principal reasons for colonization. First and foremost was the religious reason. He said that colonization would make for *"the enlargement of the gospel of Christ.''*[2] He saw that propagating the gospel would include the conversion and civilization of the Indians. *"Hakluyt lamented that he had not heard of a single infidel converted by the English explorers.''*[3]

In Chapter 20 of the *Discourse,* Hakluyt states numerous reasons for planting new colonies including: *"Wee shall by plantinge there inlarge the glory of the gospell, and from England plante sincere relligion, and provide a safe and a sure place to receave people from all partes of the worlds that are forced to flee for the truthe of Gods worde.''*[4] Many of the early settlers of America reiterated this idea. **Hakluyt was the first to proclaim the Providential purposes of America.**

Matthew Page Andrews wrote that *"Hakluyt fired the vital spark of religious purpose that played a compelling part in American colonization when England was swayed by the strong convictions of the Protestant political and religious revolution culminating in the Puritan upheaval.''*[5]

"Richard Hakluyt was not simply a historian and a collector: he was also an agitator and a prophet."[6] He imparted the vision for and directed the colonization of the greatest and most free nation in history.

Richard Hakluyt is one those heroes of Christian liberty of whom most Americans have never heard, yet, he is truly one of the founding fathers of this nation. We might even call him the first founding father, to whom God first gave the vision of America as the land of liberty, whose planting would "enlarge the glory of the gospel" and "provide a safe and a sure place to receive people from all parts of the worlds that are forced to flee for the truth of God's word." His Christian faith is revealed throughout his life, his writings, and in his death. In his last will and testament he wrote:

First I commend my soule into the hands of God from whence I received the same, trusting thorow the only merits of Jesus Christ and the sanctification of the blessed Spirit to be both in body and soule a member of His most holy and heavenly kingdome.[7]

Charter for Colonization

On April 10, 1606, a charter was issued to Sir Thomas Gates, Sir George Somers, Richard Hakluyt, Edward-Maria Wingfield, Thomas Hanham, and others who established the London and Plymouth Companies. The incorporators of this charter were resolved into two groups. One was the London Company and was entitled to establish the first colony between 34 and 38 degrees north latitude; the other was the Plymouth Company which was to establish the "second colony," between 41 and 44 degrees north latitude. The area in-between was to be open to both companies.

King James gave them authority to plant colonies in that part of America called Virginia and other parts *'which are not now actually possessed by any Christian Prince or People. "* The reason for their endeavors was stated in this first Charter of Virginia:

We, greatly commending, and graciously accepting of, their

Desires for the Furtherance of so noble a Work, which may, by the Providence of Almighty God, hereafter tend to the Glory of his Divine Majesty, in propagating of Christian Religion to such People, as yet live in Darkness and miserable Ignorance of the true Knowledge and Worship of God, and may in time bring the Infidels and Savages, living in those parts, to human Civility, and to a settled and quiet Government: DO, by these our Letters Patents, graciously accept of, and agree to, their humble and well-intended Desires.[8]

This charter extended the rights of Englishmen to any new colonies that would be established.

Orders and instructions given to the first colonists by the London Council emphasized the religious motive, as Hakluyt had been doing since his first writings in 1582. They wrote: *"We do specially ordain, charge, and require"* those concerned *"with all diligence, care and respect"* to provide that the *"Christian faith be preached, planted, and used, not only within every of the said several colonies, and plantations, but also as much as they may arouse the savage people which do or shall adjoin unto them"*; and that every one should *"use all good means to draw the savages and heathen people. . . to the true service and knowledge of God."*[9]

According to a statement published by the Virginia Company, entitled *A True and Sincere Declaration*, the *"principal and main ends,"* of the settlers, *"... were first to preach and baptize into the Christian religion, and by propagation of the Gospel, to recover out of the arms of the Devil, a number of poor and miserable souls, wrapt up unto death in almost invincible ignorance; to endeavor the fulfilling an accomplishment of the number of the elect which shall be gathered from all corners of the earth; and to add our mite to the treasury of Heaven."*[10]

Though some opposed the provision of propagating the Gospel to the natives, stating it would be their downfall, it proved to be their salvation and the key to their survival. The events that transpired show that without Hakluyt's insistence that ministers accompany the settlers, to not only perform their sacred duties for the English but also to seek to convert the Indians, Jamestown would not have survived and America could have had a different history.

In November, 1606, Hakluyt was named as the officially recognized clergyman for the new settlement and was probably intended to be the head of the church in the colony. He would have gone with the first colonists to Virginia in 1607 but age or infirmity prevented him. Hakluyt recommended that Robert Hunt go in his place.[11]

♫ *Tercentenary Monument*

In 1907 a monument was constructed at Jamestown Historical Park in honor of the 300th anniversary of the founding of Jamestown. Engraved on the monument are the concluding instructions to the colonists from the London Council's *Instructions for the Intended Voyage to Virginia:*

> *Lastly and chiefly, the way to prosper and achieve good success is to make yourselves all of one mind for the good of your country and your own, and to serve and fear God, the Giver of all goodness, for every plantation which our Heavenly Father hath not planted shall be rooted out.*[12]

♫ *Original Site of Jamestown Fort*

When the first 104 Colonists landed at Cape Henry on April 26, 1607, they erected a wooden cross where Rev. Robert Hunt led the men in prayer. Then they sailed across the bay and up a river that was named the James in honor of the king. On May 13 they reached the site they felt would be good for their settlement and called it Jamestown, also in honor of the king. Soon after going ashore, Rev. Robert Hunt *"gathered his flock around him without delay, and standing in their midst under the trees uttered, for the first time in the western world, the solemn invocation: 'The Lord is in His Holy*

Temple; Let all the earth keep silence before Him.' The new land had been claimed for an earthly potentate; he now claimed it for the King of kings.''[13]

A triangular fort was built within a month after landing. The side facing the river was 420 feet in length, the other two sides were 300 feet long, and at each of the three corners bulwarks were built which contained 3 to 5 cannons. A sixty by twenty-four foot church would be built in the center of the fort, but until it was, services were held out doors. Rev. Hunt preached from a wooden platform nailed between two trees and covered with a sail. The colonists were careful in selecting a site to settle and felt they had chosen a good location because at this spot the river was deep enough for ships to anchor right next to the land, and they felt it would be easy to defend themselves from an Indian attack by land or a Spanish attack by sea. Yet they would learn later that the swamps that surrounded Jamestown were full of mosquitoes that could cause malaria. Also, some of the water of that area that they drank was impure and would later cause typhoid fever and dysentery.

🔔 *Statue of John Smith*

The first year at Jamestown was a time of crisis due to sickness, lack of food, and lack of strong leadership. Captain John Smith, explorer, soldier and author, provided the strong leadership needed for survival. When he was chosen President of the Virginia Council in September, 1608, one of the things that he required of everyone was to go to church. Rev. Hunt had died in July of that year and the church had fallen into disrepair. Smith had it restored and said that *"...we had daily common prayer... and surely God did most mercifully hear us.''*[14]

Smith is called the "Father of Virginia" due to his significant contributions in the establishment and survival of Jamestown. He made a detailed map of Virginia and wrote an early history called *A True Relation.* When threatened, he fought the Indians, yet also made the breakthroughs in peaceful relations with them that were essential for survival. His courage, honesty, good sense, and skill as Governor set an example that the colonists needed, and his insistence that everyone work hard was an essential ingredient for their survival. Since the Jamestown colonists were not a covenanted group of people from one church congregation (as were the majority of the Pilgrims of Plymouth), unity was very difficult. At first they lacked the character and unselfishness to put work before adventure and material gain. As a result, they almost starved to death.

Smith made a rule based on the Bible: *"if you don't work, you don't eat."* He refused lodging for himself until all others had it first. Due to an injury in 1609, Smith had to return to England, but his one year of leadership made the difference.

John Smith also contributed to the success of the Pilgrims in Plymouth by carrying Squanto back to his home on a voyage Smith made from England to New England in 1619. Two years later Squanto providentially helped the Pilgrims to survive.

Pocahontas Saves John Smith

The Indians' initial reaction to the settlers at Jamestown was fear, suspicion, and hostility. Two weeks after the English arrived, 200 Indians attacked the settlement killing two and wounding 10 others. During the summer, when musket or cannon fire signaled the death of a settler, the Indians would celebrate the misfortune of the English by dancing and yelling in nearby marsh grass. They would let out horrendous shrieks and cries of "Yah, ha, ha!" and "Whe, Whe, Whe, Tewittowah" and call upon their devil-god to plague and destroy the English. This savage action of the Indians is what caused the Jamestown colonists to call them "naked slaves of the devill." This picture of the Powhatan Indians makes the action of Pocahontas even more miraculous and affirms John Smith's words that "God made Pocahontas."[15]

John Smith said that Pocahontas was *"...next under God... the instrument to preserve this colony from death, famine, and utter confusion."*[16] This young daughter of the Indian Chief Powhatan befriended the colonists from the beginning.

While exploring far up the Chickahominy River in December 1607, John Smith was captured by a band of Indians and eventually taken to Powhatan's village. That Smith was taken to the village and not killed right away was quite providential. Other colonists that accompanied him on the trip were captured and killed, some in torturous ways. Smith was held captive for weeks, during which time he diverted a surprise attack on the fort at Jamestown, and eventually procured his release. In his writings, Smith describes various events during his capture, including their "hellish" singing, yelling, and dancing.[17]

Upon arrival at the chief's, or Powhatan's, village, Smith was treated as a special guest and was given a big dinner. But in short time he was ordered to be put to death. His head was placed on a large stone where Indians with clubs prepared *"to beat out his braines,"* but at this moment Pocahontas laid her head on his and pleaded for his life, which her father granted. Smith wrote that she took his *"head in her armes and laid her owne upon his to save him from death."*[18]

Pocahontas not only saved Smith, but also helped save the Jamestown settlers from death. During their first winter all their food ran out and Pocahontas was instrumental in getting the Indians to bring new supplies. One writer of that period said that *"...God the patron of all good indevours, in that desperate extremitie, so changed the hearts of the Salvages, that they brought such plenty of their fruits, and provision, as no man wanted."*[19] She brought food to the starving colonists at other times as well, and also helped obtain peace treaties with the Indians. John Fiske writes of Pocahontas: *"But for her friendly services on more than one occasion, the tiny settlement would probably have perished"*[20]

🔔 *Robert Hunt Shrine*

After the settlers arrived in May 1607, they put up tents until houses could be built and they stretched a sail between two trees as a place for worship. According to John Smith, *"For a Church we did hang an awning (which is an old sail) to three or foure trees to shadow us from the sunne. Our walls were rales of wood, our seats unhewed trees, till we cut plankes, our Pulpit a bar of wood nailed to two neighboring trees.*"[21]

It was here that the founder of the first Protestant church in America, Rev. Robert Hunt, conducted services until the church was built. This good and courageous clergyman preached twice each Sunday, read the morning and evening prayers, and celebrated communion once every three months. Rev. Hunt composed a special prayer for the colonists that was repeated each morning:

> *Almighty God, . . . we beseech Thee to bless us and this plantation which we and our nation have begun in Thy fear and for Thy glory. . . and seeing Lord, the highest end of our plantation here is to set up the standard and display the banner of Jesus Christ, even here where Satan's throne is, Lord let our labour be blessed in labouring for the conversion of the heathen. . . . Lord sanctify our spirits and give us holy hearts, that so we may be Thy instruments in this most glorious work.*[22]

Each time the guards were changed in the center of the fort, Rev. Hunt would lead in this prayer:

> *We know, O Lord, we have the Devil and all the gates of Hell against us, but if Thou, O Lord, be on our side, we care not who be against us. And, seeing by Thy motion and work in our hearts, we have left our warm rests at home and put our lives into Thy hands, principally to honor Thy name and advance the kingdom of Thy Son, Lord, give us leave to commit our lives into Thy hands.*[23]

Rev. Hunt was not only the minister of Jamestown, but also one of the nine original Council members chosen by the Virginia Company to rule the Colony. He set the example of hard work for others, personally building the grist mill and taking care of the sick when at times there was only he and a handful to take care of all the rest. He preached against the proud and lazy and helped heal many divisions among the people. John Smith marveled at *"that honest, religious, courageous divine,"* who in his service at Jamestown lost *"all but the clothes on his back, [but] none did ever hear him repine his loss."*[24]

Rev. Hunt fulfilled the desires of the London Council by not only conducting services in the New World, but also by working to convert the Indians. His first convert was an Indian named Navirans, who was very helpful to the early colonists.[25]

Hunt died in July of 1608. John Smith wrote that *"till he could not speak, he never ceased to his utmost to animate us constantly to persist; whose soul, questionless, is with God."*[26] On his memorial is written:

> *He preferred the service of God to every thought of ease at home. He endured every privation, yet none ever heard him repine. . . He planted the first Protestant church in America, and laid down his life in the foundation of Virginia.*

⌂ *Memorial Cross*

"Staving Time," 1609-1610

After Smith returned to England, George Percy became Governor in his place until Lord Delaware arrived from England. Percy was a man of fine character but was not a decisive leader as Smith had been. When the Indians learned that Smith had left, they broke the peace and *"did spoile and murther all they incountered."*[27] Due to lack of discipline, and weakness on Percy's part to enforce the laws of the colony, many people stopped working and recklessly ate up all the supplies. Epidemics also broke out and many began to die. All of this brought much disorder. Houses and parts of the fort were torn down and used for fire wood. By this time Pocahontas had also been forbidden by Powhatan to communicate with or assist the colonists on penalty of death, so their greatest link with the Indians had been cut off.

This winter of 1609-10 was known as the "Starving Time." The settlers ate horses, snakes, cats, rats, roots and boiled leather and book covers to survive. One early historian wrote: *"So great was our famine, that. . . one amongst the rest did kill his wife, powdered [salted] her, and had eaten part of her before it was knowne; for which hee was executed, as hee well deserved."*[28] Of the 490 colonists in Jamestown in September 1609, only 59 were left alive six months later. The Memorial Cross marks the site where some 300 of them were hastily buried at night so that the Indians would not know how many were still alive.

In May of 1610, Sir Thomas Gates sailed into Jamestown with two ships he, and other settlers heading for Jamestown, had built while shipwrecked in Bermuda. Gates was to be the interim governor until Lord Delaware's arrival. While they had some supplies, it was not enough to last everyone for very long. Therefore, the thin, half-naked, and desperate settlers decided to abandon Jamestown and return to England. Some of them wanted to burn what was left of Jamestown, but Gates, John Rolfe, and others stopped them. An early Virginia historian wrote: *"God, who did not intend that this excellent country should be abandoned, put it into the heart of Sir T. Gates to save it."*[29]

They boarded their boats and sailed to the mouth of the James River where they dropped anchor for the night. The next morning, as they continued their voyage, they met Lord Delaware who had come with three well-stocked ships from England. There were cries of joy from the colonists who thanked God that help had come in time. Since Jamestown had not been burned, they were able to return with renewed hope that the colony would succeed.

On Sunday, June 10, 1610, the colonists stood amid the remains of Jamestown as Lord Delaware stepped from his boat. *"The new governor of Virginia knelt and prayed, thanking God that he had come in time to save the colony. He then led the settlers to the church where, at his request, a sermon of thanksgiving was preached,"*[30] by the new Chaplain Rev. Richard Bucke (1573-1623) who had come with the fleet.

Lord Delaware, 1610-1611

Lord Delaware was prepared and inspired to fulfill his role as the new supreme governor of the colony. After receiving his appointment while in England, he had listened to the sermon delivered by the Reverend William Crashaw in honor of his obtaining the position:

> *And thou most noble Lord, whom God hath stirred up to neglect the pleasures of England, and with Abraham to go from thy country, and forsake thy kindred and thy father's house, to go to a land which God will show thee, give me leave to speak the truth. Thy ancestor many hundred years ago gained great honour to thy house but by this action thou augmenst it.... Remember, thou art a general of English men, nay a general of Christian men; therefore principally look to religion. You go to commend it to the Heathen, then practice it yourselves; make the name of Christ honourable, not hateful unto them.[31]*

A history textbook formerly used in Virginia schools states:

> *Lord Delaware was a religious man, and he was determined that the colonists should have the opportunity to worship God. A bell was rung for prayers every day at ten in the morning and at four in the afternoon. All were required to attend church. Two sermons were preached on Sunday, and one on Thursday. The little church was decorated with flowers, and the colonists enjoyed the periods of peace and quiet spent there.[32]*

The Second Virginia Charter of 1609 declared *"that it shall be necessary for all such as inhabit within the precincts of Virginia to determine to live together in the fear and true worship of Almighty God, Christian peace, and civil quietness;"* and that *"the principal effect which we [the crown] can desire or expect of this action is the conversion and reduction of the people in those parts unto the true worship of God and the Christian religion.[33]*

The charter made provision for *"the true word of God and the Christian faith"* to be *"...preached, planted and used, not only within the colonies, but as much as they may, amongst the Savage People."* The Charter also provided for private enterprise. Before poor health forced him to return to England in March of 1611, Delaware encouraged this private enterprise by abolishing communal farming and giving each colonist his own plot of ground to cultivate.

Sir Thomas Dale replaced Delaware as governor. He arrived in May, 1611, with other settlers, including the Rev. Alexander Whitaker. Dale imposed nearly totalitarian rule, which he felt necessary to see the colony survive. His rule helped assure the lasting success of the new colony. Rev. Whitaker said of Dale that he was *"a man of great knowledge in Divinity, and of a good conscience in all his doings: both which Bee rare in a martial man."*[34]

Alexander Whitaker was a minister in the colony for 6 years, until his death in 1617. He not only served the English settlers but also the native Indians, and hence he is known as the "apostle to the Indians." He wrote a famous essay entitled *Good News From Virginia* which influenced Europeans to colonize America for the glory of God. He asserted that the survival of Jamestown through those difficult years was proof *"that the finger of God hath been the only true worker here; that God first showed us the place, God called us hither, and here God by His special Providence hath maintained us."*

Lawes Divine, Morall and Martiall

The Second Virginia Charter provided for *"Laws Divine, Morall, and Martiall, etc."* which were written between 1609 and 1612 by Sir Thomas Gates, Sir Thomas West (Lord Delaware), and Sir Thomas Dale. According to Professor David Flaherty, these laws "represented the first written manifestations of the common law in America."[35] Following are a few of the laws:[36]

1. First since we owe our highest and supreme duty, our greatest and all our allegeance to him, from whom all power and authoritie is derived,... we must alone expect our successe from him, who is onely the blesser of all good attempts, the King of kings, the commaunder of commaunders, and Lord of Hostes, I do strictly commaund and charge all Captaines and Officers,... to have a care that the Almightie God bee duly and daily served, and that they call upon their people to heare Sermons, as that

also they diligently frequent Morning and Evening praier them-
selves by their owne exemplar and daily life...

2. *That no man speake impiously or maliciously, against the*
holy and blessed Trinitie, or any of the three persons, that is to
say, against God the Father, God the Son, and God the holy
Ghost, or against the knowne Articles of the Christian faith,
upon paine of death.

3. *That no man blaspheme Gods holy name upon paine of*
death, or use unlawful oathes, taking the name of God in vaine,
curse, or banne [an imprecation of a curse], upon paine of se-
vere punishment...

4. *No man shall use any traiterous words against his Majes-*
ties Person, or royall authority upon paine of death.

5. *No man shall speake any word, or do any act, which may*
tend to the derision, or despight [open defiance] of Gods holy
word upon paine of death...

6. *Everie man and woman duly twice a day upon the first*
towling of the Bell shall upon the working daies repaire unto the
Church, to hear divine Service...

♤ *Statue of Pocahontas*

During Dale's governorship, Pocahontas was treacherously sold
by some Indians to an English sea captain, who took her to Jamestown
as a hostage. Dale tried to trade her to Powhatan for some English
hostages he held, but he refused. Pocahontas was then placed in the
care of Rev. Alexander Whitaker, who took her to his farm near
Henrico.

It is interesting to note that the Rev. William Symonds when
preaching to Jamestown-bound colonists as they were leaving England in May, 1609, concluded his sermon by reminding them that *''a*
captive girl brought Naaman to the Prophet. A captive woman was

the means of converting Iberia.... God makes the weake things of the worlde confound the mighty, and getteth himself praise by the mouth of babes and sucklings.'[37]

During this period, Rev. Whitaker, Sir Thomas Dale, and Captain John Rolfe taught Pocahontas about Christianity and also taught her how to read. She memorized the Apostle's Creed, the Lord's Prayer, and the Ten Commandments, and she learned the answers to the questions of the short catechism. "In the spring of 1614, Whitaker reviewed her in the catechism, received her renunciation of paganism, heard her confession of faith in Jesus Christ,"[38] and baptized her from a font made from the trunk of a tree. She took the name Rebecca. In April of that year, at the age of about 17, she was married to Rolfe in the Jamestown Church at a service performed by Rev. Bucke. Rolfe wrote that the marriage would be for the *"good of this plantation, for the honour of our countrie, for the glory of God."*[39]

In 1616 Pocahontas, John Rolfe, and their son, Thomas, traveled to England to visit. She died there in March, 1617, and was buried at St. George's Parish Church in Gravesend. John Smith later was said to have commented: *"Poor little maid. I sorrowed much for her thus early death, and even now cannot think of it without grief, for I felt toward her as if she were mine own daughter.'*[40]

Thomas would later return to America where he married an Englishwoman, Jane Poythress. *"From their union descended seven successive generations of educators, ministers, statesmen, and law-makers, among whom were the Blairs, the Bollings, the Lewises, and the Randolphs. One of Thomas' – and therefore Pocahontas' – most distinguished descendants was John Randolph of Roanoke, who represented Virginia in the United States House of Representatives and in the United States Senate. Thus, through her son and his descendants, Pocahontas lived on in American history.'*[41]

🔔 *The Church*

The Old Church Tower, built in 1647, is an addition to the first brick church of 1639. It is one of the oldest English edifices standing in the United States. While the tower dates from 1647, the present Memorial Church was built in 1907 over the foundation of the 1639 brick church. This was probably built on the same site as the church of 1617. (This is the one reconstructed in the Jamestown Settlement.) The 1617 church was the cradle of self-government in the new world.

In 1612 Virginia was granted a new charter which gave the Virginia Company the right to select its own officers independent of Parliament or King. In 1618 Virginia was granted yet another charter which gave Virginians the right to choose their own representatives who would make their own laws. It was known as the General Assembly of Virginia and was composed of two houses — the Council chosen by the Virginia Company and the House of Burgesses chosen by the people. It was the beginning of representative government in the New World. The Virginia General Assembly abolished Dale's laws, gave toleration to dissenters, and created elected vestries.

First Representative Assembly, 1619

The first General Assembly met in the church at Jamestown on July 30, 1619. The burgesses sat in the choir and the Council sat in the front pews. A Virginia public school textbook of the 1960s states: *"The men who came together in this first meeting of the first representative government in America wanted God to guide them in their work.'*[42] They recognized that *"...men's affairs do little prosper where God's service is neglected."* Their minister, the Rev. Richard Buck, opened the meeting with prayer. He prayed earnestly *"that it would please God to guide and to make free from sin all our proceedings to His glory and to the good of this plantation.'*[43]

One of the representatives was a clergyman, the Rev. William Wickham. This representative government was brought into being due in part to the efforts of Edwin Sandys, a vocal Puritan leader in the House of Commons who became the treasurer of the Virginia Company in 1619.

King James took the charter away from Virginia in 1624 and made it a royal colony where the King appointed its Governor. This lasted up to the American Revolution. Virginia's period of complete self-government only lasted five years. However, the people still elected representatives to the House of Burgesses, even though the royal appointed governor had veto power over any legislation they enacted and could dissolve them at any time. Although the governor held a great amount of power, he needed the consent of the House of Burgesses for the governing of the colony. Without them he could not enact laws or collect taxes that the people would agree to. Consequently, the elected members of the House of Burgesses were able to protect and promote the interests of the people.

King James also made the Anglican Church the established church of Virginia. By law it was supported by the system of tithes. This arrangement led to persecution against dissenters (those Christians not a part of the established church) in later years. Efforts of dissenters would eventually bring about the disestablishment of the Episcopal Church in Virginia. Although the established religion was Episcopal, the church that grew up in Virginia for the next 150 years was quite different from the High Church Anglicanism of England. In fact, it looked more like the Puritanism of New England with each church expressing its own individuality and non-conformist ideas. The churches were not hierarchical or lavish and never had an English bishop. Church authority rested with the local church vestries that acted like boards of elders. Vestrymen were often elected by the church members.

Other important events occurred in 1619 as well. The first Thanksgiving celebrated in the new world took place in that year at the Berkeley plantation near Jamestown. This was a couple of years before the more famous Thanksgiving the Pilgrims celebrated in Plymouth. Late in 1619 the plan was made to send almost a hundred young women to Jamestown to provide wives for the colonists because at the time there were only a few women and many lonely men in Virginia. More families would add further stability and permanence to the society.

During the five days the first General Assembly met, they made various laws. They decided that everyone must attend church and that the form of worship would be the same as the Church of England. Everyone who owned weapons would have to bring them to church to protect against any Indian raids. Laws also prohibited the settlers from selling guns to the Indians or from harming or injuring them in any way. The towns and plantations were also required to educate a certain number of Indian children *"in true religion and civil course of life."*[44] This turned out to be crucial to the salvation of Jamestown in 1622.

Henricus School and College, 1619

In 1618 the Virginia Company obtained a charter and a large tract of land from King James I for a college and school in Virginia. Its purpose was *"education for the training of the Indians in the true knowledge of God and in some useful employment and to educate the children of the settlers who are now deprived of formal education."*[45]

By 1622 money had been raised, a teaching staff was chosen, and construction was begun on campus buildings. The Virginia Company published a book by Rev. John Brinsley on educational methods and a course of study appropriate for the school. In the *Dedicatorie* of the book Brinsley writes, *"...To this purpose God having ordained schooles of learning to be a principall meanes to reduce a barbarous people to civilitie, and thereby to prepare them the better to receive the glorious Gospel of Jesus Christ; as also for the breeding and nourishing of such a holie Ministerie, with a wise and godlie Magistracie, and people to be perpetuallie preserved..."*[46]

While the college buildings were being constructed Chief Opechancanough lead an Indian attack against the settlers resulting in the "Great Massacre." This stopped the efforts for Henrico College.

The Massacre of 1622, Chanco Saves Jamestown

By 1618 both Pocahontas and her father, Chief Powhatan, had died. Without them the peace treaty was at risk, especially considering that the new chief Opechancanough blamed the English for the death by war, disease, and starvation of a large percentage of his people. (Over a 20 year period about 85% of his people died.) In 1621 the new governor of Virginia, Sir Francis Wyatt, heard that Opechancanough was planning to break the peace, and so he sent a messenger to renew the treaty. The Chief acted as if he planned to fully keep the peace, but was really secretly plotting to kill all the colonists.

Opechancanough's plot was so well planned and his secret so well kept that the English continued to trust the Indians completely. Two days before the massacre, the colonists were allowing the Indians to guide them through the forests. They were lending boats to the Indians. They did not know that the boats would be used by the Indians to cross the James River in order to make bloody plans with their friends. On Friday morning, March 22, 1622, the very day of the massacre, the Indians came as usual to the houses of the settlers with game and food to sell. Some of the Indians even sat down and ate breakfast with those they expected to murder.

By eight o'clock in the morning, on that fearful Friday, the Indians had posted themselves in or near the homes of the English settlers. Then they fell upon the colonists all at the same time. The attack was so unexpected that many persons were unable to defend themselves. The Indians killed men, women, and children alike, sparing no one. They brutally killed their English friends and enemies alike.... John Rolfe was one of the victims.[47]

Of the more than 1200 persons living in Virginia at this time at least 357 were killed on this day of March 22, 1622. This "Great Massacre" would have been even worse if God had not intervened through an Indian boy named Chanco.

Chanco had become a Christian, and he was grateful for the kindness the settlers had shown him. When his brother told him of the plans for the massacre, he passed on the dreadful news to his godfather and employer, Richard Pace. Pace, who lived across from Jamestown, slipped away in the night and warned Governor Wyatt at Jamestown. Because of this warning, the capital of Virginia and the plantations nearby had time to pre-pare for defense. The attacking Indians were unable to enter the town or to surprise the people and the settlements near it.[48]

One early historian wrote: *"The slaughter had been universal, if God had not put it into the heart of an Indian belonging to one Mr. Pace, to disclose it."* Unfortunately, after the massacre little more was done by the colonists to spread the Christian faith among the Indians, the very thing that saved them.

Slavery in Virginia

A few weeks after the meeting of the first representative assembly in 1619, a load of 20 negroes from a Dutch pirate ship landed at Jamestown. While the institution of slavery was common all the world over, the early settlers had no intention of propagating slavery in Virginia. To purchase someone's labor as an indentured servant for a limited period of time was more acceptable, since that is how many of the early English settlers came to the new world. Very few other blacks came or were brought to Virginia until after 1670 when slavery began to be a more accepted means of labor.

Slavery was a cruel system and was a disgrace to the Christians who birthed the nation. It reveals a failure on behalf of the church to properly deal with this sin. However, God is His providence and mercy, used this sinful situation to introduce the blacks who came to America in bondage to true liberty, that which only Christ Jesus can bring.

One event that contributed to the rise of slavery in Virginia was the civil war in England. When Oliver Cromwell won the war against the King in 1649, thousands of refugees and supporters of the King and the established church fled to Virginia, causing the population to almost triple within ten years. These "Cavaliers" were enemies of the puritans and were generally less devout in their faith. They insisted on Virginians conforming to the Anglican faith. The Cavaliers were "gentlemen" who were not used to working for themselves, which led to a greater acceptance of slavery as a means of labor.

Only 300 negroes were in Virginia as of 1650, but by 1671 there were 2000. There were 6000 by 1701 when the General Assembly tried to stop slave ships from coming to Virginia by placing a heavy tax on them. The English Parliament, however, overruled Virginia's law and the slave trade continued. By 1730 there were 28,500 blacks in Virginia, one fourth of the population.

Nathaniel Bacon, 1676

During Cromwell's tenure in England, which ended in 1660, Virginia enjoyed some increased powers for its General Assembly. Yet, with the restoration of the king in England came the king-appointed governor to Virginia. Governor Berkeley refused to call for elections of the House of Burgesses and generally denied all opportunity for the people to have any voice in the government for sixteen years.

In 1676 one of the members of the Council, Nathaniel Bacon, was chosen by the people to lead a volunteer company to defend themselves against recent Indian attacks. This action was taken because Governor Berkeley would not do anything about the problem, not wanting to risk his profitable personal trade with the Indians. When the new House of Burgesses was chosen that year, Bacon was elected one of its members. When he arrived at Jamestown to take his seat in the government, Berkeley had him arrested, saying his action against the Indians was illegal. After reprimanding him, Governor Berkeley released him to take his seat on the Council, but Berkeley still refused to give him a commission to fight the Indians, who had killed hundreds of settlers.

When the colonists heard of this, hundreds of them rallied around Bacon and marched with him to the State House, where they demanded five new laws be enacted concerning a commission to fight the Indians, electing representatives, and fair taxation. Bacon wanted a just and democratic government in Virginia. Governor Berkeley later tried to violate these laws and attempted to get the militia to attack Bacon. This prompted Bacon and many people to march against Jamestown. There was a fight against the governor's troops, who fled, and upon entering the town, Bacon burned it. Before organizing a more democratic government, Bacon died of malaria and a weakened body resulting from hunger and cold and long marches through swamps and forests. Nathaniel Bacon was a patriot who gave his life to protect the rights of the people against tyranny, a struggle that would not be won until one hundred years later.

The site of the third state house, which was burnt in this year of 1676, can be seen just behind the Memorial Cross in Jamestown Historic Park.

🔔 *Jamestown Settlement*

Located next to Jamestown Historical park, Jamestown Settlement is a living history museum that was established in 1957 to celebrate the 350th anniversary of Jamestown. It contains a reconstructed fort and village as Jamestown would have appeared in the 1620s, full-scale replicas of the three ships (named *Susan Constant, Godspeed,* and *Discovery*) that brought the first settlers, and a re-created Powhatan Indian Village. Costumed characters demonstrate life in early Virginia for natives and colonists. Also at the Settlement are Museum Galleries that tell the early story of Jamestown and the Powhatan Indians.

Section 5

Williamsburg: The Colonial Capital

The capital of Virginia was moved in 1699 from Jamestown to Williamsburg and remained there most of the next century, until 1780. When the capital was moved to its new location, the town, which had been called Middle Plantation, was renamed in honor of the reigning English King, William III.

For 80 years, Williamsburg was the center of the political, social, and cultural life of Virginia. Twice each year when the general court met, the population of Williamsburg swelled to double its normal 2000 inhabitants.

In the 1920s Rev. W.A.R. Goodwin, rector of Bruton Parish Church, inspired John D. Rockefeller to give time and money to the restoration of eighteenth-century Williamsburg. Today there are 88 original structures and numerous rebuilt structures that are a part of the 175-acre Colonial Williamsburg Historic Area.

☖ The College of William and Mary

The College of William and Mary was started mainly due to the efforts of Rev. James Blair in order, according to its charter of 1691, *"that the Church of Virginia may be furnished with a seminary of ministers of the Gospel, and that the youth may be piously educated in good letters and manners, and that the Christian religion may be propagated among the Western Indians to the glory Almighty God."[1]*

☖ Wren Building

The College is the second oldest in America and its first structure, the Wren Building, is the oldest building in continuous use in America, built between 1695 and 1698. In 1732 a Chapel wing was added where all would gather daily for morning and evening prayers. Presidents Jefferson, Monroe, Tyler, and Benjamin Harrison were educated here, as well as John Marshall, the famous Chief Justice of the Supreme Court.

A few years after the Wren Building was completed a separate house was built for the president of the college, and Brafferton Hall was built for Indian students. Each year numerous Indian children were educated and cared for at the college. The desire was that through education the Indian students could be converted to Christianity. This same motive led to the attempted beginning of the College at Henrico in the early years of the Jamestown settlement.[2]

The people of Virginia believed it was the duty of parents, not the government, to provide primary education. Most children were educated in their homes but some free schools supported by private persons were started. These were not only for the settlers but also for the children of the Indians. Benjamin Symmes started the first free school in America in 1634 in Elizabeth City. Six other similar schools were started in Virginia by 1721.

Academies were also started to provide more advanced education in preparation for college. These developed in homes as parents hired tutors to supplement their children's education. Children from nearby homes also came to study under these tutors. This was how Thomas Jefferson was prepared for college at William and Mary.

As pioneers moved to the western parts of Virginia, they did not forget education. The Bible and ministers were their main source of education. Almost everyone owned a Bible and most people could read it. Its ideas shaped their character and thinking more than anything else.

Grammar School Room

Boys of about age 12 were taught in this room in preparation for college. They learned Greek, Latin, mathematics, geography, penmanship, and the Church of England catechism. Studies lasted about 4 years.

Moral Philosophy Room

The basis of the curriculum in the school of philosophy was the study of the nature of God, man, and the cosmos. Other courses in the four year program leading to a Bachelor of Arts degree included logic, rhetoric, ethics, and natural philosophy (mathematics, physics, and metaphysics). Those receiving a degree had to submit a written thesis and make an oral defense of it.

The Chapel

From the time it was built in 1732, the chapel was used for daily prayer. Students typically began their day at 6 or 7 o'clock with a morning prayer service in the chapel. Classes followed breakfast and the midday dinner, with evening prayer at 5 P.M. A light supper and a final counting and blessing of the students ended the day before bed.

People buried in the crypt include: Sir John Randolph and his sons, Peyton and John, Governor Botetourt, and Bishop James Madison.

The Great Hall

This room served as a dining hall and a place for large meetings, lectures, and balls. The House of Burgesses and General Court met here from 1700-1704 while the Capitol was being built and in 1747 when the Capitol burned. This room served as the chapel until 1732. Paintings on the north wall include Robert Boyle (whose estate executors contributed money to the college after Boyle's death in 1691), William and Mary, and James Blair.

🔔 *John Blair House*

Signer of the United States Constitution

This house is not open to the public but it is important to note as the residence of one of the signers of the U.S. Constitution. John Blair, Jr., was born in Williamsburg in 1732. His maternal grandfather was a minister. Blair was the great-nephew of James Blair, the founder of the College of William and Mary.

John attended William and Mary and studied law in London and upon returning to America established a successful practice of law in Williamsburg. His achievements were many: Member of the House of Burgesses, 1766-1770; Clerk of the Council, 1770-1775; a member of Virginia's Constitutional Convention, serving on the committee that drew up the first state constitution and Virginia's Declaration of Rights; selected as a judge of the General Court of Virginia, becoming Chief Justice in 1779; member of the Constitutional Convention and signer of the Constitution, 1787; Associate Justice of the United States Supreme Court, 1789-1796.

John Blair, Jr., spent his last four years at his home in Williamsburg, where he died in 1800. He is buried in the graveyard of Bruton Parish Church, which is where he worshipped all his life.

🔔 *Public Hospital*

Opened in 1773, the Public Hospital was the first such institution built in North America solely for the care and treatment of the mentally ill. The church generally provided such care in a community. At the urging of Governor Fauquier (1758-1768) in 1766, to help those "Persons who are so unhappy as to be deprived of their reason," the General Assembly passed an act (in 1770) to "make Provision for the Support and Maintenance of Ideots, Lunaticks, and other Persons of unsound Minds."

♤ *Bruton Parish Church*

In 1715 Bruton Parish Church was completed. The governor, the General Assembly, the students of William and Mary College, and most of the people of the town met here to worship together. Notables who worshipped here included George Washington, Thomas Jefferson, James Monroe, and John Tyler. This Church was the scene of many significant events in the life of the capital and the colony. The Church bell rang out to signal many important events: the repeal of the Stamp Act in 1766; Virginia's proclamation as an independent state in 1776, two months before the Declaration of Independence was agreed to in Philadelphia; the surrender of Cornwallis in 1781 at Yorktown; and the peace with Great Britain in 1783. It is said that the stone baptismal font was brought from an earlier church at Jamestown.

The Anglican Church was the established church in colonial Virginia and therefore was supported by the state. Every white was a member (except for a small numbers of dissenters — which grew greatly after the Great Awakening and around the time of the Revolution. The influence of Baptist and Presbyterian dissenters brought about the disestablishment of the Episcopal Church in the 1780s via Jefferson's and Madison's work.) Those people not attending divine service at least once a month could be fined. A Sunday service included readings from the Book of Common Prayer, a sermon, and, four times a year, communion. Ministers would also deliver sermons on election days or other special days.

Blacks who lived in the area also attended services. They sat in the north gallery. Over 1000 blacks were baptized in Bruton Church after the mid 1700s. After the Revolution a number of blacks established their own church. In 1793 "the Baptist Church of black people at Williamsburg" was received, with its 500 members, into the Dover Baptist Association.

The Great Awakening of the 1740's and 1750's had an impact in

Virginia as it did throughout the colonies. Its leading figure, Rev. George Whitefield of England, visited and preached to large crowds in Williamsburg. This movement had a profound impact on the future leaders of the Revolution who were young men at the time of the awakening. Christian groups not part of the established church in Virginia, like the Presbyterians and Baptists, began to grow rapidly. One Presbyterian minister who came to Virginia during this time, Rev. Samuel Davies, had a profound impact on Patrick Henry, who regularly attended his services. James Madison was tutored at home by a Presbyterian minister and he eventually went to the College of New Jersey (Princeton), a Presbyterian University founded during the first Great Awakening. Madison also greatly admired the Baptists in his town who were imprisoned for preaching without a license. They helped elect him to office to promote religious freedom in Virginia and the United States.

The Bruton Parish Church was the site of many days of prayer and fasting. When the colonists called for a day of prayer and fasting in June of 1774 for Boston,

> . . .the House of Burgesses assembled at their place of meet-ing; went in procession, with the speaker at their head, to the church and listened to a discourse. 'Never,' a lady wrote, 'since my residence in Virginia have I seen so large a congregation as was this day assembled to hear divine service.' The preacher se-lected for his text the words: 'be strong and of good courage, fear not, nor be afraid of them; for the Lord thy God, He it is that doth go with thee. He will not fail thee nor forsake thee.' 'The people,' Jefferson says, 'met generally, with anxiety and alarm in their countenances; and the effect of the day, through the whole colony, was like a shock of electricity, arousing every man and placing him erect and solidly on his centre.[3]

This act initiated by Virginia and imitated in other colonies brought about the greatest miracle of the Revolution: that colonies with different nationalities, religious opinions, and modes of colonial government would be able to unite in the same principles of theory and actions in so short a time. As Rosalie Slater states:

> *It ... was, perhaps, a singular example in the history of mankind — thirteen clocks were made to strike together; a perfection of mechanism which no artist had ever before effected. Within the space of two months, for the first time in Christian history, three million people achieved Biblical Christian Unity.*[4]

Our national motto reflects this miracle: *E Pluribus Unum — From Many, One.*

🔔 *George Wythe House*

Signer of Declaration and Constitution

George Wythe (1726-1806) — a lawyer, teacher, legislator, and judge — was one of the most influential men in America during his life. He was one of only eight men to sign both the *Declaration* and the *Constitution.*

Some of Wythe's political activities included: first elected to the House of Burgesses in 1754 and served most of the years until 1769; from 1769 to 1775, he was clerk of the House; signer of the *Declaration of Independence*; elected speaker of the House of Delegates in 1777; elected in 1778 as one of the three judges of Virginia's High Court; signer of the *U.S. Constitution.*

Wythe aided in revising the laws of Virginia along with Jefferson and Edmund Pendleton. He was America's first titled "Professor of Law" (1779), training such people as Jefferson (who studied law in Wythe's office prior to his professorship), John Marshall, James Monroe, and Henry Clay. Jefferson referred to Wythe as "my faithful and beloved Mentor in youth, and my most affectionate friend through life."

Wythe died in 1806 when he was poisoned, probably by his grandnephew George Sweeney who hoped to profit financially from his death. Wythe lived long enough to disinherit him. While a slave witnessed the act, Sweeney was never convicted because at that time a slaves' testimony was not admissible in Virginia courts. Like many Virginians of his time, Wythe opposed slavery and freed his slaves in his will at his death. Wythe is buried in St. John's Churchyard in Richmond.

Jefferson stayed in the Wythe House in 1776 and George Washington made it his headquarters just before the battle of Yorktown in 1781.

🔔 *The Governor's Palace*

The Governor's Palace, which was begun to be built in 1706, served as the home for seven royal governors and the first two governors of independent Virginia, Patrick Henry (Governor from 1776-1779) and Thomas Jefferson (Governor from 1779-1781). When the palace was completed in 1722 it was one of the finest such buildings in colonial America. Alexander Spotswood was the first royal governor to live in the palace, moving into it in 1716, six years before it was completed. Redecorations, repairs, and additions were made over the years by various governors. Jefferson was living in the Governor's Palace when Richmond became the capital of Virginia in 1780. He was the last governor to reside in this building as the governor's residence moved to Richmond in that year. In December 1781 the Palace burnt to the ground.

On November 11, 1779, while Jefferson was governor and living in the Palace, he issued a proclamation appointing *"a day of publick and solemn thanksgiving and prayer to Almighty God, earnestly recommending to all the good people of this commonwealth, to set apart the said day for those purposes, and to the several Ministers of religion to meet their respective societies thereon, to assist them in their prayers, edify them with their discourses, and generally to perform the sacred duties of their function, proper for the occasion."* The proclamation contained a number of items for which the people were asked to pray, including:

. . . for the continuance of his favour and protection to these United States; . . .that He would. . . spread the light of christian knowledge through the remotest corners of the earth;. . . . That he would in mercy look down upon us, pardon all our sins, and receive us into his favour; and finally, that he would establish the independence of these United States upon the basis of religion and virtue, and support and protect them in the enjoyment of peace, liberty and safety.[5]

The present Palace was reconstructed, beginning in 1930, from various colonial records as a replica of the original. The Parlor Room, or waiting room on the front and right, has 34 Scripture prints hanging on the walls. These drawings are of scenes from the life of Christ.

🔔 *Market Square*

This green open space was used by nearby farmers to sell their wares on market day — which in the later part of the eighteenth century often took place six times per week. People often shopped daily to get fresh food items.

The local militia would also train in the square several times a year. The militia was composed of every able-bodied white male between the age of 16 and 60. This training was often watched by many of the local residents.

Market square was used for the two annual fairs, public announcements, and elections and celebrations. Men would gather in front of the Courthouse to choose their local officials. Ministers would deliver special sermons from the area, or at times in front of the church.

♨ *Courthouse*

Both the county and city courts met once per month in the Courthouse, at times lasting several days if there were enough cases. All types of cases were heard here, except the more serious ones involving life and limb which were heard by the General Court that met in the Capitol. Court days attracted many visitors to the town to not only hear the news at court, but to also witness the punishment of the offenders, which was often carried out in public immediately after the verdict. This might be a public flogging at the whipping post located by the courthouse, or time spent in the stocks exposed to public shame.

♨ *Peyton Randolph House*

President of the First Continental Congress

Peyton Randolph (1721-1775) was elected to the House of Burgesses in 1748 and served as the Speaker from 1766-1775. He was unanimously elected to be the President of the first Continental Congress which met in Philadelphia in 1774. He was described by a colleague as a "venerable man,. . . an honest man; has knowledge, temper, experience, judgment, above all, integrity,"

Peyton's cousin, Thomas Jefferson, wrote in a letter to his grandson, that in his early years, when faced with difficult situations, he would ask himself how Peyton Randolph would act and if his intended course would meet with Randolph's approval.

As a law-examiner, Randolph was one of the men who interviewed Patrick Henry for a law license in 1760. Randolph signed Henry's license, though Henry had only read law for six weeks. Thomas Jefferson said Randolph acknowledged Henry was very ignorant of law, but that Randolph "perceived that he was a man of genius, and did not doubt he would soon qualify himself."[6]

Jefferson bought Randolph's library after his death in 1775. These books became part of Jefferson's collection which formed the nucleus for the Library of Congress.

♨ *Public Gaol*

The Public Gaol is where persons accused of felonies would be held until court was convened to hear their case. Debtors also were held here. Punishment for convicted criminals in colonial Virginia was swift and sometimes harsh. The death penalty was not only invoked for murder but also, at times, for such offenses as horse stealing, arson, forgery, burglary, and piracy. First time offenders might be granted clemency.

♨ *The Capitol*

When the State House burned in Jamestown in 1698 it was decided to move the capital to Williamsburg. The foundation for the Capitol Building was laid in 1701 and it was first occupied in 1704. The west end was used by the General Court, the Governor and his Council. The east end was used by the House of Burgesses and after independence, the General Assembly, up until 1780 when the capital moved to Richmond.

The Council was composed of 12 leading colonists who were appointed by the king for life. The House of Burgesses consisted of two members elected from each county in Virginia, plus one member each from Jamestown, Williamsburg, Norfolk, and the College of William and Mary. The Council not only served as the upper house of the legislature but also assisted the governor by acting as a council of state and serving with him on the General Court. Sessions of the General Assembly were convened periodically by the governor and would last from a few days to several weeks. The General Court met in the spring and fall, and the criminal court would meet in the summer and winter if necessary.

The Capitol is shaped like an H with a large conference room connecting the two wings on the upper floor. This provided a convenient place for joint conferences of the General Assembly to work our any differences of opinions. Morning prayers were also conducted here.

It was in the conference room that Patrick Henry spoke out boldly against the Stamp Act in 1765 saying that only the legislatures of the colonies had the right to tax the American people. On the floor of the House of Burgesses he went on to say:

"Caesar had his Brutus; Charles the First, his Cromwell; and George the Third..."

"Treason! Treason!" shouted the Speaker of the House.

"Treason! Treason!" echoed from every part of the room.

Without faltering for an instant, and fixing on the Speaker an eye that flashed fire, the orator added —

"...may profit by their example. If this be treason, make the most of it."

It was in the Capitol that the first call was made to the Continental Congress to declare the colonies free and independent states. On May 15, 1776, the burgesses unanimously adopted a resolution for American independence. Acting on this resolution, Richard Henry Lee, on June 7, introduced a motion for independence on the floor of the Continental Congress in Philadelphia. This led to the writing and adoption of the *Declaration of Independence* in July.

It was in the Capitol on June 12 that the Virginia Convention adopted the *Virginia Declaration of Rights* written by George Mason. This *Declaration* became the basis of the Federal *Bill of Rights* that later was added to the *U.S. Constitution* in 1791. The *Virginia Declaration of Rights* states that:

. . . All men are by nature equally free and independent and

have certain inherent rights. . . . namely, the enjoyment of life and liberty, with the means of acquiring and possessing property, and pursuing and obtaining happiness and safety. That all power is vested in, and consequently derived from, the people; that magistrates are their trustees and servants and at all times amenable to them. . . . That no free government, or the blessings of liberty, can be preserved to any people but by a firm adherence to justice, moderation, temperance, frugality, and virtue, and by frequent recurrence to fundamental principles. . . . That all men are equally entitled to the free exercise of religion, according to the dictates of conscience; and that it is the mutual duty of all to practice Christian forbearance, love, and charity toward each other.

The Virginia Constitution was also adopted on the 29th of June in the Capitol Building.

🔔 *Raleigh Tavern*

Taverns in Colonial times were nothing like the taverns of today, which are primarily drinking establishments. Rather, they were more like a motel with a restaurant where people stayed over night, ate meals, and socialized.

Raleigh Tavern was the favorite meeting place for many of our Founding Fathers while in the capital city. It was even used for meetings by the House of Burgesses when the Governor dissolved that body of elected officials. It was here that the proposal for a colony-wide day of prayer was suggested by Thomas Jefferson in 1774 *"...to invoke the divine interposition to give to the American people one heart and one mind to oppose by all just means every injury to American rights.*"[8]

This tavern was also the place where Jefferson's close friend, Dabney Carr, proposed, in 1773, that the colonies organize Committees of Correspondence. Jefferson, Patrick Henry, and the Lees were in full support of this idea and helped in forming Virginia's Committee. While meeting at the Raleigh Tavern in 1774, the Virginia delegates called for the first Continental Congress and also agreed to boycott importing British goods as a way to protest the tyrannical action of Britain.

🔔 *The Powder Magazine*

The Magazine was built in 1715 to store arms and ammunition that were used to protect the colony. In addition to muskets, shot, powder, and flints, other military equipment — such as tents, swords, canteens, tools — were also kept here. After the Civil War the building was used as a market, a Baptist meeting house, a dancing school, and a livery stable.

An event at the Powder Magazine was the spark that ignited the revolution in Virginia. In March, 1775, at the meeting of the Second Virginia Convention held at St. John's Church in Richmond, Patrick Henry urged Virginians to prepare to defend themselves militarily against the tyranny of Britain in his famous "give me liberty or give me death" speech. When Governor Dunmore learned of their resolve to use force if necessary, he secretly sent men in the night preceding the 21st of April to capture the colonist's supply of gunpowder and arms being stored in the Powder Magazine. Believing the governor should return the arms or pay for them, Patrick Henry assembled a body of the Hanover County Militia to march to Williamsburg to demand this take place.

Before setting out, Henry not only spoke to the militia leaders but also to the county committee, seeking their approval in order to give greater authority to his intended action. William Wirt relates Henry's remarks:

> *When assembled, he addressed them with all the powers of his eloquence; laid open the plan on which the British ministry had fallen to reduce the colonies to subjection, by robbing them*

of all the means of defending their rights; spread before their eyes, in colours of vivid description, the fields of Lexington and Concord, still floating with the blood of their countrymen, gloriously shed in the general cause; showed them that the recent plunder of the magazine in Williamsburg was nothing more than a part of the general system of subjugation; that the moment was now come in which they were called upon to decide, whether they chose to live free, and hand down the noble inheritance to their children, or to become hewers of wood, and drawers of water to those lordlings, who were themselves the tools of a corrupt and tyrannical ministry – he painted the country in a state of subjugation, and drew such pictures of wretched debasement and abject vassalage, as filled their souls with horror and indignation – on the other hand, he carried them, by the powers of his eloquence, to an eminence like Mount Pisgah; showed them the land of promise, which was to be won by their valour, under the support and guidance of heaven; and sketched a vision of America, enjoying the smiles of liberty and peace, the rich productions of her agriculture waving on every field, her commerce whitening every sea, in tints so bright, so strong, so glowing, as set the souls of his hearers on fire. He had no doubt, he said, that that God, who in former ages had hardened Pharaoh's heart, that he might show forth his power and glory in the redemption of his chosen people, had, for similar purposes, permitted the flagrant outrages which had occurred in Williamsburg, and throughout the continent. It was for them now to determine, whether they were worthy of this divine interference; whether they would accept the high boon now held out to them by heaven – that if they would, though it might lead them through a sea of blood, they were to remember that the same God whose power divided the Red Sea for the deliverance of Israel, still reigned in all his glory, unchanged and unchangeable – was still the enemy of the oppressor, and the friend of the oppressed – that he would cover them from their enemies by a pillar of fire – that for his own part, he was anxious that his native county should distinguish itself in this grand career of liberty and glory, and snatch the noble prize which was now offered to their grasp. . . .

The effect was equal to his wishes. The meeting was in a flame, and the decision immediately taken, that the powder should be retrieved, or counterbalanced by a reprisal.[9]

Dunmore paid for the arms and powder, but afterwards declared Henry an outlaw.

During this time more news of the fighting in Lexington and Concord reached Virginia. The Virginia Gazette covered the battles in Massachusetts, ending their story in these words: *"The sword is now drawn. God knows when it will be sheathed."*[10] The war for independence had begun.

Section 6

Yorktown: The Final Battlefield of the Revolution

Yorktown was the scene of the last major battle of the Revolutionary War. It was also the scene of a "Tea Party" similar to the one in Boston in 1773. In November of 1774, in response to the arrival of a ship carrying unjustly taxed tea, the citizens of Yorktown dumped the tea into the York River. The Committee of Safety for York County boarded the ship at 10 AM, declaring to be taking such action in response to the unjust laws of England. They were standing with Boston in their resistance.

Once the War for Independence commenced in 1775, it would be five years before any major battles were fought on Virginia soil. However, Virginia made significant contributions to the war from the beginning, the most notable being the Commanding General of the American troops, George Washington, who served 8 years without pay. Others Virginians who were brave leaders in the war included: Captain John Paul Jones from Fredericksburg who founded the American Navy; George Rogers Clark who conquered the Northwest Territory; Daniel Morgan; and General Peter Muhlenberg who was a clergyman in Woodstock before leading the men of his church off to war.

☖ *Yorktown Battlefield Visitors Center*

In October of 1781, British General Cornwallis had his troops stationed at Yorktown, Virginia. While Cornwallis waited for reinforcements, Washington marched his troops from New York to Yorktown. Unknown to Washington or Cornwallis, a French fleet under Admiral De Grasse arrived just in time to defeat the British fleet sent to relieve General Cornwallis at Yorktown.

☖ Redoubts 9 and 10

Without reinforcements, Cornwallis was barely holding out against the siege of the American and French forces. Redoubts number 9 and 10 were all that kept Washington from an open avenue to fire upon the British forces in Yorktown. On the night of October 14, Washington sent two detachments to take these two British fortifications. Four hundred French troops attacked Redoubt 9, while the same number of American troops attacked Redoubt 10. Lt. Col. Alexander Hamilton led the American troops, who overcame the 70 British and German defenders in fierce, hand-to-hand fighting in the space of 10 minutes. The French forces overtook the 120 defenders of Redoubt 9 in about half an hour. The second siege line that the Allies built from these points enabled them to easily fire into the British position. It was now merely a matter of time before Cornwallis would have to surrender.

As a last resort Cornwallis decided to attempt a retreat across the York River. At 10 o'clock on the night of October 17th, sixteen large boats were loaded with troops and embarked for Gloucester. After the first few boats had landed a great turn of events occurred. In the official dispatch to his superior, Cornwallis wrote:

> . . .But at this critical moment, the weather, from being moderate and calm, changed to a violent storm of wind and rain, and drove all the boats, some of which had troops on board, down the river.

Due to this miraculous weather change, Cornwallis was unable to complete his intended retreat and found his force divided when Washington's batteries opened at daybreak. When the boats finally returned he ordered them to bring back the troops that had passed during the night. Later that day he surrendered his forces to General Washington. This essentially marked the end of the war.

General Washington and our Congress recognized the Providence of God in the battle of Yorktown. The Journals of the Continental Congress record this entry:

> *Resolved, that Congress will, at two o'clock this day, go in procession to the Dutch Lutheran Church, and return thanks to Almighty God, for crowning the allied arms of the United States and France, with success, by the surrender of the Earl of Cornwallis.*

And in his congratulatory order to the allied army on the day after the surrender, General Washington concluded:

> *The General congratulates the army upon the glorious event of yesterday... Divine service is to be performed tomorrow in the several brigades and divisions. The commander-in-chief recommends that the troops not on duty should universally attend with that seriousness of deportment and gratitude of heart which the recognition of such reiterated and astonishing interpositions of Providence demand of us.[1]*

☖ *The Nelson House*

Thomas Nelson Jr. was born in Yorktown on December 26, 1738. His father, William Nelson was a native of England and after emigrating to America made a large fortune through his industry. One year old Thomas was with his father, William, when he laid the foundation of the Nelson House in 1740. Thomas would later become a signer of the *Declaration of Independence*, a General in the Revolutionary War, and Governor of Virginia.

When Thomas married at age 23 he and his wife, Lucy, moved into this house. Their home was noted for hospitality. From the beginning of the conflict with England, Thomas Nelson was a leader of the patriots. He was a member of the 1774 House of Burgesses that Governor Dunmore dissolved. Nelson was one of the 89 men who met the next day at Raleigh Tavern. The action they took led to the meeting of the First Continental Congress in September 1774. When the Virginia delegates met in March, 1775, at St. John's Church in Richmond, Nelson introduced the proposal to organize the militia of the State for their defense. Governor Dunmore considered this act treasonous. Patrick Henry strongly supported the measure, delivering his famous "Give Me Liberty" speech.

Nelson was a member of the Continental Congress in 1775, 1776, and 1777. As a member of the Congress in 1776, he signed the *Declaration of Independence*. Failing health forced him to retire from public service in 1777, but not long after he was asked by the Governor of Virginia to assume command of the forces of the state to prepare for an attack by the British. This attack did not materialize. Not long afterwards, Nelson raised a volunteer corps at his own expense to assist the Continental Army under Washington's command.

In June, 1781, Nelson was elected governor of Virginia. He sought to borrow two million dollars for the state from some friends, but they would not lend "the governor a shilling on the security of the commonwealth; but would lend *him* all they could possibly raise."[2]

As governor and head of the Virginia militia he led troops to Yorktown in the fall of 1781 to assist in defeating the British. One writer records what happened at the battle:

> *During the siege, observing his own house uninjured by the artillery of the American batteries he inquired the cause. A respect for his property, was assigned. Nelson. . . requested that the artillerists would not spare his house more than any other, especially as he knew it to be occupied by the principal officers*

of the British Army. Two pieces were accordingly pointed against it. The first shot went through the house and killed two... officers. . . . Others balls soon dislodged the hostile tenants.[3]

It has been said that Nelson gave 10 guineas to the man who fired the first shot. His home was not badly damaged, but some holes caused by the cannon fire can still be seen today on one outside wall.

In his general orders, George Washington acknowledged Nelson and the militia saying "the highest praises are due" them "for the difficulties and dangers which they met with so much firmness and patriotism."[4]

In November, 1781, Nelson was forced to resign as governor due to ill health. He lived seven more years, but three of these were in relative poverty because he was forced to sell most of his property to pay for debts incurred due to the war. He had payed two regiments out of his own pocket and personally secured state loans for two million dollars needed to carry on the war. One writer says of these acts of generosity:

He had spent a princely fortune in his country's service; his horses had been taken from the plough, and sent to drag the munitions of war; his granaries had been thrown open to a starving soldiery, and his ample purse had been drained to its last dollar, when the credit of Virginia could not bring a sixpence into her treasury.

Neither Nelson in his life, nor his widow in the 30 years following his death, received reimbursement for his expenses. Nelson never complained. Colonel Innis of Virginia said of Nelson, "This was a man."[5]

Nelson's simple gravestone at Grace Church graveyard in Yorktown summarizes the price he paid:

Thomas Nelson
Governor of Virginia.
He Gave All for Liberty

♧ *Yorktown Victory Center*

The Yorktown Victory Center is a living museum that presents the story of the American Revolution through a road to the Revolution walk way, audio-visual exhibits, a film, and an outdoor Continental Army camp.

Section 7

Patrick Henry and His Homes at Scotchtown and Red Hill

🔔 Scotchtown

Patrick Henry, with his wife Sarah Shelton and their six children, moved into Scotchtown House in April 1771. This house, located northeast of Richmond near Beaverdam, Virginia, was built around 1719 and is one of the oldest Virginia plantation houses. Henry lived here for about seven years — seven of his most politically active years. It was during these years that Henry served in the First Continental Congress in Philadelphia in 1774, gave his famous "Liberty or Death" speech on March 23, 1775, at the meeting of the Virginia legislature at St. John's Church in Richmond, and, on June 29, 1776, was elected the first governor of the independent Commonwealth of Virginia.

🔔 Red Hill, Last Home and Burial Site

Henry lived in a dozen different places in Virginia, but his last home at Red Hill was his favorite. He called it "the garden spot of the world." He and his second wife, Dorothea, moved to Red Hill in 1794. Sarah died in 1775 and two years later Patrick married Dorothea Dandridge, granddaughter of Royal Governor Alexander Spotswood. He and Dorothea had eleven children, giving Patrick 17 in all. Two of his children were born at Red Hill. Red Hill is located southeast of Lynchburg, Virginia, near Brookneal.

Henry moved to Red Hill with the intent of retiring from public service. Therefore, he refused offers from President Washington to serve as Secretary of State in 1795 and as Chief Justice of the Supreme Court in 1796. In 1796 he also refused an offer from the General Assembly of Virginia to serve as Governor. In 1799 he refused an offer from President Adams to serve on a Mission to France. He was pressed into running for the House of Delegates in the spring of 1799. Though elected he was unable to take office, dying on June 6 at the age of 63. He is buried at Red Hill in the family graveyard where his stone bears the inscription: "His fame his best epitaph."

Patrick Henry, Orator of the American Revolution

As a great orator and man of vision, Patrick Henry was one of the first and foremost leaders in the cause of independence. Henry's words and actions in the Virginia House of Burgesses in 1765 were the first steps taken in opposing the unjust taxation policies of Britain. He set in motion events that resulted in America's independence. His ability to inspire and lead through his oratorical skills were evident from his first service in public life. Thomas Jefferson said, *"He was the greatest orator that ever lived."*[1] But Henry was not only a voice of liberty and a man of vision, he was also a man of virtue. This is what provided the great strength of his words and the ability to persuade men. He was able to lead in the cause of liberty because he loved and valued liberty.

George Mason said of Henry:

He is by far the most powerful speaker I ever heard; every word he says not only engages but commands the attention; and your passions are no longer your own when he addresses them. But his eloquence is the smallest part of his merit. He is in my opinion the first man upon this continent, as well in abilities as public virtues, and had he lived in Rome about the time of the

first Punic War, when the Roman people had arrived at their me-
ridian glory and their virtue not tarnished, Mr. Henry's talents
must have put him at the head of that glorious commonwealth.[2]

Early Life and Education

Patrick Henry was born May 29, 1736 in Hanover County,
Virginia. He was the second of nine children born to Colonel John
Henry and Sarah Winston Syme Henry. He was educated at home by
his father and in a local common school. His brother-in-law, Colonel
Samuel Meredith, says:

> *He was sent to a common English school until about the age*
> *of ten years.... He never went to any other school, public or pri-*
> *vate, but remained with his father, who was his only tutor. With*
> *him he acquired a knowledge of the Latin language, and a smat-*
> *tering of the Greek. He became well acquainted with mathemat-*
> *ics, of which he was very fond. At the age of fifteen he was well*
> *versed in both ancient and modern history. . . . There was noth-*
> *ing in early life for which he was remarkable, except his invari-*
> *able habit of close and attentive observation. . . . Nothing*
> *escaped his attention. . . . His father often said that he was one*
> *of the most dutiful sons that ever lived, and his sister, Mrs.*
> *Meredith, states, that he was never known in his life to utter the*
> *name of God, except on a necessary or proper occasion.*[3]

Besides his parents, Patrick was positively influenced by a variety
of people, including his cousins, his uncle the Rev. Patrick Henry,
who was the rector of the local Church of England parish, local
magnates and their stump speeches, and numerous people whom he
listened and spoke to at the nearby stores and churchyard. No one
influenced his oratorical development more than Samuel Davies, the
local Presbyterian leader.

Rev. Samuel Davies was a bold ambassador for Christ. In his
desire to see the Kingdom of God come *on earth as it is in heaven*
he served not only as a pastor but also as a lawyer, an ambassador to
England, and President of Princeton College. E.L. Magoon writes of

Davies that:

> *[H]e had made himself a thorough master of English law, civil and ecclesiastical, and always chose to meet every persecuting indictment in the highest courts with his own plea. . . . [H]e went to England and obtained the explicit sanction of the highest authority with respect to the extension of the Toleration law to Virginia. It was during this mission that. . . George II and many of his court were in the congregation of this American Dissenter. His majesty, struck with admiration, or forgetting the proprieties of the occasion, spoke several times to those around him and smiled. Davies paused a moment, and then looking sternly at the king, exclaimed, "When the lion roars, the beasts of the forest all tremble; and when King Jesus speaks, the princes of earth should keep silence."*[4]

Davies, one of the greatest orators in colonial America, served as the mentor for "the greatest orator that ever lived" — Patrick Henry. When Patrick was around 12 years old his mother joined the church where Samuel Davies preached. Mrs. Henry would attend regularly and would always take Patrick, who from the first showed a high appreciation for the preacher. Each Sunday as they rode home in their buggy, Mrs. Henry and Patrick would review the sermon. This greatly influenced Patrick's thinking and the development of his oratorical skills. Patrick ever declared that Davies was "the greatest orator he ever heard."[5] But Patrick Henry also learned from Davies a sound Biblical theology, one which has produced some of the leading men in all history. William Wirt Henry writes: "His early example of eloquence. . . was Mr. Davies, and the effect of his teaching upon his after life may be plainly traced."[6] This is a great example for Pastors today to be mentors for our youth, inspiring and equipping them to lead in all areas of life.

Henry's association with dissenters via his mother's Presbyterian faith, caused him to greatly aid the cause of religious liberty among various groups, especially the Baptists. Mr. Semple records in his *History of the Baptists in Virginia* how Henry often proved their ally:

. . . being always a friend of liberty, he only needed to be informed of their oppression; without hesitation he stepped forward to their relief. From that time, until the day of their complete emancipation from the shackles of tyranny, the Baptists found in Patrick Henry an unwavering friend. May his name descend to posterity with unsallied honor![7]

Henry often represented Baptist ministers when they were imprisoned for ''the heinous charge of worshipping God according to the dictates of their own consciences.'' Henry secured the release of one minister who had been imprisoned five months on the charge of creating a disturbance by preaching. When the jailer refused to release the man until his jail fees, which were substantial, were paid, Henry secretly covered this cost out of his own pocket. The minister learned of the event over 20 years later.[8]

Examples of Henry's Oratorical Skills

After some failed attempts at business and farming, Patrick weighed his abilities and desires and, at age 23, decided to read law and prepare himself for a life before the bar. After a few months of self-study, Henry went to Williamsburg to be examined by George Wythe and other leading lawyers. He obtained his license in 1760 and was successful from the start. This was a profession for which he was well suited. It not only provided ample income for his growing family, but it also brought him fame. The first case that brought his oratorical skills to light came to be known as ''the Parsons' Cause.''

Parsons' Cause

For many years the Anglican ministers in Virginia were paid with a certain weight of tobacco. When the crop was scarce, the value increased and the people began adjusting the payment to the ministers accordingly. A number of ministers led by Rev. James Maury brought suit for back pay. Patrick Henry took over the defense from another gentleman, but this only after the case was in essence over. As the law was clear, the case was decided in favor of the plaintiff. All that remained was to decide the amount of the settlement. After the counsel for the plaintiff rested his case, Patrick Henry took up the case for the defense. William Wirt Henry writes:

He rose to reply to Mr. Lyons with apparent embarrassment and some awkwardness, and began a faltering exordium. The people hung their heads at the unpromising commencement, and the clergy were observed to exchange sly looks with each other, while his father [who sat on the bench] sank back in his chair in evident confusion. All this was of short duration however. As he proceeded and warmed up with his subject, a wonderous change came over him. His attitude became erect and lofty, his face lighted up with genius, and his eyes seemed to flash fire; his gesture became graceful and impressive, his voice and his emphasis peculiarly charming. His appeals to the passions were overpowering. In the language of those who heard him, "he made their blood to run cold, and their hair to rise on end." In a word, to the astonishment of all, he suddenly burst upon them as an orator of the highest order. The surprise of the people was only equalled by their delight, and so overcome was his father that tears flowed profusely down his cheeks.[9]

During his argument, Henry addressed the plaintiff's attorney's attempt to show the benevolence of the clergy. Captain Trevilian related the words of Henry :

We have heard a great deal about the benevolence and holy zeal of our reverend clergy, but how is this manifested? Do they manifest their zeal in the cause of religion and humanity by practising the mild and benevolent precepts of the Gospel of Jesus? Do they feed the hungry and clothe the naked? Oh, no, gentlemen! Instead of feeding the hungry and clothing the naked, these rapacious harpies would, were their powers equal to their will, snatch from the hearth of their honest parishioner his last hoecake, from the widow and her orphan children their last milch cow! the last bed, nay, the last blanket from the lying-in woman![10]

In his defense, Henry also *"powerfully attacked the tyranny in Church and State, which all felt and yet no one had been bold enough to denounce."*[11]

To close, Henry said the jury had to find in favor of the plaintiff under the ruling of the court, but they need not find more than one farthing. After less than five minutes of deliberation the jury returned with a verdict of one penny damages for the plaintiff. At the conclusion of the trial, *"the feelings of the excited people, which with difficulty had been restrained, now overleaped all bounds, and, wild with delight, they seized their champion and bore him on their shoulders in triumph around the court-yard. . . . It is said that the people who heard this famous speech never tired of talking of it, and they could pay no higher compliment to a speaker afterward than to say of him, 'He is almost equal to Patrick Henry when he plead against the parsons.'"*[12]

Beef!

During the American Revolution, John Hook, a wealthy Scotsman and one suspected of being unfriendly to the American cause, lived in Virginia. When Cornwallis invaded Virginia in 1781, an army commissary, Mr. Venable, took two of Hook's steers for food for the troops. This action was not strictly legal, so after the war Hook brought charges against Venable. Patrick Henry defended Mr. Venable; Mr. Cowan, a prominent lawyer, was for the plaintiff. Wirt relates that during the trial,

[Henry] appeared to have complete control over the passions of his audience: at one time he excited their indignation against Hook: vengeance was visible in every countenance: again, when he chose to relax and ridicule him, the whole audience was in a roar of laughter. He painted the distresses of the American army, exposed almost naked to the rigour of a winter's sky, and marking the frozen ground over which they marched, with the blood of their unshod feet; where was the man, he said, who had an American heart in his bosom, who

*would not have thrown open his fields, his barns, his cellars, the
doors of his house, the portals of his breast, to have received
with open arms, the meanest soldier in that little band of fam-
ished patriots? Where is the man? — There he stands — but
whether the heart of an American beats in his bosom, you, gentlemen, are to judge. He then carried the jury, by the powers of
his imagination, to the plains around York[town], the surrender
of which had followed shortly after the act complained of: he de-
picted the surrender in the most glowing and noble colours of
his eloquence—the audience saw before their eyes the humiliation and dejection of the British, as they marched out of their
trenches—they saw the triumph which lighted up every patriot
face, and heard the shouts of victory, and the cry of Washington
and liberty, as it rung and echoed through the American ranks,
and was reverberated from the hills and shores of the neighbour-
ing river — "but, hark, what notes of discord are these which
disturb the general joy, and silence the acclamations of victory
— they are the notes of John Hook, hoarsely bawling through
the American camp, **beef! beef! beef!**"*

*The whole audience were convulsed: a particular incident
will give a better idea of the effect, than any general description.
The clerk of the court, unable to command himself, and unwill-
ing to commit any breach of decorum in his place, rushed out of
the court house, and threw himself on the grass, in the most violent paroxysm of laughter, where he was rolling, when Hook,
with very different feelings, came our for relief, into the yard
also. "Jemmy Steptoe," said he to the clerk, "what the devil
ails ye, mon?" Mr. Steptoe was only able to say, that he could
not help it. "Never mind ye," said Hook, "wait till billy Cowan
gets up: he'll show him the la'." Mr. Cowan, however, was so
completely overwhelmed by the torrent which bore upon his cli-
ent, that when he rose to reply to Mr. Henry, he was scarcely
able to make an intelligible or audible remark. The cause was
decided almost by acclamation. The jury retired for form sake,
and instantly returned with a verdict for the defendant.[13]*

"If This Be Treason"

In May, 1765, Patrick Henry was elected to the House of Burgesses from Louisa County. The topic of foremost concern for the Virginia legislature was the newly passed stamp act. Though Henry was a novice at the assembly, when he found no one willing to oppose the tax he felt compelled to take action, so he wrote down some resolutions on his own. He would later write of the events:

> *Upon offering them to the house, violent debates ensued. Many threats were uttered, and much abuse cast on me, by the party for submission. After a long and warm contest, the resolutions passed by a very small majority, perhaps of one or two only. The alarm spread throughout America with astonishing quickness, and the ministerial party were overwhelmed. The great point of resistance to British taxation was universally established in the colonies. This brought on the war, which finally separated the two countries, and gave independence to ours. Whether this will prove a blessing or a curse, will depend upon the use our people make of the blessings which a gracious God hath bestowed on us. If they are wise, they will be great and happy. If they are of a contrary character, they will be miserable. — Righteousness alone can exalt them as a nation. Reader! whoever thou art, remember this; and in thy sphere, practise virtue thyself, and encourage it in others.*[14]

During the debates on his resolutions, Patrick Henry spoke out boldly against the Stamp Act saying that only the legislatures of the colonies had the right to tax the American people. On the floor of the House of Burgesses he went on to say:

> *"Caesar had his Brutus; Charles the First, his Cromwell; and George the Third..."*

> *"Treason! Treason!" shouted the Speaker of the House.*

> *"Treason! Treason!" echoed from every part of the room.*

> *Without faltering for an instant, and fixing on the Speaker an*

eye that flashed fire, the orator added —

"...may profit by their example. If this be treason, make the most of it."[15]

In his autobiography, Jefferson said of Henry's speech: *"I attended the debate at the door of the lobby of the House of Burgesses, and heard the splendid display of Mr. Henry's talents as a popular orator. They were great indeed; such as I have never heard from any other man. He appeared to me to speak as Homer wrote."[16]*

Patrick Henry wrote on his copies of the resolutions that *"they formed the first opposition to the stamp act, and the scheme of taxing America by the British parliament."[17]*

Numerous leaders in America attributed to Henry the leading role in the great revolution. William Wirt Henry writes: "America was filled with Mr. Henry's fame, and he was recognized on both sides of the Atlantic as the man who rang the alarm bell which had aroused the continent. His wonderful powers of oratory engaged the attention and excited the admiration of men, and the more so as they were not considered the result of laborious training, but as the direct gift of Heaven. Long before the British poet applied the description to him, he was recognized as—*the forest-born Demosthenes, Whose thunder shook the Philip of the seas."[18]* Patrick Henry "was hailed as the leader raised up by Providence for the occasion."[19]

"Give Me Liberty or Give Me Death"

In March of 1775 the Virginia House of Burgesses convened at St. John's Church in Richmond. They were meeting here instead of in the capital city of Williamsburg to be free from interference of the governor. The tongue (Patrick Henry), the pen (Thomas Jefferson), and the sword (George Washington) of the American Revolution all were a part of this very historic meeting.

The convention members were debating whether to began to prepare themselves militarily in response to the growing conflict between Britain and the colonies. Henry led those advocating immediate preparation. He was supported by George Washington, Thomas Jefferson, Richard Henry Lee, Thomas Nelson, Jr., and others. The opposition, which included Edmund Pendleton, Benjamin Harrison, and Richard Bland, supported a more moderate response of postponing action.

The convention culminated on March 23 with Patrick Henry's now-famous speech. (See *Section 10* on *Richmond, St. John's Church*, for the concluding portions of this speech.) All who heard his speech were awe-struck, and the majority were swayed to agree to his call for a "well-regulated militia."

Address to Hanover County Militia and Leaders

When Governor Dunmore learned that the Virginia legislature had resolved to prepare to defend themselves militarily, he secretly sent men in the night preceding the 21st of April to capture the colonist's supply of gunpowder and arms being stored in the Powder Magazine in Williamsburg. Believing the governor should return the arms or pay for them, Patrick Henry assembled a body of the Hanover County Militia to march to Williamsburg to demand this take place. (Other counties had sent men before this to take action, but they stopped after being assured the problem would be resolved peaceably.)

Before setting out, Henry not only spoke to the militia leaders but also to the county committee, seeking their approval in order to give greater authority to his intended action. (Henry's remarks are given in *Section 5, Williamsburg*, under the *Powder Magazine*.)

Dunmore declared Henry an outlaw, but this only helped to highlight the cause and bring more esteem to Henry in the eyes of Virginians. Henry's action resulted in Dunmore paying for the arms and powder. Wirt writes that *"the same man, whose genius had in the year 1765 given the first political impulse to the revolution, had now the additional honour of heading the first military movement in Virginia, in support of the same cause."* [20]

As most Virginians believed their rights were being trampled upon and saw Patrick Henry as one who would not just talk but act to defend them, *"the heart of Virginia began to go forth to him in expressions of love, of gratitude, and of homage, such as no American colonist perhaps had ever before received."*[21] After the Governor declared Henry a rebel, many counties wrote to him pledging their support. When he set out on May 11 to attend the second Continental Congress, a volunteer guard accompanied him to the border of Virginia to assure the Governor did not use the opportunity to arrest him. All along the way, the people expressed their thanks to him.

Common Virginian's Esteem for Henry

In 1780 the British captured Richmond forcing the General Assembly to meet in Charlottesville. In June of 1781 British General Cornwallis sent a detachment of troops to attack Charlottesville and capture Governor Jefferson and the General Assembly. An incident occurring as the legislators fled from Charlottesville to Staunton, reveals how highly esteemed the common people of Virginia held Patrick Henry:

> *It is said that as Patrick Henry, Benjamin Harrison, Judge Tyler, and Colonel Christian were hurrying along, they saw a little hut in the forest. An old woman was chopping wood by the door. The men were hungry, and stopped to ask her for food.*
>
> *"Who are you?" she asked.*
>
> *"We are members of the legislature," said Patrick Henry; "we have just been compelled to leave Charlottesville on account of the British."*
>
> *"Ride on, then, ye cowardly knaves!" she said in wrath. "Here are my husband and sons just gone to Charlottesville to fight for ye, and you running away with all your might. Clear out! Ye shall have nothing here."*
>
> *"But," replied Mr. Henry, "we were obliged to flee. It would not do for the legislature to be broken up by the enemy. Here is Mr. Benjamin Harrison; you don't think he would have*

fled had it not been necessary?''

"I always thought a great deal of Mr. Harrison till now,'' answered the old woman, *''but he'd no business to run from the enemy.''* And she started to shut the door in their faces.

"Wait a moment, my good woman,'' cried Mr. Henry; *''would you believe that Judge Tyler or Colonel Christian would take to flight if there were not good cause for so doing?''*

"No, indeed that I wouldn't.''

"But,'' he said, *"Judge Tyler and Colonel Christian are here.''*

"They are? Well, I would never have thought it. I didn't suppose they would ever run from the British; but since they have, they shall have nothing to eat in my house. You may ride along.''

Things were getting desperate. Then Judge Tyler stepped forward: "What would you say, my good woman, if I were to tell you that Patrick Henry fled with the rest of us?''

"Patrick Henry!'' she answered angrily, *"I should tell you there wasn't a word of truth in it! Patrick Henry would never do such a cowardly thing.''*

"But this is Patrick Henry,'' said Judge Tyler.

The old woman was astonished; but she stammered and pulled at her apron string, and said: "Well, if that's Patrick Henry, it must be all right. Come in, and ye shall have the best I have in the house.''[22]

The Power of Henry's Life and Speech: Faith and Christian Character

Patrick Henry knew that the strength of free men and free nations is rooted in Christianity. He recognized the importance of Christian principles forming the foundation of free nations. That is why he supported ''a bill, establishing a provision for teachers of the Christian religion." Its preamble stated: "Whereas the general diffusion of Christian knowledge hath a natural tendency to correct the morals of men, restrain their vices, and preserve the peace of society." The bill failed to pass, but not because the people did not believe the purpose was good, but rather they felt the means of accomplishing the goals was not proper.

Henry recognized the Providence of God in the events of history. He wrote in a letter to General Henry Lee, June 27, 1795:

> *The American revolution was the grand operation, which seemed to be assigned by the Deity to the men of this age in our country, over and above the common duties of life. I ever prized at a high rate the superior privilege of being one in that chosen age, to which Providence intrusted its favorite work..*[23]

In a letter to Archibald Blair, January 8, 1799, Henry spoke of the great pillars of American society:

> *And, whilst I see the dangers that threaten ours from her [France's] intrigues and her arms, I am not so much alarmed as at the apprehension of her destroying the great pillars of all government and of social life, — I mean virtue, morality, and religion. This is the armor, my friend, and this alone, that renders us invincible. These are the tactics we should study. If we lose these, we are conquered, fallen indeed.*[24]

According to his daughter, Sarah Butler, Henry read the Bible every morning and after his retirement he devoted much time to its study.[25] He wrote: *"The Bible is worth all the books that ever were printed, and it has been my misfortune that I have never found time to read it with the proper attention and feeling till lately. I trust in the mercy of heaven that it is not yet too late."*[26]

William Wirt wrote: *"Mr. Henry's conversation was remarkably pure and chaste. He never swore. He was never heard to take the name of his Maker in vain. He was a sincere Christian."*[27]

The following incident reveals the humility of Patrick Henry.

Though he had retired from public life many years before, in the spring of 1799, seeing certain dangers threatening his state, he presented himself in Charlotte county as a candidate for the house of delegates. Wirt writes:

> *On the day of the election, as soon as he appeared on the ground, he was surrounded by the admiring and adoring crowd, and whithersoever he moved, the concourse followed him. A preacher of the Baptist church, whose piety was wounded by this homage paid to a mortal, asked the people aloud, "Why they thus followed Mr. Henry about? — Mr. Henry," said he, "is not a god!" "No," said Mr. Henry, deeply affected both by the scene and the remark; "no, indeed, my friend; I am but a poor worm of the dust — as fleeting and unsubstantial as the shadow of the cloud that flies over your fields, and is remembered no more." The tone with which this was uttered, and the look which accompanied it, affected every heart, and silenced every voice. Envy and opposition were disarmed by his humility; the recollection of his past services rushed upon every memory, and he "read his history" in their swimming eyes.* [28]

Moses Coit Tyler records the following from Henry's later years:

> *From one of his grandsons, who was much with him in those days, the tradition is derived that, besides "setting a good example of honesty, benevolence, hospitality, and every social virtue," he assisted "in the education of his younger children," and especially devoted much time "to earnest efforts to establish true Christianity in our country." He gave himself more than ever to the study of the Bible, as well as of two or three of the great English divines, particularly Tillotson, Butler, and Sherlock. The sermons of the latter, he declared, had removed "all doubts of the truth of Christianity"; and from a volume which contained them, and which was full of his penciled notes, he was accustomed to read "every Sunday evening to his family; after which they all joined in sacred music, while he accompanied them on the violin."*

*There seems to have been no time in his life, after his arrival
at manhood, when Patrick Henry was not regarded by his private acquaintances as a positive religious person.... [F]rom a
grandson who spent many years in his household comes the tradition that "his parents were members of the Protestant Episcopal Church [his mother was actually Presbyterian according to
others], of which his uncle, Patrick Henry, was a minister;" that
"he was baptized and made a member of it in early life;" and
that "he lived and died an exemplary member of it." Further-
more, in 1830, the Reverend Charles Dresser, rector of Antrim
Parish, Halifax County, Virginia, wrote that the widow of Patrick Henry told him that her husband used to receive "the communion as often as an opportunity was offered, and on such
occasions always fasted until after he had communicated, and
spent the day in the greatest retirement. This he did both while
governor and afterward." In a letter to one of his daughters,
written in 1796, he makes this touching confession: "Amongst
other strange things said of me, I hear it is said by the deists that
I am one of the number; and, indeed, that some good people
think I am no Christian. This thought gives me much more pain
than the appellation of Tory; because I think religion of infi-
nitely higher importance than politics; and I find much cause to
reproach myself that I have lived so long, and have given no decided and public proofs of my being a Christian. But, indeed, my
dear child, this is a character which I prize far above all this
world has, or can boast."[29]*

While some in public life may have not known of his devote
Christian life, those who saw him in private well knew of his
devotion. Tyler writes:

*For years before his retirement from the law, it had been his
custom, we are told, to spend "one hour every day... in private
devotion. His hour of prayer was the close of the day, including
sunset;... and during that sacred hour, none of his family in-
truded upon his privacy."*

As regards his religious faith, Patrick Henry, while never os-

tentatious of it, was always ready to avow it, and to defend it. [30]

After America gained her independence, some French writers began to try to convince some Americans to cast off "the religious ideas of their childhood, and even the morality which had found its strongest sanctions in those ideas. Upon all this, Patrick Henry looked with grief and alarm." He set out to confront French skepticism; "and he then deliberately made himself, while still a Virginia lawyer and politician, a missionary also, — a missionary on behalf of rational and enlightened Christian faith. Thus during his second term as governor he caused to be printed, on his own account, an edition of Soame Jenyns's *View of the Internal Evidence of Christianity."* He distributed this pamphlet wherever he went. [31]

Tyler writes:

When, during the first two years of his retirement, Thomas Paine's "Age of Reason" made its appearance, the old states-man was moved to write out a somewhat elaborate treatise in defense of the truth of Christianity. This treatise it was his purpose to have published. "He read the manuscript to his family as he progressed with it, and completed it a short time before his death." When it was finished, however, being "diffident about his own work," and impressed, also, by the great ability of the replies to Paine, which were then appearing in England, "he directed his wife to destroy," what he had written. She "complied literally with his directions," and thus put beyond the chance of publication a work which seemed, to some who heard it, to be "the most eloquent and unanswerable argument in the defence of the Bible which was ever written."

Finally, in his last will and testament, bearing the date of November 20, 1798, and written throughout, as he says, "with my own hand," he chose to insert a touching affirmation of his own deep faith in Christianity. After distributing his estate among his descendants, he thus concludes: "This is all the inheritance I can give to my dear family. The religion of Christ can give them one which will make them rich indeed." [32]

Patrick Henry's firm Christian faith was evident up to the end of his life. Confined to bed for many weeks with an illness that was rapidly killing him, his doctor prescribed as a last resort a dose of liquid mercury with the hope that it might stop the acute inflammation of the intestine. If it did not give immediate relief it would prove fatal. His doctor said he would surely die in a short time without it. Before taking the dose Henry "prayed, in clear words, a simple childlike prayer, for his family, for his country, and for his own soul then in the presence of death." After swallowing the medicine, Henry spoke "words of love and peace to his family, who were weeping around his chair. Among other things, he told them that he was thankful for that goodness of God, which, having blessed him through all his life, was then permitting him to die without any pain." He then asked his doctor and dear friend, Mr. Cabell, with whom "he had formerly held many arguments respecting the Christian religion. . . to observe how great a reality and benefit that religion was to a man about to die. And after Patrick Henry had spoken to his beloved physician these few words, in praise of something which, having never failed him in all his life before, did not then fail him in his very last need of it, he continued to breathe very softly for some moments; after which they who were looking upon him saw that his life had departed."[33] Thus ended the life of the voice of liberty, the orator of the American Revolution, "the greatest orator that ever lived."

Section 8

James Madison and Montpelier

Though small in person, being only 5 feet 6 inches tall, James Madison was big in his influence on establishing a new government in the United States. He was soft in speech, but the force of his governmental ideas were great. His health was generally poor throughout his life, but he lived longer than any other framer, dying in 1836.

◬ Montpelier, Madison's Lifetime Home

Born at his maternal grandparents home in Port Conway, Virginia, on March 16, 1751, James Madison was the first of 10 children born to James and Eleanor Madison, who were moderately wealthy planters. James, Sr. was a vestryman of the Episcopal Church and a lay delegate to the Episcopal Convention of 1776. James, Jr. was baptized in the family church three weeks after his birth.

At an early age James moved to his father's house, Montpelier, which was the first brick house built in Orange County, Virginia. This would be his home for all his life. Madison would spend many years in Washington, D.C., but he visited Montpelier whenever he had a chance, and was delighted to retire there in 1817 after his second term as President. Montpelier was about 30 miles from Thomas Jefferson's home, and after they met, when Madison was seventeen years old, they developed a deep friendship which lasted their entire lives. Over the years, Jefferson and Madison frequently visited one another.

When Madison married Dorothy Payne Todd, a widow from Philadelphia, in 1794, he and Dolly moved into Montpelier with his parents. Over time the house was enlarged to accommodate both families. They lived together in perfect harmony. James, Sr. saw his son become President, and Eleanor, who lived to the age of ninety-eight, was "a central point in the life of her distinguished son, and the object of his most devoted care to the end of her days."[1]

Education

James was taught at home until age 12. His mother and paternal grandmother were his primary teachers. The Madison library, though not extensive, did contain many excellent works, and included such Christian writings as the *Holy Bible*, the *Book of Common Prayer, Gospel Mystery of Sanctification*, and *Life of God in the Soul of Man*.[2]

Around age 11 or 12, Madison was sent to the boarding school of Scottish minister, Donald Robertson. He studied a variety of subjects — Latin, Greek, arithmetic, geography, algebra, geometry, literature, French — and read many great authors — including Virgil, Horace, Justinian, Montaigne, Locke, Montesquieu, Smollet, Thomas Kempis. Madison said of Robertson: "All that I have been in life I owe largely to that man."[3]

After five years of study under Robertson, Madison was then tutored at his home by Episcopal minister Thomas Martin, the rector of his parish church. Rev. Martin was a recent graduate of the College of New Jersey and he urged the Madison's to send their son there.

At age 18 Madison enrolled in college, but not at the Episcopal college of William and Mary, where most college bound Virginians would go. His mother especially thought that the Presbyterian College of New Jersey (Princeton) better reflected their views on religious liberty, American independence, and Christian orthodoxy. The President and principal instructor at the college in 1769 was the Scottish Presbyterian John Witherspoon. Witherspoon's ideas greatly affected Madison's religious and political ideas. He studied divinity and theology along with the classics, history, philosophy, writing, and speech. Madison had a great interest in Christianity and considered a career in the ministry. Bishop Meade, who had visited in Madison's home, said of him:

> *Mr. Madison was sent to Princeton College—perhaps through fear of the skeptical principles then so prevalent at William and Mary. During his stay at Princeton a great revival took place, and it was believed that he partook of its spirit. On his return home he conducted worship in his father's house. He soon after offered for the Legislature, and it was objected to him, by his opponents, that he was better suited to the pulpit than to the legislative hall.[4]*

Madison's friends at college were Christians. Many became ministers (Samuel Stanhope Smith, John Blair Smith), others went into public service as government officials (William Bradford), and some did both (Caleb Wallace). After Madison graduated in 1771, he stayed another half year in Princeton to study further under Witherspoon. Upon returning home to Virginia, Madison still pursued his theological studies. Some of his Bible study notes are preserved today.

Examples include:

> *Mat. Ch 1st*
> *Jesus is an Hebrew name and signifies a Saviour v. 1.*
> *Christ is a Greek name and signifies Anointed. v. 1*
> *Pollution Christ did by the power of his Godhead purify our nature from all the pollution of our Ancestors v. 5. . .*
> *Acts Chapter 20*
> *Sunday, why kept by the Christians, for the Sabbath v.7. . .*
> *Humility, the better any man is, the lower thoughts he has of himself v. 19.[5]*

One historian writes of his study of the Bible:

> *After the manner of the Bereans he seems to have searched the Scriptures daily and diligently. . . . He explored the whole*

history and evidences of Christianity on every side, through
clouds of witnesses and champions for and against, from the Fa-
thers and schoolmen down to the infidel philosophers of the
eighteenth century. No one not a professed theologian, and but
few even of those who are, have ever gone through more labori-
ous and extensive inquiries to arrive at the truth.[6]

While considering his career future he wrote to his friend, William Bradford. In one letter of November 9, 1772, he said "a watchful eye must be kept on ourselves lest while we are building ideal monuments of Renown and Bliss here we neglect to have our names enrolled in the Annals of Heaven."[7] When Bradford notified Madison of his decision to become a lawyer (August 1773), Madison commended him but urged him to "keep the Ministry obliquely in View whatever your profession be." He said "there could not be a stronger testimony in favor of Religion. . . than for men who occupy the most honorable and gainful departments and are rising in reputation and wealth, publicly to declare their unsatisfactoriness by becoming fervent Advocates in the cause of Christ, & I wish you may give in your Evidence in this way."[8]

Around this time Madison viewed first hand the persecution of religious dissenters. Several "well-meaning men," as Madison described them, were put in jail for their religious views. This was not the first time such a thing had occurred either. In 1771, just prior to Madison's return from college, one Baptist minister, Elijah Craig, was imprisoned for preaching without a license. Craig continued preaching through the jail windows until he was released. Not long after his release, Rev. Craig and others conducted a series of meetings at Blue Run Baptist Church, which was founded by Craig and was just down the road from Madison's home, Montpelier. A crowd of 5000 people gathered and camped for days to hear the preaching.

These events helped to solidify in Madison his lifelong support of religious freedom. From these early years, he began defending the Baptists in his area against acts of persecution. He continued to work for many years to end state religious taxes, licensing of preachers by the state, special privileges for the Episcopal clergy, and any compelling by the state in religious affairs.

His views would be expressed in the Constitution of Virginia of 1776. He drafted the article dealing with religious freedom:

> *That Religion, or the duty which we owe to our CREATOR, and the manner of discharging it, can be directed only by reason and conviction, not by force or violence: and therefore, that all men should enjoy the fullest toleration in the exercise of religion, according to the dictates of conscience, unpunished, and unrestrained by the magistrate, unless under colour of religion, any man disturb the peace, the happiness, or safety of Society. And that it is the mutual duty of all to practice Christian forbearance, love, and charity, towards each other.[9]*

During the time Madison witnessed religious persecution in his area, he began devoting himself to service in public life. He studied law and in 1774 was elected to serve on the Committee of Safety for Orange County. This was the beginning of public service lasting about one half a century. Madison did not give a reason for not entering the ministry. Some have suggested it was his soft voice, which was not suitable for preaching, and others suggest his poor health. His theological education did, however, affect his political ideas. Witherspoon's influence can be seen throughout his life.

Public Service

Madison spent nearly a half a century in public service. His positions included:

- Member of Orange County's Committee of Safety, 1774.
- Member of Virginia's constitutional convention, 1776, where he drew up the first draft of the article on religious freedom.
- Member of Virginia's first state legislature, the House of Delegates, 1777. Here he fought for establishment of complete religious freedom.
- Governor's Council, 1778-1780. Under Governor's Henry and Jefferson, he was responsible for preparing many state pa-

pers, thus receiving useful knowledge of the day-to-day working of government.

- Member of Congress under the Articles of Confederation, 1780-1783. This helped to give him a national point of view. Having experienced the weaknesses of the government under the Articles, he spoke for their revision and for more power in the central government.
- Virginia House of Delegates, 1784-1786. Leader in establishing religious freedom. Introduced Jefferson's bill for religious freedom.
- Member of the Constitutional Convention, 1787. His draft for a new constitution formed the framework for what became the U.S. Constitution.
- Led forces to ratify Constitution in Virginia.
- Member of the U.S. House of Representatives, 1789-1797. In the first Congress of 1789, Madison proposed 12 amendments to the Constitution, of which 10 were ratified by the states (The Bill of Rights) and became part of the Constitution on December 15, 1791.
- Secretary of State under Jefferson, 1800-1807.
- 4th President of the United States, 1808-1817.
- Virginia constitutional convention, 1829.
- Rector of the University of Virginia, 1826-1836.

Christian Faith

After entering public life, Madison wrote very little about his religious beliefs, therefore, it is difficult to accurately present his faith. His early writings reveal his orthodox beliefs. Nothing in his later writings negate these or show any doubting of his Christian faith or loss of interest in religion. He remained friendly to Christianity and attended church throughout his life.

Three factors probably affected his lack of writing on his religious beliefs. One, at this time most considered doctrinal beliefs were private matters. Two, as a public official Madison may have thought it best to remain silent or neutral so as not to divide the nation, because there was great diversity in Christian beliefs. Three, his view of separation of church and state most certainly restrained him from publicly addressing religion.[10]

His faith did affect his principles of government and law. John Witherspoon and his Calvinistic ideas are reflected in Madison's thought. Madison believed in the innate depravity of man. Since man was sinful, government not only needed to restrain sinful actions of citizens, but there also had to be restraints on governmental leaders. Madison sought to limit powers via separation of powers and a system of checks and balances. In his political thinking he started from a theological base. A biblical view of man caused Madison to say: "All men having power ought to be distrusted."[11]

His character was a product of his faith. In his Bible study notes from his post-college days he recorded: "Humility, the better any man is, the lower thoughts he has of himself." Madison portrayed this humble character. Paul Jennings, a former slave born and raised at Montpelier, wrote of Madison in 1865:

> *Mr. Madison, I think, was one of the best men that ever lived. I never saw him in a passion, and never knew him to strike a slave, although he had over one hundred; neither would he allow an overseer to do it. Whenever any slaves were reported to him as stealing or 'cutting up' badly, he would send for them and admonish them privately, and never mortify them by doing it before others. They generally served him very faithfully. I don't think he drank a quart of brandy in his whole life. . . . For the last fifteen years of his life he drank no wine at all.*[12]

Madison acknowledged the hand of God and His providence in his First Inaugural Address, March 4th, 1809:

> *. . . we have all been encouraged to feel in the guardianship and guidance of that Almighty Being, whose power regulates the destiny of nations, whose blessings have been so conspicuously dispensed to this rising republic, and to whom we are bound to*

*address our devout gratitude for the past, as well as our fervent
supplications and best hopes for the future.[13]*

In Federalist 20.24 he gave thanks to God and called others to do
so:

*...let our gratitude mingle an ejaculation to Heaven, for the
propitious concord which has distinguished the consultations for
our political happiness.[14]*

In the *Federalist Papers* he also acknowledged God spoke to man
in written communication, saying: "When the Almighty himself
condescends to address mankind in their own language. . . "[15]

Constitutional Convention

Madison was a central force behind promoting a whole new
Constitution instead of simply revising the Articles of Confederation.
His letter to Washington formed the basis of the "Virginia Plan" —
"Fifteen Resolves" drawn up by Madison and the other Virginia
delegates. These were introduced at the Constitutional Convention
of 1787 by Randolph of Virginia and became the framework of the
agenda of the convention as they worked to frame a new constitution.
Madison spoke 161 times at the convention, more than anyone,
except Gouverneur Morris and James Wilson. He kept the most
complete record of the convention and helped broker many compro-
mises. He was also on the Committee on Style which determined the
final wording. This is why he is called the "father of the Constitution."

A Georgia delegate to the convention said of Madison:

*Mr. Maddison is a character who has long been in public
life; but what is very remarkable every Person seems to acknow-
lege his greatness. He blends together the profound politician,
with the scholar. In the management of every great question he
evidently took the lead in the Convention, and tho' he cannot be
called an Orator, he is a most agreeable, eloquent, and convincing speaker. From a spirit of industry and application which he*

possesses in a most eminent degree, he always comes forward the best informed Man of any point in debate. The affairs of the United States, he perhaps has the most correct knowledge of, of any Man in the Union. . . . Mr. Maddison is . . . a Gentleman of great modesty, — with a remarkably sweet temper. He is easy and unreserved among his acquaintances, and has a most agreeable style of conversation.[16]

So many problems were overcome at the convention and with such unanimity that Madison said the adoption of the Constitution was nothing "less than a miracle."[17] He also stated:

It is impossible for the man of pious reflection not to perceive in it a finger of that Almighty hand which has been so frequently and signally extended to our relief in the critical stages of the revolution.[18]

Madison saw no need for a listing of rights or a provision protecting religious freedom in the Constitution because such a provision of rights was already guaranteed by each of the states. He also believed that if a listing were attempted it might be construed to limit individuals to only those rights. As far as a national religious establishment, Madison felt there were so many denominations in the United States that their rivalry would keep any one from gaining precedence. However, when a Bill of Rights was demanded by the people, Madison took up the charge to see these through, including in the First Amendment a provision for religious freedom.

Political Writings and Speeches

Some of Madison's most significant writings and speeches include:

- *Memorial and Remonstrance against Religious Assessments* (1784)
- The Virginia plan which formed the framework of the U.S. Constitution
- *Notes of Debates in the Federal Convention of 1787*

- Speech to the Convention of Virginia to ratify the Constitution (June 6, 1788), on the nature of the union and power of the Federal Government to raise money.
- *The Federalist Papers.* He wrote 29 of the 85 essays using the pseudonym, "Publius."
- "Mr. Madison's Report" to the Virginia General Assembly, January 7, 1800, on the state and federal relationship.
- Madison's War Message (1812)

Governmental Philosophy

A reading of the *Federalist Papers* provides an excellent look at James Madison's governmental philosophy, which was greatly shaped by his Biblical worldview. His Biblical view of man is evident in Federalist 51:

> *But what is government itself, but the greatest of all reflections on human nature? If men were angels, no government would be necessary. If angels were to govern men, neither external nor internal controls on government would be necessary. In framing a government which is to be administered by men over men, the great difficulty lies in this: you must first enable the government to control the governed; and in the next place oblige it to control itself.*[19]

Following are some of Madison's governmental principles as seen in the *Federalist*:

1. Power derived from the people. Right to elect magistrates.

- "A dependence on the people is, no doubt, the primary control on the government." (Federalist 51.7)
- Free and frequent elections are one means for this (see Federalist 39, 52, 53, 37.8)
- People must be self-governed for republic to work (Federalist 39.2 — "... to rest all our political experiments on the capacity of mankind for self-government.")

2. Constitutional government. The rule of law.

- A constitution is necessary to specify the **limited powers of the government.** The people should delegate power to the government through a written constitution. This will limit what power the people give to government. (Federalist 39.16, 41.25, 41.26, 52.3, 53.4, 53.5)
- The people's representatives drew up the constitution and ratified it. (Federalist 39.13)

3. A republic is best, rather than democracy.

- Federalist 39. Elected representatives and a constitution is basis of republic.

4. Separation of powers between legislative, executive, and judicial branches (Federalist 47, 51.2, 51.4, 51.5, 37.1)

5. Checks and balances between branches (Federalist 48)

6. Legislative authority is predominate but should be divided into two houses.

- These diffuse power and provide checks. Checks also from other branches. (Fed. 51.9, 51.10)

7. Federal nature of United States

- Two separate governmental authorities (state and national) would further diffuse power and protect individuals. Each of these were separated, had checks and balances, etc. (Fed. 51.13. 14.10, 37.10)
- The general powers of the national government were limited by and enumerated in the Constitution. The States retained their sovereign and independent jurisdiction (Federalist 40.13). Madison saw the States as more powerful and influential (see Federalist 45).

8. Minority rights guarded

- A constitutional republic would guard the rights of minorities. Madison wrote: "It is of great importance in a republic not only to guard the society against the oppression of its rulers, but to guard one part of the society against the injustice of the other part." (Federalist, 51.14)

9. Civil and religious rights equally protected (Federalist 51.15)

10. Protection of property rights is the first object of government (Fed. 10.9)

11. "Justice is the end of government" (Federalist 51.16).

- "... the safety and happiness of society are the objects at which all political institutions aim." (Federalist 43.30)
- This is a biblical view of the purpose of government – to protect the righteous and punish evil-doers. Government is not to regulate everything into a utopia, or control things necessary to better the lives of citizens, such as education, health, welfare, retirement. It is to provide peace and justice so people can pursue these on their own.

12. God's authority supersedes man's

- Madison believed that the Constitution and governmental institutions could not contravene "the transcendent law of nature and nature's God." (Federalist 43.30)

Though Madison was initially a strong federalist (nationalist), he gradually shifted his position during his years in Congress. He became the congressional leader of the Jeffersonian Democratic Republicans.

Madison and the Cod Fishery Bill

In 1792 Congress considered a bill that would have given subsidies to cod fishermen in New England. Some few argued Congress had power to do so under the general welfare clause. Speaking against the bill, James Madison noted that this is a limited government with only the specified powers listed in the *Constitution* belonging to Congress, the executive, and judiciary. He then said:

> *If Congress can employ money indefinitely to the general welfare, and are the sole and supreme judges of the general welfare, they may take the care of religion into their own hands; they may appoint teachers in every state, county, and parish, and pay them out of their public treasury; they may take into their own hands the education of children, establishing in like*

manner schools throughout the Union; they may assume the pro-
vision for the poor; they may undertake the regulation of all
roads other than post-roads;.... [20]

Madison wrote in the Federalist: "The powers delegated by the... Constitution to the federal government are few and defined. Those which are to remain in the State governments are numerous and indefinite."

Madison would be greatly dismayed at the reach of the national government today.

Defense of Religious Liberty

From the example of his family, the views he learned from tutors and at college, and from the persecutions he witnessed first hand, Madison had developed a firm belief in religious freedom. As a young man he wrote to his college friend, William Bradford, on January 24, 1774:

That diabolical, hell-conceived principle of persecution rages among some; and to their eternal infamy, the clergy can furnish their quota of imps for such business. This vexes me the worst of anything whatever. There are at this time in the adjacent county not less than five or six well-meaning men in close jail for publishing their religious sentiments, which in the main are very orthodox. [21]

He continued to follow closely religious freedom issues in his state. He wrote to Bradford on April 1, 1774, that the next Assembly was likely to hear petitions from dissenters for more religious freedom. Madison did not think they would be successful at that time due to the opposition of the established clergy who had much power and influence. He did express his belief that "the rights of conscience... is one of the characteristics of a free people." He also wrote that religious liberty promoted advancement and industry in every sphere of life, while "religious bondage shackles and debilitates the mind, and unfits it for every noble enterprise, every expanded prospect." [22]

Madison took up the fight as a delegate to the Virginia Constitutional Convention, authoring the first draft of the article dealing with religious freedom.

Madison lead opposition to other attempts of state establishment, including Patrick Henry's proposal in 1784 for a tax to support teachers of the Christian religion. As an argument against this proposal, Madison wrote a *Memorial and Remonstrance* in 1785. This helped in the defeat of the bill. His opposition had nothing to do with any hostility to Christianity. It really expresses his belief that Christianity is of divine origin and, hence, does not need the support of the state for it to flourish.

In the *Memorial* Madison calls Christianity "the Religion which we believe to be of divine origin." He says "that this Religion both existed and flourished, not only without the support of human laws, but in spite of every opposition from them. . . . [A] Religion not invented by human policy, must have pre-existed and been supported, before it was established by human policy." Christianity has an "innate excellence" and enjoys "the patronage of its Author." In other words, since Christianity is of divine origin, it is supported by God and does not need the support of men to exist and flourish.

Madison said that every man has a duty to God. He wrote:

> *It is the duty of every man to render to the Creator such homage, and such only, as he believes to be acceptable to him. This duty is precedent both in order of time and degree of obligation, to the claims of Civil Society. Before any man can be considered as a member of Civil Society, he must be considered as a subject of the Governor of the Universe.*[23]

Another argument Madison used against the bill was that it would discourage "the number still remaining under the dominion of false Religions" from coming to Christian dominions and having the opportunity of being converted. He also saw that the effect of such a bill would put the state in a position of determining what was and was not Christian. He understood that the defining of Christianity was outside the jurisdiction of civil government.

Jefferson's Statute for Religious Freedom, 1786

In 1779 Jefferson authored a bill that would have disestablished the Episcopal Church as the official state church in Virginia. It did not pass. In 1785 and 1786, while Jefferson was in Europe, Madison took up the cause and saw the passage of the *Statute for Religious Freedom.* The principles contained in this statute are similar to those Madison had espoused in his *Memorial and Remonstrance.* The *Statute for Religious Freedom* proved to be a model for the First Amendment, as well as for other states considering religious freedom. In it Jefferson wrote:

> *Almighty God hath created the mind free; that all attempts to influence it by temporal punishments or burthens, or by civil incapacitations, tend only to begat habits of hypocrisy and meaness, and are a departure from the plan of the Holy Author of our religion, who being Lord both of body and mind, yet chose not to propagate it by coercions on either, as was in his Almighty Power to do;. . . to compel a man to furnish contributions of money for the propagation of opinions which he disbelieves is sinful and tyrannical.*[24]

Madison's firm belief in religious freedom was the basis for his drafting the First Amendment. He wanted Christianity to flourish and saw that in order for this to occur, there should be no state religion. His original wording of this amendment, submitted to the House of Representatives of June 7, 1789, read:

> *The Civil Rights of none shall be abridged on account of religious belief or worship, nor shall any national religion be established, nor shall the full and equal rights of conscience be in any manner, nor on any pretext infringed.*

Floyd's summary of the House debate gives Madison's meaning:

> *Mr. Madison said, he apprehended the meaning of the words to be, that Congress should not establish a religion and enforce the legal observation of it by law, nor compel men to worship God in any manner contrary to their conscience.*[25]

As time went on, Madison embraced more of a separation view, like Jefferson, though not to the same extent. Consequently, as President, he was limited in his public support of religion. This was because he thought it outside the jurisdiction of government. In 1811 he vetoed "An Act incorporating the Protestant Episcopal church in the town of Alexandria, in the District of Columbia." To him government had no jurisdiction in such matters. Two different times, when Congress asked him to proclaim a day of prayer, he took a middle ground. Washington and Adams had readily proclaimed such days; Jefferson chose not to for jurisdictional reasons. On July 9, 1812, Madison issued a proclamation saying that all those religious "societies so disposed, to offer, at one and the same time, their common vows and adorations to Almighty God." His 1813 proclamation had similar wording, and gave the reason why he did not call on all the American people to pray but merely those "piously disposed" to do so:

> *If the public homage of a people can ever be worthy the favorable regard of the Holy and Omniscient Being to whom it is addressed, it must be that in which those who join in it are guided only by their free choice, by the impulse of their hearts and the dictates of their consciences. [God should be given those prayers and offerings which] alone can be acceptable to Him whom no hypocrisy can deceive and no forced sacrifices propitiate.[26]*

Madison did recognize, though, that belief in God was essential for the happiness of mankind. He wrote: ". . . the belief in a God All Powerful wise and good, is so essential to the moral order of the World and to the happiness of man."[27] While he saw this as essential, he not believe government should compel in matters of religion for the church flourished most without government support. Madison did see that this line is not always easy to discern — "I must admit. . . that it may not be easy, in every possible case, to trace the line of separation, between the rights of the religious and the civil authority, with such distinctness, as to avoid collisions and doubts on unessential points."[28]

Madison and Slavery

Madison was against slavery, though he owned over 100 slaves during his life and gave freedom only to a few. He grew up playing with slaves and was close to many throughout his life. He always treated them with respect, which was attested to by many. His opposition was based on his principles of justice and individual rights. He said that "the whole Bible is against negro slavery; but that the clergy do no preach this, and the people do not see it."[29]

If he opposed slavery why did he continue to have slaves? He thought that emancipation should take place gradually, giving the nation time to overcome any prejudices and prepare the blacks to live as freemen in society. Without this he feared the freed slaves would not be able to live alongside the whites experiencing the same freedoms. He thought their conditions would even be worse without this preparation. They would suffer "the degrading privation of equal rights political or social."[30]

Thinking it was in the best interest of all, Madison favored repatriation of the freed black population to a new nation in West Africa called Liberia. In 1816 the American Colonization Society was formed to promote this purpose. Madison was a lifetime member, even serving as President at one point.

Madison wrote that those who opposed the Constitution because of its policies on slavery, in particular prohibiting the importation of slaves until 1808, were misrepresenting the purpose of the framers. He wrote:

> *It ought to be considered as a great point gained in favor of humanity, that a period of twenty years may terminate forever, within these States, a traffic which has so long and so loudly upbraided the barbarism of modern policy; that within that period, it will receive a considerable discouragement from the federal government, and may be totally abolished.*[31]

He saw this action as a great step forward in ending slavery. In Federalist 42, he went on to point out that slaves in Europe had no such prospect in their future. The founders were leading the way in the world in taking steps to end slavery. Since independence, each state had the freedom to deal with slavery and many began to outlaw it.

Retirement at Montpelier

When Madison's second term as President ended, he and Dolly gladly returned to Montpelier, their home near Orange, Virginia. In the next 20 years they experienced much joy at their home, which Dolly said was "within a squirrel's jump of heaven."[32] They did not have much of an opportunity to be alone, though, for guests and friends continually visited. At times there were so many guests that they had to set up tables out doors to accommodate them. Madison wrote in 1820: "Yesterday we had ninety persons to dine with us at our table, fixed on the lawn, under a large arbor.... Half a dozen only staid all night."[33] The guests that visited Madison's home were reminded of his Christian faith when they walked into the entrance hall, because on the wall was a huge painting (8 by 12 feet) of Jesus with His twelve disciples.

In his later years, in addition to entertaining visitors at his home, Madison served as Rector of the University of Virginia, collected his correspondence, edited some of his previous writings, and occasionally wrote his thoughts on current political events. On June 28, 1836, the last surviving Framer died at home and was buried in the cemetery at Montpelier.

Section 9

George Mason and Gunston Hall

George Mason (1725-1792) was author of the *Virginia Declaration of Rights*, and since this document formed the basis of the first ten amendments to the *United States Constitution*, he has been called the "Father of the Bills of Rights." A French philosopher wrote of Mason: "the first Declaration of Rights that is entitled to be called such is that of Virginia. Its author is entitled to the eternal gratitude of mankind." Mason also drafted the first Constitution of Virginia and was a member of the United States Constitutional Convention. Thomas Jefferson called Mason "one of our really great men, and of the first order of greatness."[1]

🔔 Gunston Hall

George Mason built Gunston Hall in 1758 on land he inherited from his father. Mason's home was located four miles down the Potomac River from Mt. Vernon. Mason and Washington were not only neighbors, but warm friends. They often visited one another and frequently sent gifts back and forth. For a period of time they both served on the vestry of Truro parish.

Mason's service as a vestryman for 36 years shows the esteem he held in the eyes of his neighbors, his leadership skills, and his devout Christian faith. He and his wife, Anne, imparted their faith to their children. Over a twenty year period they had 12 children, with nine surviving. From a young age, the Mason's taught them to pray at meals and before bedtime. Before going to bed, the children would kneel down before their mother, put their hands in her lap, and say their prayers. The children received Christian love and discipline, which had great effect on family relations. One of the sons, John, said: "There was never, to the best of my knowledge, a single quarrel or even a transient coolness that ever took place between any of us."[2]

Mason penned many vital proposals and documents during America's time of crisis between 1765 and 1790. The most famous he began to write on May 20, 1776, in Williamsburg with these words: "That all Men are born equally free and independent and have certain inherent natural Rights." Six weeks later, Jefferson would echo these words in the *Declaration of Independence*. Mason wrote the *Virginia Declaration of Rights* in less than a week, but he had prepared himself for over 50 years.

This preparation was begun by his father, George (who was actually the third George Mason), and mother, Ann. As the oldest son of a wealthy planter, George IV had the advantages of this position; but his parents knew that much work was required to impart character and leadership skills to their son. From a young age his father would take George with him to the county court or to various homes and meeting places to listen to discussions. George would daily witness his father running their large plantation. When George was ten, his father died in an accident. From that point his mother, his relatives, and various tutors assumed a larger role in his education.

His uncle and guardian, John Mercer, was a brilliant lawyer who tutored George in law and allowed him to use his personal library with over 1500 books, half on law. While George was under his guardianship, Mercer wrote an abridgment of the laws of Virginia. These things were invaluable for Mason's future work on governmental documents.

Those who taught Mason reflected Mercer's views of what a tutor should be: "My opinion of a Tutor is, that besides instructing his pupil in such branches of learning as his is designed for, he should also be particularly careful of his Religion, morals, & behavior, in short he should be a gentleman."[3] As was typical in early America, one of Mason's tutors was a minister, Rev. Alexander Scott.

In 1749 Mason, just 24 years old, was first elected as a vestryman in Truro parish. Vestrymen did much more than just govern in church matters. They handled the major social concerns in the community, including providing for the poor and needy, securing medical help for the poor, finding homes and arranging apprenticeships for orphans, and assisting the elderly. They also made sure that all families were teaching their children and their slaves, if they owned any, the catechism.[4]

While Mason served in various local, state, and national government positions throughout his life, he much preferred being home with his family. After the death of his wife in 1773, it became more difficult for him to serve politically, knowing his nine children needed him even more. With the increasing conflict with Britain, Mason felt he had to go to Williamsburg when elected in 1774 to the Virginia House of Burgesses. Even while away, he continued to train his children. The delegates had declared "a day of Fasting, Humiliation, and Prayer" for June 1. Mason was in Williamsburg at the time but wanted to make sure his family observed this day. In a letter to his neighbor, he wrote: "Please to tell my dear little family that I charge them to pay strict attention to it, and that I desire my three eldest sons, and my two eldest daughters, may attend church in mourning."[5]

In 1776 Mason drafted the *Virginia Declaration of Rights* and the state's first constitution. Both served as a model for many state constitutions, for the *Declaration of Independence*, and for the future *Bill of Rights*. These contained ideas considered invaluable to the American people, such as: the right to life, liberty, and property; all power comes from the people; separation of powers; freedom of the press and religion. Borrowing the idea from John Locke, Mason called Virginia a commonwealth, instead of a state. In such a government the legislature is supreme.

At the Virginia Constitutional convention, Mason also helped to draw up the "Great Seal for the Commonwealth of Virginia." On it Virginia is represented by a female figure that has TYRANNY, represented by a prostrate man with a crown fallen from his head, under her feet, with the words *Sic semper tyrannis*, "thus always to tyrants."

Mason was a member of the Virginia House of Delegates from 1776 to 1788, during which time he helped to organize the new state government. He was also instrumental in assisting George Rogers Clark in his efforts to secure the Northwest country for America. Because of this, when the Treaty of Peace was signed with Britain, America's western border was recognized to extend to the Mississippi River.

In 1787 Mason traveled to Philadelphia as a member of the Virginia delegation to the Constitutional Convention. Preferring to remain home, his sense of duty and recognition of the great need to change the existing national union, were what motivated him to go. He realized that their actions would effect "the Happiness or Misery of Millions yet unborn."[6] He was very active in the Convention, speaking 136 times and serving on eleven committees.

Although Mason believed a new federal government was needed, he did not sign or support the Constitution the delegates approved in September 1787. He thought the proposed constitution went too far in centralizing power in the national government, concluding "that it would end either in monarchy, or a tyrannical aristocracy."[7] He felt it should contain a bill of rights for the protection of individual liberties.

As a lifelong opponent of slavery, he also believed the compromise reached to continue the slave trade until 1808 was wrong. Believing that equal rights belonged to all, including blacks, he dubbed the slave trade as disgraceful to mankind. He spoke out strongly against slavery at the Convention declaring:

> *Every master of slaves is born a petty tyrant. They bring the judgment of heaven on a Country. As nations can not be rewarded or punished in the next world they must be in this. By an inevitable chain of causes & effects providence punishes national sins, by national calamities.*[8]

For these reasons George Mason refused to sign the Constitution "declaring that he would sooner chop off his right hand than put it to the Constitution as it now stands."[9]

Upon his return to Virginia, Mason was chosen as a member of the Virginia convention considering the ratification of the United States Constitution. He and Patrick Henry led the opposition, insisting on a bill of rights and other changes. The Constitution was ratified, but Mason's opposition was a great force in the eventual adoption of the Federal *Bill of Rights*, which were influenced greatly by the *Virginia Declaration of Rights* which Mason had written earlier.

After this Mason retired to Gunston Hall, refusing to accept future political positions, including appointment as one of Virginia's first two United States Senators. He died on October 7, 1792, less than one year after the *Bill of Rights* became part of the Constitution, securing the inherent natural rights of man.

Richmond

The Richmond area was first explored in 1607 by Captain Christopher Newport, Capt. John Smith, and twenty others, sent from Jamestown to discover the head of the James River. These explorers planted a cross on an island near the Falls of the James. Today, a large stone cross in Gamble's Hill Park commemorates this event, when Newport and Smith claimed this area for the Kingdom of God.

Richmond was founded by William Byrd II in 1733 and it was laid out in 1737 by his friend Major William Mayo. They named it for the town in England because "its situation was like that of Richmond-on-the-Thames." It was incorporated by the General Assembly in 1742. The General Assembly voted in 1779 for Richmond to become the new capital of Virginia. The government physically moved from Williamsburg to Richmond in April 1780.

St. John's Church

St. John's is the oldest church in Richmond, dating from 1741. The present building has been enlarged a few times since then. About 30 of the original pews still remain, though they were lowered in the 1830's. St. John's was one of the earlier churches of Henrico Parish. This parish began in 1611, with Alexander Whitaker as its first rector. Whitaker helped in the conversion of Pocahontas to Christianity and baptized her in the spring of 1614.

Henry's "Give Me Liberty" Speech

In March of 1775 elected representatives from throughout Virginia gathered for a meeting in St. John's Church. They were meeting in Richmond, then a small village, instead of the capital city Williamsburg, to be free from interference of the governor, who had dissolved Virginia's House of Burgesses. The rector of St. John's Church, the Rev. Mr. Miles Selden, opened his church to the delegates and served as their chaplain.

The tongue (Patrick Henry), the pen (Thomas Jefferson), and the sword (George Washington) of the American Revolution all were a part of this very historic meeting. Six of the 120 delegates would be future signers of the Declaration of Independence — Jefferson, Benjamin Harrison, Richard Henry Lee, Carter Braxton, Francis Lightfoot Lee, and Thomas Nelson, Jr. Two would be future Presidents of the United States — Washington and Jefferson.

The convention members were debating whether to began to prepare themselves militarily in response to the growing conflict between Britain and the colonies. Henry led those advocating immediate preparation. He was supported by George Washington, Thomas Jefferson, Richard Henry Lee, Thomas Nelson, Jr., and others. The opposition, which included Edmund Pendleton, Benjamin Harrison, and Richard Bland, supported a more moderate response of postponing action.

The convention culminated on March 23 with Patrick Henry's now-famous speech:

> ... Sir, we have done everything that could be done to avert the storm which is now coming on. We have petitioned – we have remonstrated – we have supplicated – we have prostrated – ourselves before the throne, and have implored its interposition to arrest the tyrannical hands of the ministry and Parliament. Our petitions have been slighted; our remonstrances have produced additional violence and insult; our supplications have been disregarded; and we have been spurned, with contempt,

*from the foot of the throne. In vain, after these things, may we in-
dulge the fond hope of peace and reconciliation. There is no
longer any room for hope. If we wish to be free – if we mean to
preserve inviolate those inestimable privileges for which we
have been so long contending – if we mean not basely to abandon the noble struggle in which we have been so long engaged,
and which we have pledged ourselves never to abandon until the
glorious object of our contest shall be obtained – we must fight!
I repeat it, sir, we must fight!! An appeal to arms and to the God
of Hosts is all that is left us!*

*They tell us, sir, that we are weak – unable to cope with so
formidable an adversary. But when shall we be stronger? Will it
be the next week, or the next year? Will it be when we are totally
disarmed, and when a British guard shall be stationed in every
house? Shall we gather strength by irresolution and inaction?
Shall we acquire the means of effectual resistance by lying su-
pinely on our backs, and hugging the delusive phantom of Hope,
until our enemies shall have bound us hand and foot? Sir, we
are not weak, if we make a proper use of those means which the
God of nature hath placed in our power. Three millions of people, armed in the holy cause of liberty, and in such a country as
that which we possess, are invincible by any force which our enemy can send against us. Besides, sir, we shall not fight our battles alone. There is a just God who presides over the destinies of
nations, and who will raise up friends to fight our battles for us.
The battle, sir, is not to the strong alone; it is to the vigilant, the
active, the brave. Besides, sir, we have no election. If we were
base enough to desire it, it is now too late to retire from the contest. There is no retreat, but in submission and slavery! Our
chains are forged, their clanking may be heard on the plains of
Boston! The war is inevitable – and let it come!! I repeat it, sir,
let it come!!!*

*It is in vain, sir, to extenuate the matter. Gentlemen may cry,
peace, peace – but there is no peace. The war is actually begun.
The next gale that sweeps from the North will bring to our ears*

the clash of resounding arms! Our brethren are already in the field! Why stand we here idle? What is it that gentlemen wish? What would they have? Is life so dear, or peace so sweet, as to be purchased at the price of chains and slavery? Forbid it, Almighty God! I know not what course others may take; but as for me, give me liberty or give me death![1]

All who heard his speech were awe-struck. Colonel Edward Carrington broke the silence following Henry's speech by exclaiming, "Right here I wish to be buried!"[2] (He is buried just outside the church.) Henry swayed the majority to agree to his call for a "well-regulated militia."

In response to this action, Governor Dunmore secretly sent troops to raid the Powder Magazine in Williamsburg, which prompted Patrick Henry to assembly a militia unit to march to Williamsburg to demand the Governor return the arms and powder or pay for them. This was the first military movement in Virginia related to independence.

Six years later, St. John's Church became associated with the infamous American traitor, Benedict Arnold. After his defection to the British, Arnold led a force of British troops into Virginia. When he took possession of Richmond in 1781, he quartered his troops in the church.

Today, there are 1340 graves in the churchyard of St. John's, dating from the mid-eighteenth century. The more famous include: George Wythe (1726-1806), signer of the Declaration and first law professor in America, training Jefferson, James Monroe, John Marshall, and Henry Clay; two governors of Virginia, James Wood Jr. and John Page; and Elizabeth Arnold, mother of Edgar Allan Poe.

🔔 *The Virginia State Capitol*

Construction began on the Virginia State Capitol in 1785. It was in the fall of 1788 that the Virginia General Assembly first met in this building. It has been in continuous use since that time, making it the second oldest working Capitol in the United States. Jefferson chose a Roman temple built in France during the first century as the model for the Capitol. This was the first building built in the new world in the Classical Revival style of architecture. A visitor in 1796 wrote that "the building is, beyond comparison, the finest, the most noble, and the greatest, in all America." [3]

The original structure now forms the central part of the Capitol. East and west wings were added between 1904 and 1906, which house the House of Delegates and the Senate respectively.

The Rotunda of the Capitol contains Virginia's most treasured work of art — a marble life-size statue of George Washington. Commissioned by the Virginia General Assembly, Frenchmen Jean Antoine Houdon completed this sculpture in France in 1788. He had visited Washington at Mt. Vernon in 1785 and made a plaster bust of his head and took detailed measurements of his body to assist him in making the only sculpture of Washington made from life. People who knew Washington said the statue was a perfect likeness. Lafayette said: "That is the man, himself. I can almost realize he is going to move." [4]

Also displayed in the Rotunda are busts of the seven other Presidents who were born in Virginia: Thomas Jefferson, James Madison, James Monroe, William Henry Harrison, John Tyler, Zachary Taylor, and Woodrow Wilson. An Houdon marble bust of the Marquis de Lafayette can be seen in the Rotunda as well.

Church services were held regularly in the Capitol, often in the House of Delegates chamber. For a period of time, Episcopal and Presbyterian churches alternated meeting Sundays in the chamber.

Busts of many famous Virginians are displayed in the old House chamber. These include: George Mason, Richard Henry Lee, Patrick Henry, George Wythe, Matthew Fontain Maury, Cyrus McCormick, John Marshall, Sam Houston, Stonewall Jackson, J.E.B. Stuart, Joseph E. Johnson, and Fitshugh Lee. A bronze statue of Robert E.

Lee stands where he stood on April 23, 1861, when he accepted command of the Confederate forces of Virginia with these words:

> *Mr. President and Gentlemen of the Convention, — Profoundly impressed with the solemnity of the occasion, for which I must say I was not prepared, I accept the position assigned me by your partiality. I would have much preferred had your choice fallen on an abler man. Trusting in Almighty God, an approving conscience, and the aid of my fellow-citizens, I devote myself to the service of my native State, in whose behalf alone will ever again draw my sword.[5]*

Monument of Early Virginia Leaders

Northwest of the Capitol is a monument topped by the figure of George Washington on a horse. The monument depicts the role of Virginia in the birth of the United States, with six of her prominent citizens standing in front of allegorical figures representing different contributions to the cause: Andrew Lewis, Colonial Times; Thomas Jefferson, Independence; Patrick Henry, Revolution; Thomas Nelson, Finance; George Mason, Bill of Rights; John Marshall, Justice. The monument was begun in 1850 and completed in 1869.

The John Marshall House

Chief Justice of the United States Supreme Court for 34 years, John Marshall was born in Fauquier County, Virginia, on September 24, 1755. After being educated by his parents at home for some years, an Episcopal clergyman from Scotland, Rev. James Thompson, was hired to carry on his education. At age 14 John attended a school for one year, then returned home to continue his studies under Rev. Thompson. He never attended college, but still received an excellent education.

Marshall began the study of law when he was 18 years old, using the newly published Blackstone's *Commentaries*. His study was interrupted by the events of the Revolution. John joined a regiment of the Virginia militia in 1775, receiving an appointment as lieutenant. The hunting shirts of these minutemen bore the motto "Liberty or death!" and the emblem on their banner was a coiled rattlesnake, with the inscription "Don't tread on me!" The next year Marshall enlisted in the Continental Army and participated in most of the principal battles of the war until the end of 1779, including Brandywine, Germantown, and Monmouth. He also endured the hardships of Valley Forge during the winter of 1777-1778.

When his term of service expired, Marshall returned to Virginia and the study of law, which included listening to the law lectures of George Wythe at the College of William and Mary. He received a license to practice law in the summer of 1780. From this time he became increasingly involved in state government. Following is a summary of Marshall's public service.

Areas of Public Service

- Virginia militia lieutenant, 1775
- Officer in the Continental Army, 1775-1779
- Member of the Virginia legislature, first elected in 1782 and served various terms during the 1780's and 1790's
- Member of the Virginia executive council, 1782-84
- Member of the Virginia constitutional ratifying convention of 1788. He strongly supported ratification and, with James Madison, led the way for adoption
- Commissioner to France, 1797-1798
- Member of the U.S. House of Representatives, 1799
- Secretary of State under John Adams
- Beginning in 1801, he served 34 years as Chief Justice of Supreme Court

As Supreme Court Chief Justice, Marshall set in place principles and policies upon which a strong national government emerged. It has been said the he "oversaw the transition of the country from a confederation to a nation."[6] Madison was instrumental in shaping the powers of the Supreme Court.

The most famous case that Madison presided over — *Marbury v. Madison*, 1803 — has been used by modern jurists and law schools to promote the idea of "judicial review." This is the view that the Judiciary, and ultimately the Supreme Court, has the power to determine the constitutionality of laws, or of acts of the other two branches of government. This was not the view of the founders nor was it applied in the outcome of the *Marbury* case. The Court's opinion stated that it had no authority over this case constitutionally, but gave its opinion on what should be done anyway. Jefferson and Madison ignored the Court's decision, and no one was outraged at this.[7]

Concerning the founders view of who should decide the constitutionality of laws and actions, they felt this rested with the Congress, who was regularly accountable to the people through elections, rather than with a few unelected members of the court.[8]

Private Life

John Marshall has been described as "a man of unassuming piety and amiability of temper. He was tall, plain of dress, and somewhat awkward in appearance, but had a keen black eye, and overflowed with geniality and kind feeling. He was the object of the warmest love and veneration of all his children and grandchildren."[9] "His dress was plain even to negligence. He marketed for himself and might be seen at an early hour returning home with a pair of fowls, or a basket of eggs in his hand, not with ostentatious humility, but for mere convenience."[10]

A few incidences in Marshall's life reveal his humble and loving nature. One author writes:

It is related by Flanders that Marshall "was one morning

strolling through the streets of Richmond, attired in a plain linen roundabout and shorts, with his hat under his arm, from which he was eating cherries, when he stopped in the porch of the Eagle Hotel, indulged in some little pleasantry with the land-lord, and then passed on." Just then a man from the country, who wished a lawyer to appear for him in court, was referred by the landlord to Marshall, as the best advocate he could have, but the countryman declined to have anything to do with the careless young man. In court he asked the clerk for a lawyer, and was once more recommended to take John Marshall. Again he refused. Just then a dignified old man in powdered wig and black coat entered. He was at once engaged, on his appearance. After a time the inferiority of the black-coated lawyer was so apparent that the country-man sought Marshall, told him of the mistake he had made, said that he had left but five dollars of the one hundred dollars he had set aside for lawyers' fees, and asked Marshall if he would assist on the case. The lawyer laugh-ingly agreed. [11]

John Marshall married Mary Willis Ambler on January 3, 1783. When they met about a year and 1/2 earlier, it is said to have been "a case of love at first sight." [12] The newly married couple lived for a number of years in a small two-room frame building in Richmond, which was then merely a village. Marshall practiced law between times of public service. In 1793 they moved into a nine-room brick house he had built on Shockoe Hill.

For many years Mary was a "nervous invalid," and according to Bishop Meade, "the least noise was sometimes agony to her whole frame, and his [John's] perpetual endeavor was to keep the house and yard and out-houses from the slightest cause of distressing her; walking himself at times about the house and yard without shoes." [13]

Justice Marshall was Vice-President of the American Bible Society and an officer in the American Sunday School Union. He frequently attended the Monumental Church in Richmond. This was a Protestant Episcopal Church built between 1812-1814 on the site where a theater had burned in 1811, killing 61 people, including the governor of the state. In remembrance of this event it was agreed to build "an edifice to be set apart and consecrated for the worship of God." The church was the monument.[14] Since Marshall was tall, the pews cramped his legs. "Not finding room enough for his whole body within the pew, he used to take his seat nearest the door of his pew, and, throwing it open, let his legs stretch a little into the aisle."[15]

When his wife died at the end of 1831, it was a great loss to him. A year later he wrote, "Never can I cease to feel the loss and to deplore it."[16] In 1835 Marshall traveled to Philadelphia seeking medical advice. He died while there, on July 6, 1835.

Section 11

Jefferson's Home: Monticello and Charlottesville

☖ *Albemarle County Courthouse*

The settlement of the Virginia Piedmont was significantly different than that of the Valley and the Tidewater regions. Albemarle County, formed officially in 1745, was settled in the 1730s by a blend of European nationalities, whereas the other regions were predominantly settled by one group — either English, Scotch-Irish, or German. Likewise, while the other regions were settled predominantly by one religious sect, such as the Presbyterians in the Valley and the Anglicans in the Tidewater area, in Albemarle County and surrounding areas, these groups converged during the first settlement period and grew up together, producing a very unique tradition of religious diversity, tolerance, and interdenominational cooperation.

In 1762 the General Assembly of Virginia established the town of Charlottesville in honor of Queen Charlotte, wife of King George III of England. The founder of the town was Dr. Thomas Walker, a leading layman in the Anglican Church. In 1750, after founding Charlottesville, Walker led the first expedition to Kentucky and blazed the Cumberland Gap.

Thomas Jefferson called the Albemarle County Courthouse the "Common Temple" because the major denominations all met here together for their regular Sunday services for many decades. No church buildings were erected in town until 1826.

Jack Jouett's Ride

In 1781 the Courthouse became the meeting place of the Virginia General Assembly when it was forced out of Richmond by Benedict Arnold's raids. Since Charlottesville was the temporary capital of Virginia, British General Cornwallis sent Tarleton to raid the city hoping to capture the Legislature and Governor Jefferson. The plan would have likely succeeded if it were not for the "Paul Revere of Virginia," Jack Jouett.

On the evening of June 3, 1781, the young Virginia Captain Jack Jouett was at Cuckoo Tavern in Louisa County, when he noticed some 250 British troops ride past. He guessed where they were going and immediately set off on a daring ride to Charlottesville to warn Jefferson and the lawmakers. He rode as fast as he could for about 40 miles over back roads, taking short cuts through pastures and over narrow paths. It was so dark in the woods that he could not see low branches which hit his face and tore his clothes. He carried scars with him for life from this ride.

Jouett arrived at Monticello at dawn and after warning Jefferson that British troops were coming, he rode down the little mountain to Charlottesville to let the General Assembly know as well. Before Jefferson fled Monticello he saw the redcoats riding into Charlottesville with his spyglass. But thanks to Jack Jouett, most of the Virginia leaders (including Patrick Henry, Richard Henry Lee, Thomas Nelson, Benjamin Harrison, and future president John Tyler) escaped capture by Tarleton. Had they been captured, the war might have been lost. (Daniel Boone was one of the legislators who was captured.)

One block from the Courthouse is the site of James Monroe's first home, which later became a hotel. It was at that hotel that Meriwether Lewis celebrated when he returned to his home town from his historic trip to explore the west.

☖ *Lewis and Clark Monument*

Meriwether Lewis was born near Charlottesville in 1774. From an early age he loved to explore, and being from the same town, he also knew Thomas Jefferson. After President Jefferson purchased the Louisiana Territory from France for 15 million dollars, he selected Lewis to lead an expedition to explore and map this new edition to America. Lewis picked William Clark, younger brother of George Rogers Clark, to help lead the group of 43 men who set out from St. Louis in May, 1804. By October they had traveled 1600 miles to what is now North Dakota, where they camped until Spring. Continuing west, they met an Indian woman named Sacagawea who led them over the Rocky Mountains. On November 7, 1805, they arrived at the Pacific Ocean. They started home in March and arrived back in St. Louis over two years after leaving that town. They brought back notebooks filled with information and maps of the territory as well as many artifacts collected on the way. This monument, showing Lewis and Clark gazing into the distance and Sacagawea kneeling beside them, honors the courage of these explorers.

☖ *Jefferson and Monticello*

Albemarle County's most famous resident, Thomas Jefferson, started building his home in 1768 on a "little mountain" overlooking Charlottesville. It would take decades for Jefferson to complete the building of Monticello as it stands today.

The great breadth of Thomas Jefferson — from farmer to philosopher — can been seen in visiting his home, Monticello. Best known as the author of the *Declaration of Independence* and the third President of the United States, Jefferson was involved in much more than just government. A French visitor in 1782 described Jefferson as a "Musician, Draftsman, Surveyor, Astronomer, Natural Philosopher, Jurist, and Statesman." His library reveals his great range of interest, from the Greek classics to science, architecture, theology, political science, and agriculture.

Thomas Jefferson was born on April 13, 1743, on his father's plantation in Shadwell, Virginia, almost at the foot of the "little mountain" where he would later build Monticello. In fact, as a child, Jefferson would often play on the mountain that would become his home. He always loved the place and early determined to build his home on the mountain.

Thomas was the third of ten children born to Peter and Jane Jefferson. Peter was a large land-owner and a leader in his community, both in the church (as vestryman) and state (as justice of the peace and member of the colonial legislature). Thomas inherited from his father, both physical and intellectual strength. After his father's death in 1757, Thomas, at age fourteen, inherited a large amount of land, including the site of Monticello.

Jefferson's father took great care in his education. Home instruction was interspersed with tutoring from Rev. William Douglass, a Scotchman, and Rev. James Maury, a Huguenot. Jefferson and Rev. Maury remained friends for life. Dr. Maury "exercised a powerful influence in shaping the character of the brilliant youth, who always regarded him with confidence and affection."[1] Thomas's family was very musical, and he practiced the violin assiduously from boyhood, becoming an accomplished player, which he continued throughout his life.

At age 17, Jefferson entered the College of William and Mary, in accordance with the wishes of his father. Within months of arriving in Williamsburg, Jefferson somehow became the frequent companion of some of the leading men in the state — Francis Fauquier, the royal Governor of Virginia, Dr. William Small, professor of natural philosophy (science) and mathematics at the college, and George Wythe, law instructor — which had a great impact on him. Jefferson said that Dr. Small "fixed the destinies of my life."[2] Thomas was very diligent in his work at school, for a season studying 15 hours a day. After graduating from William and Mary in 1762, Jefferson studied law under George Wythe and was admitted to the bar five years later.

During the time of his study of law, Jefferson, at age 21, assumed the management of his father's estate. While in Williamsburg he also witnessed the memorable scenes in the House of Burgesses following the passage of the stamp act. In later years he would enjoy recalling "the torrent of language" that flowed from Patrick Henry's lips when he spoke in the House, amidst cries of treason, against the stamp act (see section on Patrick Henry and the Capitol in Williamsburg). From the time Jefferson heard this speech of Henry, he became a changed man.[3]

After being admitted to the bar, Jefferson practiced law for about eight years before events of the Revolution summoned him elsewhere. His law practice grew from 68 cases the first year, to nearly 500 cases in a single year. Though not a fluent or forcible speaker, he did acquit himself well in the cases he tried.

Just a few days after Jefferson married Martha Skelton on January 1, 1772, he took her to live at his new home at Monticello. Jefferson recorded in his diary that there was more than two feet of snow on the ground and that his horse had a difficult time hauling them through. They first lived in a guest house, while the main house was built. Over the years he designed, built, added on, redesigned, and rebuilt Monticello. The remodeling continued until about the time he retired his second term as President in 1809.

Marriage to the beautiful widow brought him much happiness, and when her wealthy father died in 1773, 40,000 acres and 135 slaves were added to their fortune. Jefferson also soon became a father with the birth of Martha. She was the first of six daughters, but only two survived infancy. Thomas and Martha were married for 10 delightful years. On September 6, 1782, Martha died from complications following the birth of their sixth child. The death of his wife was a shocking blow to him. On her death bed, Thomas promised her he would not remarry; and he never did.

Public Service

Jefferson's public life began at age 26 when he was elected as a member of the Virginia House of Burgesses on May 11, 1769. This began nearly 50 years of service in politics, which he always considered as a "duty." Jefferson made a resolution "never to engage, while in public office, in any kind of enterprise for the improvement of my fortune, nor to wear any other character than that of a farmer."[4]

Summary of Jefferson's Public Service follows:

- Member of Virginia's House of Burgesses, 1769-1775
- Member of the Virginia Committee of Correspondence
- In 1774 wrote *Summary View of the Rights of British America*
- Delegate to the Continental Congress, 1775-1776
- Author of the original draft of the *Declaration of Independence*, 1776, and a signer of the final document
- Member of the Virginia House of Delegates, 1776, where he helped revise the laws of Virginia. His proposals for religious freedom and abolition of the slave trade would be adopted within ten years.
- Governor of Virginia, 1779-1780
- Returned as a member of Congress in 1783
- Sent to France in 1784 to negotiate treaties
- In 1785 became U.S. minister to France
- Served as the first U.S. Secretary of State, 1790-1793
- Elected Vice-President of the United States in 1796. Drafted the *Kentucky Resolves* in 1798.
- Served two terms as President of the United States beginning in 1801. During his Presidency he oversaw the Louisiana Purchase and the exploration of the vast new lands via the Lewis and Clark expedition.
- Founded the University of Virginia, 1819, and served as first rector.

Religious Beliefs

Jefferson's religious beliefs are one of the most misunderstood things about him. William Gould said: "Thomas Jefferson. . . was probably the object of more unjust attacks than any other American statesman before or since his time. Pamphleteers misrepresented his religious opinions, and many of his enemies spread false accusations concerning his personal life. As a result, the belief became wide-spread that he was an infidel." However, Gould says that "despite his liberal leanings, Jefferson was a lifelong member of the Episcopal Church. . . [and] he was especially well pleased with the religious situation which existed in Charlottesville, where Episcopalians, Pres-byterians, Methodists, and Baptists met together every Sunday in the courthouse."[5]

Jefferson's religious life can be divided into three periods, with his time living in France as the first turning point in his thinking. Before going to France, his religious beliefs seemed to follow the orthodox Anglican faith and Calvinism. After his experience in France, he adopted more inter-denominational or non-creedal Chris-tian beliefs. Around 1813, approximately twenty-five years later, he became more of a Unitarian Christian.

He went to France in 1784 when he was 41 years old. For the first 44 years of his life, there is no clear evidence that Jefferson held to anything other than orthodox Anglican Christian tenets. He grew up in the Anglican Church and attended schools run by Anglican cler-gymen. As an adult he worshipped regularly and served on the vestry of his church.[6] Beginning around 1773, Jefferson also regularly attended the services held in the courthouse that were led by other denominations. Jefferson's regular exposure to the diversity of Chris-tian worship and religious awakening occurring at this time in central Virginia helps us to understand his keen interest in leading the fight for religious freedom.

Jefferson put both his own children and a nephew in private Christian schools and commended other Christian schools as well.[7]

He consistently referred to God and His higher law in public settings, from the time of an early court case in 1767 to the end of his life. His personal motto on his seal was "Rebellion To Tyrants Is Obedience to God"[8] Two thirds of the paintings and sculptures in his home at Monticello were from Biblical or Christian history. Throughout his life Jefferson studied the Bible for his own personal benefit and also gave money to Bible societies to distribute them to others.[9]

Jefferson's religious life underwent a critical change following the deaths of his wife, in 1782, and of his two year old daughter, in 1784, and during his public service in France. The deaths of his wife and daughter left Jefferson devastated and emotionally despondent and may have contributed to his questioning of Christianity.

Events occurring in France likely affected his religious views as well. There was a strong anti-clerical feeling among the French people due to the strong support of the Catholic church for the politically corrupt and unpopular monarchs. This caused some thinkers in France to become anti-Christian. Although Jefferson rejected this latter stance, the next 25 years of his life was marked by a period of sincere questioning and analysis of orthodox Christianity (1788-1812), followed by the avowal of unorthodox Unitarianism for his final 14 years (1813-1826).

Jefferson never explicitly agreed with Unitarianism until 1813 (and then only privately to a few friends).[10] In 1803 he had deliberately distributed to his family and closest friends a paper he called "my religious creed" in order to clearly affirm his Christian faith. It was entitled *A Syllabus of the Merits of the Doctrines of Jesus*.[11] In that same year, Jefferson wrote to Benjamin Rush: "My views are very different from that anti-Christian system imputed to me by those who know nothing on my opinions. To the corruptions of Christianity I am indeed, opposed, but not to the genuine precepts of Jesus himself. I am a Christian. . ."[12]

As a Unitarian Christian, he still worshipped in trinitarian churches and faithfully supported orthodox ministers and Bible societies.[13] Even when Jefferson adopted Unitarian views, he believed that he was becoming a more purely Biblical believer, like the first century Christians. Unitarianism at this point, as taught at Harvard's Divinity School, was still rooted in Scripture and the person of Jesus. It was not detached from these until after Jefferson's death when it merged with Universalist thought. Unitarianism today, therefore, differs greatly from Jefferson's beliefs. Jefferson's adoption of unitarian views followed the leading of some Evangelical churches in his community that became non-trinitarian.

It is his writings of his last 14 years that are most frequently cited and quoted by modern scholars as somehow indicative of his whole life. Letters to five Unitarian clergymen are quoted frequently, while the other 110 orthodox clergymen in his life and his more orthodox writings are ignored or down-played. The modern historians' bias toward the views Jefferson held when he was in his 70s and 80s tends to color their perception of his whole life and contributes to misconceptions of Jefferson in many areas.

Common Misconceptions of Jefferson's Religious Life

Following are common misconceptions of Jefferson's religious life.

1. Some people believe Jefferson was opposed to organized religion and was not a regular participant of any church.

In reality, Jefferson worshipped regularly all his life and even served on the vestry of his church twice. He financially supported his Anglican/Episcopalian pastors as well as other clergy, churches, Bible societies, and Christian schools and colleges.[14] He was married in the church and had his family baptized, married and buried with its services.[15] He arranged for organized chapel services and nondenominational religious instruction in schools and at his university in Virginia.[16] He made many statements in support of Christianity and expressed delight when he heard of churches growing in size.[17]

When his Anglican church lost its financial and popular support during the Revolutionary War, he personally led in an effort to start a new church called the Calvinistical Reformed Church.[18] He put forth his own money to secure as its pastor Charles Clay who, significantly, was a notable evangelical.[19] Jefferson donated his architectural services to design a plan for the first Charlottesville Episcopal church building.[20]

He worshipped frequently with other denominations in the Albemarle County courthouse which he called the "common temple."[21] Jefferson also frequently attended Baptist church services at the Lewis Mountain Meeting house.[22] While President, Jefferson worshipped regularly with various denominations that used the U.S. Capitol building for church services.[23] In 1774 he drafted a resolution for the Virginia legislature appointing a *Day of Fasting and Prayer*, and then he made a special effort to organize a worship service with Albemarle County citizens to observe that day.[24] In 1779, while governor of Virginia, Jefferson proclaimed a *Day of Thanksgiving* to be observed throughout the state.

2. Some people believe Jefferson and the clergy were antagonistic to each other.

In reality, Jefferson admired, supported, commended and worked in partnership with well over 100 different Christian clergymen. They admired and supported him as well. This included the national leadership of the major denominations in America. He was personal friends and allies with the following: two moderators of the Presbyterian General Assembly; three Presidents of Princeton University and other Presbyterian Divinity schools; John Leland and Luther Rice of the Baptists; Ezra Stiles, a leader of the Congregationalists and President of Yale; the Muhlenbergs of the Lutheran Church; the Bishop of the Episcopal Church in Virginia; and Catholic Archbishops in both America and France. Although he never personally met the national leaders of the Methodist Church or the Disciples of Christ, they publicly praised him.

Many clergy gave Jefferson their political support. Jefferson supported many clergy in various ways. He helped to get clergy appointed as chaplains in the government and as professors at the College of William and Mary.[25] He attempted to move the entire faculty of John Calvin's University of Geneva to Virginia to form the foundations of a state university (although he was thwarted by the legislature).[26] He appointed some clergy to government posts while he was President. He secretly commissioned and donated funds to a Baptist minister to start anti-slavery churches in Illinois.[27] He used his influence while President to get the Commissioners of the District of Columbia to allow land to be purchased by the Catholic Church.[28]

There were a few clergymen who disliked Jefferson. Some were those who had lost their jobs when the Episcopal church was disestablished after Jefferson's *Statute for Religious Freedom* was approved in 1786. Others were clergymen who favored the Federalist party when Jefferson was the Republican candidate for President. While some attacked Jefferson during the campaign, many came to his aid. Rev. Samuel Knox wrote a well known tract in 1800 entitled *A Vindication of the Religion of Mr. Jefferson.*[29] The clergy who supported Jefferson greatly outnumbered those who did not. In fact, Jefferson was considered the pre-eminent champion of the evangelicals in early America.[30]

Eight clergymen in central Virginia (Charles Clay, Charles Wingfield, William Woods, John Waller, Henry Fry, John Goss, Peter Muhlenberg, and John Leland) ran for public office as overt Jeffersonians, and some did so as a result of his outward support and urging.[31] His letter of 1779 publicly commending his pastor Rev. Charles Clay, or his multiple letters to churches while President, clearly show the way Jefferson felt about most clergymen and churches.[32] Only in a few letters, out of the 20,000 written during his long life, did Jefferson ever express animosity toward any clergy, and it was understandable when he did so.

3. Some people believe Jefferson was not only for separation of church and state, but also separation of all religion from public life, that is, he was for a secular state.

Jefferson did support the separation of church and state, but to him this meant that there be no single official state-favored denomination supported by tax dollars. In his famous 1802 letter to the

Baptists in Danbury, Connecticut, Jefferson spoke of a ''wall of separation'' between the church and the state.[33] Jefferson was paraphrasing the words of the famous Baptist Roger Williams who spoke of a wall being needed to protect the church from government interference. Jefferson believed that the Constitution's First Amendment was a legal wall that prevented the national government from setting up a favored national church. It is interesting that on January 3, 1802, two days after Jefferson wrote this letter, he went for the first time to a church service held in the House Chamber at the Capitol Building. He attended these church meetings constantly for the next seven years.[34]

Another letter in 1802 said that he did not want a ''government without religion.''[35] In his *Notes on Virginia*, he said that civil liberties could never be secure if divorced from a belief in God. His 1808 letter to Rev. Samuel Miller and his *Second Inaugural Address* in 1805 emphasized that under the Constitution, religious legislation was placed under the exclusive authority of the state governments.[36] He believed that religious expression in the public sector was not prohibited by the Constitution. While he opposed government compulsion of religion, he supported government involvement in religion in many ways. Some of his actions include:

- Support for legislative and military chaplains
- Recommending a national seal using religious symbols
- Appointing official Days of Fasting and Prayer
- Writing laws that punished Sabbath breakers
- Supporting the use of Christian oaths
- Allowing government property and facilities to be used for worship
- Supporting the use of Bibles and non-denominational religious instruction in public schools
- Funding of salaries of clergymen in Indian mission school
- Exempting churches from taxation[37]

The image many people have today of Jefferson as a secularist who promoted removing religion from public life is totally unfounded. In fact, Jefferson recognized the great need for the Christian religion to be dispersed throughout a nation that desires to be free. This is one reason he contributed throughout his life to Bible societies. In 1814 he sent money to one Bible society saying: "I had not supposed there was a family in this State not possessing a Bible. . . . I, therefore, enclose you cheerfully, an order. . . for fifty dollars, for the purposes of the Society. . . . There never was a more pure and sublime system of morality delivered to man than is to be found in the four Evangelists."[38] While President, Jefferson served as the chairman of the D.C. school board from 1805-1807, and in this capacity he promoted the teaching of the Bible in the public schools of Washington, D.C. Jefferson said:

> *The Bible is the cornerstone of liberty. A student's perusal of the sacred volume will make him a better citizen, a better father, a better husband.*[39]

🔔 Gravesite

Jefferson died on July 4, 1826, the fiftieth anniversary of the Declaration of Independence. On that same day, and almost at the same hour, John Adams, whom Jefferson had communicated with frequently in later life, died in Massachusetts. Jefferson was buried just down the hill from his home in the family burial ground, next to his wife and his boyhood friend, Dabney Carr. When young, he and Carr used to play under the shade of a tree at this spot and talked of being buried here when they died. Carr had died many years earlier and was the first to be buried at this site.

A small obelisk monument has been placed over Jefferson's gravesite and contains the words that Jefferson instructed be written as his epitaph:

> *Here was buried Thomas Jefferson, Author of the Declaration of American Independence, Of the Statute of Virginia for Re-*

ligious Freedom, and Father of the University of Virginia.

Jefferson considered these three things his most important accomplishments.

🔔 *University of Virginia*

🔔 The Lawn and Rotunda

The University of Virginia was founded by Thomas Jefferson in the last years of his life. Between 1817 and 1826, Jefferson designed and oversaw the construction of his "Academical Village." He described his complex of buildings in a letter to the Board of Visitors, October 7, 1822:

> *We have completed all the buildings proposed. . . ten distinct houses or pavilions containing each a lecture room with generally four other apartments and the accommodation of a professor and his family, and with a garden, and the requisite family offices; six hotels for dieting the students, with a single room in each for a refectory, and two rooms, a garden and offices for the tenant, and an hundred and nine dormitories, sufficient each for the accommodation of two students, arranged in four distinct rows between the pavilions and hotels, and united with them by covered ways. . . The remaining building [the Rotunda], . . . which was to contain rooms for religious worship, for public examinations, for a library and other associated purposes, is not begun for want of funds.*

Construction of the Rotunda was begun in 1822 and completed in 1826, the year of Jefferson's death. One historian recorded of Jefferson that "while the buildings were being erected, his visits to them were daily; and from the northeast corner of the terrace at Monticello he frequently watched the workmen engaged on them, through a telescope."[40]

Some people have said that Jefferson started the University of

Virginia as a secular university, but it was really founded as a non-denominational Christian university. The motto of the university comes from the words of Jesus in John 8:32 — "You shall know the truth and the truth shall set you free." These words can be seen today chiseled in Greek letters across the portico of Cabell Hall (on the opposite end of *The Lawn* from the Rotunda).

The Gateway to the University, found across from "the Corner," bears the following inscription from Proverbs 24:3-4:

> *Through wisdom a house is built, and by understanding it is established; by knowledge the rooms are filled with all precious and pleasant riches.*

The Christian character of Jefferson's University was affirmed by a book written in 1921 on *The Centennial of the University.* It states that "the University of Virginia could never have been anti-Christian or even non-Christian. . . . From the beginning there was no attempt to discourage religion, but only to make it free." It further states:

> *It was for the advancement of Christian scholarship and Christian education that universities had their beginnings as denominational colleges. . . chiefly for the training of their own ministry. Thomas Jefferson. . . in his proposal for a university. . . aimed no blow at any religious influence that might be fostered by it. The blow was at sectarianism only. As a matter of fact we know that so far as concerns the religious influence of this institution, from its very inception the wind has always blown in a single direction.*[41]

From its inception, Presbyterians and Baptists supported Jefferson's idea for a college and were key in the passage of the University bill in the General Assembly. In 1817 the cornerstone of the University was laid with a religious ceremony. Jefferson, Madison, and then U.S. President James Monroe gathered at Pavilion VII. "Monroe applied the square and plumb, [and] the chaplain [Rev. William King] asked a blessing on the stone."[42]

To assure the non-denominational nature of the university, Jefferson thought there should not be a Professor of Divinity, since this person's denominational beliefs might gain ascendancy or official favors. Jefferson explained that this was not "to be understood that instruction in religious opinions and duties was meant to be precluded by the public authorities as indifferent to the interests of society; on the contrary, the relations which exist between man and his Maker and the duties resulting from those relations, are the most incumbent on his study and investigation."[43]

University historian Philip Bruce wrote:

Policy and principle alike dictated to [Jefferson] that religion, in some form or other, direct or indirect, should be recognized in his institution. . . . These methods were, (1) instruction in the Greek, Latin, and Hebrew languages, (through the professor of Ancient Languages) which would enable the student to read the 'earliest and most respected' authorities of the Christian Faith; and (2) instruction, through the professor of Moral Philosophy, in those abstract principles of virtue, in which all sects [i.e. Christian denominations] believe and which all endeavor to practice.[44]

Jefferson said that this professor would teach "the proofs of the being of a God, the creator, preserver, and supreme ruler of the universe. . . . Proceeding thus far without offense to the Constitution, we have thought it proper at this point to leave every sect to provide, as they think fittest, the means of further instruction in their own particular tenets. Our Visitors suggest that each sect establish its own independent professorship [seminary] on the confines of the University."[45]

In his plans, Jefferson suggested that there be space in a building for religious worship. "The Rotunda was built to furnish, first of all, a place for religious worship," according to the history by Patton and Doswell. They said that "the Apostle of Religious Freedom saw no inconsistency in applying public funds to the building of a chapel for unsectarian use." Jefferson wrote: "Each student would be able to attend religious exercises with the professor of their particular sect [and thus]. . . leave inviolate the constitutional freedom of religion, the most inalienable and sacred of all human rights."[46]

How could such a plan work? Jefferson pointed out a living model of it in 1822:

> *In Charlottesville there is a good degree of religion.... We have four sects, but no church or meeting house, except the court house, which is the common temple — one Sunday in the month to each, Episcopalian, Presbyterian, Methodist and Baptist, where all meet together, join in hymning their Maker, listen with attention and devotion to each other's preachers, and all mix in society with perfect harmony.*[47]

Rev. William H. McGuffey

Over the years many exemplary Christians served as chaplains and faculty at the University of Virginia. The most well known is William Holmes McGuffey, a Presbyterian clergyman who became professor of Moral Philosophy in 1845 and served for 28 years. David Culbreth writes that McGuffey's classroom teaching was "pre-eminently a Christian philosophy — one whose inspiration was gained at the foot of the Cross."[48] McGuffey gained national fame through the *McGuffey Readers*, which have been called "the most influential volumes ever published in America. . . . [and] the most significant force in the framing of our national morals and tastes" other than the Bible.[49] Over 120 million copies of the *Readers* were sold in the century following their publication in 1837.

In the Preface to his *Fourth Reader* McGuffey wrote:

> *From no source has the author drawn more copiously, in his selections, than from sacred Scriptures. For this, he certainly apprehends no censure. In a Christian country, that man is to be pitied, who at this day, can honestly object to imbuing the minds of youth with the language and spirit of the Word of God.*[50]

🔔 *Statue of George Rogers Clark*

George Rogers Clark was born in Albemarle County in 1752. As a lad he learned the ways of the woods. His love for the frontier lead him as a young man to move to the western part of Virginia, which would later become the state of Kentucky.

During the Revolutionary War, the British sent Indians to raid the homes of settlers in Kentucky, which at this time certainly resembled the meaning of the Indian word for which this territory was named – "dark and bloody ground." Many settlers had to live inside big forts or stockades to protect themselves from the Indians.

Clark sought to rid the west of this threat, so he traveled to Williamsburg, the capital of Virginia, to ask for military aid. Governor Patrick Henry made him a colonel but said he would have to recruit his own troops, since many Virginians were already engaged in battle. Col. Clark recruited about 200 men to march with him to Kaskaskia (in what is today Illinois) to attack the British fort there. The Indians called these frontiersmen "Long Knives" for the big knives they carried in their belts. They noiselessly marched for days and days and upon arriving at the British outpost on July 4, 1778, used the cover of darkness to sneak into the fort and capture the English commander and all the soldiers. This was accomplished without the lose of one life or without firing a gun.

In early August, Clark and his men captured Fort Vincennes (part of Indiana today), also without firing a shot. Clark left a small garrison at the fort and returned to Kaskaskia for the winter. When Clark received word that Vincennes was retaken by the British and Indians in December, he led a march of 180 miles across flooded land in the middle of winter to attempt to retake the fort. During much of the trip the men waded through icy water, sometimes up to their necks. The drummer boy would often float on his drum. When possible they dried out at night around a fire. They killed what food they could on the way, but often went with little, once going two days with nothing. The last seven miles of the march was almost all through deep water. Upon arriving at the fort they immediately attacked and fought all night and most of the next day. British Colonel Hamilton finally surrendered. The western lands were saved and peace came to the settlers thanks to the heroics of George Rogers Clark and the Long Knives. This action also assured that the Northwest Territory (the states of Ohio, Indiana, Illinois, Michigan, and Wisconsin) would be a part of the United States.

Conclusion

We have examined the lives of numerous men who were important in the beginning of the United States of America. Most of our founding fathers were Christians and many understood the Providential purposes of America. Many of those men God used to gain our independence believed they were giving birth to an uniquely Christian nation such has had not been seen before in history. Our sixth President, John Quincy Adams, stated:

> *Is it not that, in the chain of human events, the birthday of the nation is indissolubly linked with the birthday of the Saviour? That it forms a leading event in the progress of the gospel dispensation? Is it not that the Declaration of Independence first organized the social compact on the foundation of the Redeemer's mission upon earth? That it laid the cornerstone of human government upon the first precepts of Christianity and gave to the world the first irrevocable pledge of the fulfillment of the prophecies announced directly from Heaven at the birth of the Saviour and predicted by the greatest of the Hebrew prophets 600 years before?[1]*

What made America a Christian nation was not that everyone in the nation was a Christian, though the vast majority were, but that American was founded on Christian principles. Our founders saw these Christian principles as the source of our freedom and prosperity. The **U.S. House of Representatives** declared in 1854:

> *[T]he great vital and conservative element in our system is the belief of our people in the pure doctrines and divine truths of the gospel of Jesus Christ.[2]*

Signer of the Declaration, Benjamin Rush, wrote in 1806:

Christianity is the only true and perfect religion, and that in proportion as mankind adopt its principles and obeys its precepts, they will be wise and happy.[3]

There are many today who acknowledge that America was birthed as a Christian nation, but say we are now no longer Christian but are a pluralistic society — that we are made up of people from all different religions and so we can no longer operate our nation on the gospel of Jesus Christ. It is important to note that:

One, a pluralistic society is only possible in a Christian nation, for only Christianity is tolerant of other beliefs — Christianity does not attempt to use force to compel belief because it recognizes the power of the Holy Spirit to convert man from within. Man-made religions lack such supernatural support and need the force of government to promote the established religion and suppress contrary ideas. Consequently, there is no pluralism, or true religious freedom, in Muslim nations, in communist or marxist nations, or in humanistic nations. Those adhering to the Christian faith are usually the first ones persecuted in such nations, because the truth they espouse will ultimately undermine the state religion.

Two, the prosperity and liberty of America are a direct result of applying Biblical principles in the life of our nation. If you remove those Christian foundations, then you remove the basis for everyone's liberty and prosperity (including those who are now using their freedoms to try to remove God from every aspect of the public affairs of the United States).

America, in recent decades, has forgotten God. Even though prayer and the Bible have been removed from our schools, and the media almost completely ignores God, there is still indelibly etched within the buildings and archives of our nation, a resounding declaration that this nation only is blessed because God is Lord.

Remembering the words of Senator Byrd, "that to remove God from this country will destroy it," let us stop the destruction of our nation by infusing God and His truth into every aspect of our society.

Appendix

"In God We Trust"

Official Motto of the United States of America

On July 3, 1956, President Dwight D. Eisenhower signed a bill which was submitted as a Congressional Resolution making the phrase, "In God We Trust," the national motto of the United States.

Public Law 851, Chapter 795, Joint Resolution, July 30, 1956:

Resolved by the Senate and House of Representatives of the United States of America in Congress assembled, That the National Motto of the United States is hereby declared to be "In God We Trust." Approved July 30, 1956.

Inscribed Upon All United States Currency

Since 1865 currency of the United States has born the inscription "In God We Trust." This became official on July 11, 1955, as a bill was passed by the Senate and House of Representatives to place the inscription, "In God We Trust," on all currency and coins.

Public Law 140, Chapter 303, July 11, 1955:

To provide that all United States currency shall bear the inscription, "In God We Trust."

Be it enacted by the Senate and House of Representatives of the United States of America in Congress assembled. That at such time as new dies for the printing are adopted in connection with the current program of the Treasury Department to increase the capacity of presses utilized by the Bureau of Engraving and Printing the dies shall bear, at such place or places thereon as the Secretary of the Treasury may determine to be appropriate, the inscription, "In God We Trust," and thereafter this inscription shall appear on all United States currency and coins. Approved July 11, 1955.[1]

The Seal of the United States

The Seal of the United States (also known as "the Great Seal") is a symbol of our nation's sovereignty. It is affixed to various official national documents that are signed by the President.

Shortly after the adoption of the *Declaration of Independence* in 1776, a committee (composed of Thomas Jefferson, John Adams, and Benjamin Franklin) was appointed to formulate an official seal for the new nation. The seal was to reflect the heart of the new nation and the principles upon which she was built.

Franklin's description of his proposal for the seal was as follows:

Moses standing on the shore, and extending his hand over the sea, thereby causing the same to overwhelm Pharaoh who is sitting in an open chariot, a crown on his head and a sword in his hand. Rays from a pillar of fire in the clouds reaching to Moses, to express that he acts by command of the Deity. Motto: Rebellion to tyrants is obedience to God.[2]

Jefferson proposed that one side of the seal be *"the children of Israel in the wilderness, led by a cloud by day, and a pillar of fire by night."*[3]

Both of these men saw that the birth of America, was accomplished sovereignly and miraculously by the hand of God, as He similarly had done with ancient Israel. While almost every member of Congress agreed with this, they also felt God was doing something more with America. Consequently, Congress did not immediately adopt any official seal. It was not until 1782 that a seal was approved. Both sides of the Seal are found on the back of our one dollar bill today.

Following is a description of the reverse side given in a Department of State bulletin which was taken from the Journals of Congress:

REVERSE. A pyramid unfinished — of 13 layers of stone. In the zenith, an eye of Divine Providence, surrounded with a glory proper. Over the eye these words, "Annuit Coeptis" [Latin words that mean "He (God) has blessed our undertakings."] On the base of the pyramid the numerical letters MDCCLXXVI. And underneath, the following motto, "Novus Ordo Seclarum." [Latin for "A New Order of the Ages"]

Charles Thomson, the Secretary of the Congress that approved the Seal, wrote that "the Pyramid signifies Strength and Duration. The Eye over it and the Motto allude to the many signal interpositions of Providence in favour of the American cause."[4]

Endnotes

Section 1

Washington,D.C., the United States Capital

1. *America's God and Country Encyclopedia of Quotations*, William J. Federer (Coppell, TX: FAME Publishing, 1994), p. 311.

2. Cited in *A Christian History of the American Republic*, Walker Whitman, 1939.

3. Rosalie Slater, in Introductory article in reprint of *An American Dictionary of the English Language*, Noah Webster, 1828. Reprint by the Foundation for American Christian Education, 1980.

4. Thomas Jefferson, *Writings*, vol. 15, Letter to Mr. Hammond, 1821, pp. 330-332.

5. William Jay, *The Life of John Jay*, New York: J. & J. Harper, 1833, Vol. II, p. 376, to John Murray, Jr. on October 12, 1816. (For more on Jay, see p. 101)

6. Daniel L. Dreisbach, *Religion and Politics in the Early Republic*, Lexington, KY: The University Press of Kentucky, 1996, p. 113. (See p. 200 for more on Marshall.)

7. *The Works of Daniel Webster*, Vol. 2, Boston: Little, Brown, and Company, 1854, pp. 604-605.

8. Reproduction of Proclamation in *The Christian History of the American Revolution, Consider and Ponder*, compiled by Verna Hall (San Francisco: Foundation for American Christian Education, 1980), p. 510a.

9. *A Compilation of the Messages and Papers of the Presidents*, Vol. 1, New York: Bureau of National Literature, Inc., 1897.

10. *Christopher Columbus's Book of Prophecies*, reproduction of the Original Manuscript with English Translation by Kay Brigham (Fort Lauderdale: TSELF, 1991), p. 178-179.

11. The First Charter of Virginia, 1606, in *Sources of Our Liberties*, edited by Richard L. Perry, Chicago: American Bar Foundation, 1978, p. 40.

12. William Bradford, *Of Plymouth Plantation*, 1620-1647, a New Edition of the Complete Text, with notes and an Introduction by Samuel Eliot Morison, New York: Alfred A. Knopf, 1952, pp. 8-9.

13. Ibid., p. 25.

14. Ibid., p. 76.

15. *Remember William Penn*, compiled by the William Penn Tercentenary Committee, Harrisburg, PA: Commonwealth of Pennsylvania, 1945, p. 74

16. Ibid., pp. 85-86.

17. "Frame of Government of Pennsylvania," in *Sources of Our Liberties*, p. 210.

18. Samuel M. Janney, *The Life of William Penn: With Selections from His Correspondence and Autobiography*, Philadelphia: Lippincott, Grambo & Co., 1852, p. 407.

19. T.R. Fehrenbach, *Greatness to Spare, The heroic sacrifices of the men who signed the Declaration of Independence*, Princeton, NJ: D. Van Nostrand Co., 1968, p. 23.

20. Ibid., p. 247.

21. Mark Beliles and Stephen McDowell, *America's Providential History*, Charlottesville, VA: Providence Foundation, 1989, p. 162.

22. B.F. Morris, *Christian Life and Character of the Civil Institutions of the United States of America*, Philadelphia: George W. Childs, 1864, pp. 530-531.

23. Beliles and McDowell, p. 167.

24. Ibid.

25. George Washington, *Circular Letter Addressed to the Governors of all the States on Disbanding the Army, 1783*, Old South Leaflets, No. 15, published by the Old South Association, Old South Meeting-house, Boston, MA.

26. John M. Taylor, *Garfield of Ohio: The Available Man,* New York: W.W. Norton & Co., Inc., 1970, p. 180. Quoted from "A Century of Congress," by James A. Garfield, Atlantic, July 1877.

27. Beliles and McDowell, p. 145.

28. *Appletons' Cyclopaedia of American Biography, Vol. 4*, edited by James Grant Wilson and John Fiske, New York: D. Appleton and Co., 1888, p. 454.

29. James H. Hutson, *Religion and the Founding of the American Republic*, Washington: Library of Congress, 1998, p. 84. `

30. Hutson, p. 119, footnote 40.

31. Hutson, p. 85.

32. Hutson, p. 84.

33. Hutson, p. 84, 87.

34. Hutson, p. 84, 90.

35. Hutson, p. 86.

36. Hutson, p. 86.

37. Hutson, p. 87.

38. "A Model of Christian Charity," *Old South Leaflets*.

39. Samuel F.B. Morse, "Invention of the Telegraph," *America, Great Crises in Our History Told by Its Makers,* Vol. 6, Chicago: Veterans of Foreign Wars, 1925, p. 308.

40. Hutson, pp. 90-91.

41. Hutson, p. 91.

42. Church of the Holy Trinity v. U.S.; 143 U.S. 457, 458 (1892).

43. Hutson, p. 84.

44. Hutson, p. 91.

45. Robert Flood, *Men Who Shaped America*, Chicago: Moody Press, 1976, p. 43.

46. *The Annals of America*, Chicago: Encyclopaedia Britannica, 1968, p. 276.

47. Samuel Adams, "American Independence," An oration delivered in Philadelphia on August 1, 1776, in American Eloquence, Vol. 1, New York: D. Appleton and Co., 1858, p. 324.

48. James Madison, *Notes of Debates in the Federal Convention of 1787*, New York: W.W. Norton & Co., 1987, pp. 209-210.

49. Verna Hall, *The Christian History of the Constitution of the United States of America, Christian Self-government with Union*, San Francisco: Foundation for American Christian Education, 1979, p. 34.

50. John Eidsmoe, *Christianity and the Constitution*, Grand Rapids, MI: Baker Book House, 1987, p. 374.

51. Robert C. Winthrop, "Address to Massachusetts Bible Society Meeting, May 28, 1849," *Addresses and Speeches on Various Occassions*, Boston: Little, Brown & Co., 1852, p. 172.

52. Rosalie J. Slater, "Noah Webster, Founding Father of American Scholarship and Education," preface article in reprint of *An American Dictionary of the English Language* (1828) by Noah Webster, San Francisco: Foundation for American Christian Education, 1980, p. 14.

53. Verna Hall, *The Christian History of the Constitution of the United States, Christian Self-government*, San Francisco: F.A.C.E., 1980, p. 248A.

54. *Our Ageless Constitution*, W. David Stedman, editor, Asheboro, NC: Stedman Associates, 1987, p. 39.

55. Ibid.

56. Ibid.

57. Ibid.

58. Noah Webster, *History of the United States*, New Haven: Durrie & Peck, 1833, pp. 307-308.

59. *The Federalist* by Hamilton, Jay, & Madison, Washington, D.C.: Global Affairs Publ., 1987, p. 281.

60. *The Federalist*, no. 47.3, p. 260-261.

61. *Our Ageless Constitution*, p. 32.

62. *The Federalist*, no. 45, p. 252.

63. Benjamin Weiss, *God in American History*, South Pasadena, CA: National Educators Fellowship, 1966, p. 241.

64. William J. Johnson, *Abraham Lincoln the Christian*, reprinted by Mott Media, Milford, MI., 1976, pp. 112-114.

65. Ibid.

66. Ibid., pp. 120-121.

67. Ibid., pp. 178-179.

68. Ibid., p. 172.

69. William J. Johnson, *Robert E. Lee the Christian*, reprinted by Mott Media, Milford, MI., 1976, pp. 14-15.

70. Ibid., p. 18.

71. Ibid., p. 113-114.

72. Robert E. Lee, Jr., *Recollections and Letters of General Robert E. Lee*, Doubleday, Page and Co., 1904, p. 105.

73. Johnson, *Robert E. Lee the Christian*, pp. 118-119.

74. Gamaliel Bradford, *Lee the American*, Houghton and Mifflin Co., 1913, p. 92.

Section 2

Washington and Mount Vernon

1. *Mount Vernon, A Handbook*, The Mount Vernon Ladies' Association of the Union, Mount Vernon, Virginia, 1985, p. 11.

2. Elswyth Thane, *Mount Vernon is Ours, The Story of the Preservation and Restoration of Washington's Home*, Duell, Soan and Pearce, 1966, p. 3.

3. Philip Slaughter, *Christianity the Key to the Character and Career of Washington*, New York: Thomas Whittaker, 1886, p. 29.

4. William Wilbur, *The Making of George Washington*, Alexandria, VA: Patriotic Education, Inc., 1973, p. 21.

5. Ibid., pp. 253-254.

6. George Bancroft, *History of the United States*, Vol. 6, Boston: Little, Brown, and Co., 1878, pp. 40-41.

7. Henry Armit Brown, "Centenial Oration of Valley Forge," in *The Christian History of the American Revolution, Consider and Ponder*, Verna Hall, compiler, San Francisco: Foundation for American Christian Education, 1976, p. 61.

8. Ibid.

9. Bart McDowell, *The Revolutionary War*, Washington, D.C.: National Geographic Society, 1970, p. 128.

10. Wilbur, p. 196.

11. Brown, in *Consider and Ponder*, p. 61.

12. Wilbur, p. 195.

13. Bancroft, p. 50.

14. McDowell, p. 131.

15. Bancroft, p. 41.

16. Bancroft, p. 42.

17. Brown, p. 66.

18. Ibid., p. 68.

19. William J. Johnson, *George Washington the Christian,* reprinted by Mott Media, Milford, MI., 1976, pp. 120-121.

20. Ibid., p. 104.

21. Bruce Lancaster, *The American Revolution,* Garden City, NY: Garden City Books, 1957, p. 42.

22. Johnson, p. 113.

23. Johnson, pp. 119-120.

24. Ibid., p. 209.

25. George Washington, Letter to Colonel Lewis Nicola, Newberg, 22 May 1782, *The Writings of George Washington,* Vol. 8 Jared Sparks, editor, Boston, 1835.

26. James T. Flexner, *George Washington in the American Revolution, 1775-1783,* Boston: Little, Brown and Co., 1967, p. 507. Quoted in W. Cleon Skousen, *The Making of America,* Washington, D.C.: The National Center for Constitutional Studies, 1985, p. 106.

27. Ibid.

28. John Fiske, *The Critical Period of American History,* 1783-1789, New York: Houghton, Mifflin and Company, 1894, p. 231.

29. Wilbur, pp. 42-43.

30. Ibid., pp. 63-64.

31. Ibid., pp. 77-78.

32. Washington Irving, *The Life of Washington,* Vol. 1, New York: G.P. Putnam's Sons, 1857, p. 259.

33. Ibid., p. 352.

34. Ibid., p. 207.

35. Johnson, pp. 41-42.

36. Irving, pp. 268-269.

37. Slaughter, pp. 29-30.

Section 3

William Penn and the "City of Brotherly Love"

1. *Remember William Penn,* compiled by the William Penn Tercentenary Committee, Harrisburg, PA: Commonwealth of Pennsylvania, 1945, p. 23.

2. Ibid., p. 77.

3. Ibid., p. 20.

4. Ibid., p. 24.

5. Ibid., p. 33.

6. Elizabeth Janet Gray, *Penn,* New York: The Viking Press, 1967, p. 103.

7. John W. Graham, *William Penn, Founder of Pennsylvania*, New York: Frederick A. Stokes, 1916, p. 43.

8. *Remember William Penn*, p. 33.

9. The quotes related to this trial are from Penn's account in Samuel M. Janney, *The Life of William Penn: With Selections from His Correspondence and Autobiography*, Philadelphia: Lippincott, Grambo & Co., 1852, pp. 67-81.

10. Graham, p. 59.

11. Graham, p. 50a; *Remember William Penn*, p. 18h.

12. *Remember William Penn*, p. 23.

13. Ibid., p. 76.

14. Ibid., p. 81.

15. Graham, p. 134.

16. *Remember William Penn*, p. 158.

17. Ibid.

18. Graham, p. 134, 160.

19. Ibid., p. 11.

20. Francis Brandt and Henry Gummere, *Byways and Boulevards in and about Historic Philadelphia*, Philadelphia: Corn Exchange National Bank, 1925, p. 11.

21. *Journal of the Proceedings of the Congress Held at Philadelphia September 5, 1771*, a Facsimile of the Official Edition printed in 1774, Philadelphia: Library Company of Philadelphia, 1974, p. 24.

22. Ibid., p. 25.

23. *The Book of Abigail and John, Selected Letters of the Adams Family, 1762-1784*, edited by L.H. Butterfield, Cambridge, MA: Harvard University Press, 1975, p. 76.

24. B.F. Morris, p. 221.

25. These documents and some surrounding events were examined earlier under the section on the United States Archives. For more information see *America's Providential History*, pp. 147-150, 169-174, 186-192.

26. *Writings of Benjamin Franklin*, Albert Henry Smyth, editor, Macmillan Co., 1905-07, Vol. 9, p. 702.

27. W. Cleon Skousen, *The Making of America*, Washington, D.C.: The National Center for Constitutional Studies, 1985, p. 5.

28. Skousen, p. 162, and excerpts from newsletter.

29. John Fiske, *The Critical Period of American History*, 1783-1789, New York: Houghton, Mifflin and Co., 1902, p. 364.

30. John F. Watson, *Annals of Philadelphia and Pennsylvania*, Hart, etc. publishers, 1850, p. 398.

31. Noah Webster, *History of the United States*, New Haven: Durrie & Peck, 1833, pp. 273-274.

32. *The Autobiography of Benjamin Franklin*, compiled by John Bigelow, New York: Walter J. Black, Inc., 1932, p. 181.

33. James Madison, *Notes of Debates*, p. 210.

34. Ibid., p. 426.

35. *The Pageant of America*, Ralph Henry Gabriel, editor, New Haven: Yale University Press, Vol. 10, 1928, p. 258.

36. *The Works of Benjamin Franklin*, Jared Sparks, editor, Boston: Tappan, Whittemore, and Mason, 1840, p. 281-282.

37. *The Autobiography of Benjamin Franklin*, p. 217.

38. David Barton, *Original Intent, The Courts, the Constitution, & Religion*, Aledo, TX: WallBuilder Press, 1996, p. 118.

39. Ibid., p. 163.

40. Ibid., p. 182.

41. Ibid., p. 135.

42. *Remember William Penn*.

43. John T. Faris, *Historic Shrines of America*, New York: George H. Doran Co., 1918, p. 160.

44. Ibid., pp. 160-161.

45. Ibid., p. 161.

46. Ibid.

47. Benjamin Rush, *Thoughts Upon the Mode of Education Proper in a Republic*, Early American Imprints, 1786.

48. Benjamin Rush, *Essays, Literary, Moral and Philosophical*, Philadelphia: printed by Thomas and William Bradford, 1806, p. 113.

49. Ibid., p. 93.

50. Brandt and Gummere, p. 40.

Section 4

Jamestown: The First Permanent English Settlement

1. E.G.R. Taylor, editor, *The Original Writings and Correspondence of the Two Richard Hakluyts*, Vol. 2, London: Hakluyt Society, 1935, p. 178.

2. Ibid., p. 211.

3. Ibid.; see *The Principal Navigations, Voyages, Traffiques & Discoveries of the English Nation*, by Richard Hakluyt, Vol 12, New York: The Macmillan Co., 1905, p. 32 for more on this.

4. Taylor, p. 318 and Old South Leaflets, No. 122, *England's Title to North America*, from Hakluyt's *Discourse Concerning Westerne Planting*, p. 12, Boston: Old South Meeting-house.

5. Matthew Page Andrews, *The Soul of a Nation*, New York: Charles Scribner's Sons, 1944, p. 3.

6. *Old South Leaflets, No. 122*, p. 16.

7. *The Will of Richard Hakluyt*, 1612, in Taylor, Vol. 2, p. 506.

8. "The First Charter of Virginia," in *Sources of Our Liberties*, pp. 39-40.

9. Andrews, p. 54.

10. Benjamin Hart, *Faith and Freedom, The Christian Roots of American Liberty*, Lewis and Stanley, Dallas, 1988, p. 139.

11. George Bruner Parks, *Richard Hakluyt and the English Voyages*, New York: American Geographical Society, 1928, p. 256; and Andrews, p. 57.

12. Engraved on the Monument. Also in, John Fiske, *Old Virginia and Her Neighbors*, Vol.1, New York, Houghton, Mifflin, and Co., 1897, p. 76.

13. Hart.

14. John Smith, *Advertisements for the Unexperienced Planters of New England, or Anywhere: Or, the Path-Way to Experience to Erect a Plantation*, p. 32. cited in *Pocahontas* by Grace Steel Woodward, University of Oklahoma Press, Norman, 1969, p. 85.

15. Woodward, p. 6.

16. John Smith, *The Generall Historie of Virginia, New-England, and the Summer Isles....*, Book IV, p. 122, in *Travels and Works of Captain John Smith, Part II*, edited by Edward Arber, Edinburgh: John Grant, 1910, p. 532.

17. Ibid., pp. 395-400.

18. Ibid., p. 400.

19. Ibid., p. 392.

20. Fiske, p. 111.

21. John Smith, *Advertisements...*, in Woodward, p.52.

22. Woodward, p. 57.

23. Andrews, pp. 77-79.

24. *Travels and Works of Captain John Smith, Part II*, p. 407.

25. See Andrews, pp. 68-71, 77-79.

26. *Memorials of Methodism in Virginia* by W.W.B., 1870, p. 11.

27. *Travels and Works of Captain John Smith, Part II, p. 497.*

28. Ibid., pp. 498-499.

29. Francis B. Simkins, Spotswood H. Jones, and Sidman P. Poole, *Virginia: History, Government, Geography*, Charles Scribners's Sons, New York, 1964, pp. 68-69.

30. Simkins, pp. 69-70; Woodward, p. 125.

31. Woodward, p. 124.

32. Simkins, p. 70.

33. B.F. Morris, *Christian Life and Character of the Civil Institutions of the United States*, Philadelphia: George W. Childs, 1864, p. 93.

34. Woodward, p. 135.

35. *For the Colony in Virginea Britannia, Lawes Divine, Morall and Martiall, etc.*, compiled by William Strachey, edited by David H. Flaherty, The University Press of Virginia, Charlottesville, 1969, pp. ix.

36. Ibid., pp. 10-12.

37. Woodward, p. 152.

38. Woodward, p. 159.

39. Woodward, p. 163.

40. Woodward, p. 186.

41. Woodward, p. 191.

42. Simkins, p. 80.

43. Ibid.

44. Simkins, p. 82.

45. Pat Robertson, *America's Dates With Destiny*, Thomas Nelson Publishers, Nashville, 1986, p. 41.

46. John Brinsley, *A Consolation for Our Grammar Schooles*, Scholars' Facsimiles & Reprints, New York, reprinted in 1943 from an original copy in the New York Pubic Library.

47. Simkins, pp. 97-98.

48. Ibid., p. 99.

Section 5

Williamsburg: The Colonial Capital

1. Simkins, p. 133.

2. See Section 4, *Jamestown*, part on "Henricus School and College, 1619," p. 126.

3. Richard Frothingham, *The Rise of the Republic*, 1890, quoted in *Christian History of the Constitution*, Verna Hall, compiler, 1980, p. 337.

4. Rosalie Slater, *Teaching and Learning America's Christian History*, Foundation for American Christian Education, 1980, p. 262-263.

5. *The Virginia Gaxette, November 20, 1779*, Number 4, Williamsburg: printed by Dixon & Nicolson (Original in University of Virginia Alderman Library)

6. *Appletons' Cyclopaedia of American Biography*, edited by James Grant Wilson and John Fiske, Vol. 5, New York: D. Appleton and Co., 1888, p. 175.

7. Simkins, p. 231.

8. Frothingham, in CHOC, p. 336.

9. William Wirt, *Sketches of the Life and Character of Patrick Henry*, Philadelphia: James Webster, publisher, 1818, pp. 138-140.

10. Simkins, p. 240.

Section 6

Yorktown: the Final Battlefield of the Revolution

1. Beliles and McDowell, pp. 166-167.

2. N. Dwight, *The Lives of the Signers of the Declaration of Independence*, New York: A.S. Barnes & Burr, 1860, pp. 315-316.

3. Sanderson, *Biography of the Signers*, quoted in Faris, p. 271.

4. Quoted in Faris, p. 272.

5. T.R. Fehrenbach, *Greatness to Spare, the heroic sacrifices of the men who signed the Declaration of Independence*, Princeton, New Jersey: D. Van Nostrand Co., 1968, p. 234.

Section 7

Patrick Henry and His Homes at Scotchtown and Red Hill

1. William Wirt, *Sketches of the Life and Character of Patrick Henry*, Philadelphia: James Webster, publisher, 1818, p. 36.

2. John T. Faris, *Historic Shrines of America*, 1918, p. 283.

3. William Wirt Henry, *Patrick Henry, Life, Correspondence and Speeches*, Vol. 1, 1891, p. 8-9

4. E.L. Magoon, *Orators of the American Revolution*, New York: C. Scribner, 1857. Reprinted by Sightext Publications, El Segundo, CA, 1969, pp. 207-208.

5. William Wirt Henry, p. 15.

6. Ibid., p. 16.

7. Ibid., p. 118.

8. Ibid., p. 118-119.

9. Ibid., p. 38-39.

10. Ibid., p. 41.

11. Ibid., p. 43.

12. Ibid., p. 43.

13. Wirt, pp. 373-375.

14. Wirt., p. 58; William Wirt Henry, p. 81-82.

15. Francis Simkins et al, *Virginia: History, Government, Geography*, New York: Charles Scribner's Sons, 1964, p. 231.

16. W.W. Henry, p. 83.

17. Wirt, p. 58.

18. W.W. Henry, p. 101.

19. W.W. Henry, p. 94.

20. Ibid., p. 147.

21. *Patrick Henry*, Moses Coit Tyler, Boston: Houghton, Mifflin, and Co., 1893, p. 145.

22. Quoted in John Eidsmoe, *Christianity and the Constitution*, Grand Rapids: Baker Book House, p. 304. (See also W.W. Henry, vol. 2, p. 139-140.)

23. Tyler, p. 356-357.

24. Ibid., p. 365.

25. *Patrick's Henry's Comments on Life, Liberty and the Pursuit of Happiness*, Michael Jesse Bennett, Red Hill, VA: Patrick Henry Memorial Foundation, 1991, p. 1.

26. Bennett, p. 1 and Wirt, p. 402.

27. Wirt, p. 402.

28. Ibid., pp. 392-393.

29. Tyler, pp. 348-350. See also Wirt, p. 387.

30. Tyler, p. 350.

31. Ibid., p. 351.

32. Ibid., p. 351-352. See also copy of Patrick Henry's Will.

33. Tyler, p. 377.

Section 8

James Madison and Montpelier

1. John T. Faris, Historic Shrines of America, New York: George H. Doran, 1918, pp. 298-299.

2. Irving Brant, *James Madison*, Indianapolis: Bobbs-Merrill, 1941, I:56-57, quoted in *Christianity and the Constitution* by John Eidsmoe, Grand Rapids, MI: Baker Book House, p. 94.

3. Ibid., p. 95, from Brant, James Madison, I:60.

4. Eidsmoe, p. 96, quoting from Brant, I:113.

5. *The Papers of James Madison*, in Eidsmoe, p. 97.

6. William C. Rives, *History of the Life and Times of James Madison*, Boston: Little, Brown & Co., 1866, I:33-34, in Eidsmoe, pp. 97-98.

7. Papers, I:74-76, in Eidsmoe, p. 98.

8. Papers, I:95-97, in Eidsmoe, p. 100.

9. Norman Cousins, *'In God We Trust,' the Religious Beliefs and Ideas of the American Founding Fathers*, New York: Harper & Brothers, 1958, p. 301.

10. Eidsmoe, p. 101.

11. Eidsmoe, p. 102.

12. Quoted in Eidsmoe, p. 105.

13. Robert W. Lincoln, *Lives of the Presidents of the United States*, New York: Wm. W. Reed & Co., 1835, p. 141.

14. *The Federalist, a Collection of Essays, Written in Favor of the Constitution of the United States, as Agreed Upon by the Federal Convention,* September 17, 1787, edited by Michael Loyd Chadwick, Washington, DC: Global Affairs Publishing Co., 1987, p. 106.

15. Ibid., Federalist 37.12, p. 192.

16. Quoted by Gaillard Hunt, *The Life of James Madison,* New York: Russell & Russell, 1902, 1968, p. 134, in Eidsmoe, p. 94.

17. Madison to Jefferson, 24 October, 1787, *The Papers of James Madison,* Vol. 10, Robert A. Rutland, editor, University of Chicago Press, 1962, p. 208.

18. Federalist 37.16, *The Federalist,* edited by Chadwick, p. 193.

19. Federalist 51.6, p. 281. This and the references which follow are from *The Federalist,* edited by Chadwick,

20. *The Debates in the Several State Conventions on the Adoption of the Federal Convention,* Jonathan Elliot, New York: Burt Franklin Reprints, pp. 428-429.

21. Cousins, p. 299.

22. Cousins, p. 300.

23. *Memorial and Remonstrance,* 1785, in Cousins, pp. 308-314.

24. *Signigicant Documents in United States History,* Vol. 1, Richard B. Morris, ed., New York: Van Nostrand Reinhold Co., 1969, p. 119.

25. Eidsmoe, p. 109-110.

26. Eidsmoe, p. 111.

27. Eidsmoe, p. 110.

28. Eidsmoe, p. 110.

29. Koch, Madison's "Advice to My Country," p. 135, in Eidsmoe, p. 104.

30. Madison, 1819; quoted by Brant, *James Madison,* VI:430-431; in Eidsmoe, p. 104.

31. Federalist 42.7.

32. Faris, p. 299.

33. Ibid.

Section 9

George Mason and Gunston Hall

1. Robert A. Rutland, ed., *The Papers of George Mason 1725-1792,* 3 vols., I:296, quoted in *George Mason, Father of the Bill of Rights* by Carla R. Heymsfeld and Joan W. Lewis, Alexandria, VA: Patriotic Education Inc., 1991, p. 56.

2. Quoted in Heymsfeld and Lewis, pp. 21-22.

3. Ibid., p. 8.

4. Ibid., pp. 28-29.

5. Papers, I:190, quoted in Heymsfeld and Lewis, p. 142.

6. Papers, III:893, quoted in ibid., p. 107.

7. *Madison's Notes of Debates*, p. 651.

8. Ibid., p. 504.

9. Ibid., p. 566.

Section 10

Richmond

1. *The Proceedings of the Virginia Convention in the Town of Richmond on the 23rd of March, 1775*, Saint John's Church, 1927, pp. 12-13.

2. Faris, p. 269.

3. *The Virginia State Capitol*, booklet distibuted at the Capitol Building in Richmond, p. 2.

4. Ibid., p. 6.

5. Ibid., p. 11.

6. *Webster's American Biographies*, Charles Van Doren, editor, Springfield, MA: G. & C. Merriam Company, 1975, p. 691.

7. For more on *Marbury v. Madison*, see David Barton, *Original Intent*, pp. 259-260.

8. For more on this see Barton, pp. 253-268.

9. *Appletons' Cyclopaedia of American Biography*, Vol. IV, p. 224.

10. Faris, p. 274.

11. Faris, p. 274-275.

12. Faris, p. 275.

13. Quoted in Faris, p. 276.

14. Faris, p. 295.

15. Faris, p. 277.

16. Ibid.

Section 11

Jefferson's Home: Monticello and Charlottesville

1. William Eleroy Curtis, *The True Thomas Jefferson*, Philadelphia: J.B. Lippincott Company, 1901, p. 68.

2. Curtis, p. 69.

3. Curtis, pp. 122-123. Appletons', vol. 3, p. 416.

4. Appletons', vol. 3, p. 416.

5. William D. Gould, "Religious Opinions of Thomas Jefferson," *Mississippi Valley Historical Review*, 20, Cedar Rapids, Iowa, 1933, p. 191.

6. Julian P. Boyd, *The Papers of Thomas Jefferson*, Princeton, NJ: Princeton University Press, 1950-1993, 1:62, 63, 116; 2:6-8.

7. Ibid., 10:628; 16:88-89. James A. Bear, Jr., *Thomas Jefferson's Account Books*, pp. 767, 939, 943. Anson P. Stokes, *Church and State in the United States*, 3 vols., New York: Harper and Brothers, 1950, 1:678.

8. Dumas Malone, *Jefferson and His Time*, vol. 1, *Jefferson the Virginian*, Boston: Little, Brown, and Co., 1948, p. 242.

9. A.A. Lipscomb and A.E. Bergh, eds., *The Writings of Thomas Jefferson*, 20 vols., Washington, D.C.: The Thomas Jefferson Memorial Association, 1905, 14:81. Bear, *Account Books*, p. 860.

10. Lipscomb and Bergh, 13:352.

11. Ibid., 10:384.

12. *Thomas Jefferson's Abridgement of the Words of Jesus of Nazareth*, Mark Beliles editor, 1993, backcover.

13. Bear, *Account Books*, 902, 934 (and every year from 1820 to 1826).

14. Boyd, 3:177. And his *Account Book* entries.

15. Henry S. Randall, *The Life of Thomas Jefferson*, 3 vols., New York: Derby and Jackson, 1858, 3:555.

16. Lipscomb and Bergh, 19:450. Henry A. Washington, *The Writings of Thomas Jefferson*, 9 vols., Philadelphia: J.B. Lippincott and Co., 1864, 7:267.

17. Lipscomb and Bergh, 8:147.

18. Boyd, 2:6-8.

19. Ibid., 2:6, 3:67.

20. Henry W. Foote, *The Religion of Thomas Jefferson*, Boston: Beacon Press, 1960, pp. 6-8.

21. Lipscomb and Bergh, 15:404.

22. Thomas Armitage, *A History of the Baptists*, New York: Bryan, Taylor, and Co., 1890, p. 799. Charles Buck, *A Theological Dictionary*, Philadelphia, 1833, p. 469.

23. Dumas Malone, *Jefferson the President* (vol. 4 of *Jefferson and His Time*), Boston: Little, Brown, and Co., 1970, p. 199. See also Hutson, p. 84.

24. Boyd, 1:105, 116.

25. Lipscomb and Bergh, 9: 291, 297; 19:109, 112.

26. Curtis, p. 323.

27. William W. Sweet, *Religion on the American Frontier: The Baptists*, New York: Henry Holt and Co., 1931, pp. 88-91.

28. Malone, p. 191.

29. Samuel Knox, *A Vindiction of the Religion of Mr. Jefferson*, Baltimore, n.d.

30. Alan Heimert, *Religion and the American Mind*, Cambridge, MA: Cambridge University Press, 1966, pp. 510-552.

31. Boyd, 3:67; and unpublished research of Mark Beliles.

32. Lipscomb and Bergh, 15:60; 11:32.

33. Lipscomb and Bergh, 16:281.

34. Hutson, p. 93,

35. Letter to John Bacon, April 1802.

36. Washington, *Writings*, 5:236-237; and Jefferson's *Second Inaugural Address*.

37. For references on these and other items, see *Thomas Jefferson's Abridgement of the Words of Jesus of Nazareth*, Mark Beliles editor, 1993, p. 11,

38. Lipscomb and Bergh, 14:81.

39. *Thomas Jefferson's Abridgement*, p. 21.

40. Faris, p. 327.

41. Mark Beliles, "Religious Freedom and Jefferson's University," in *Providential Perspective*, Vol. 4, No. 2, May 1989, Charlottesville, VA: Providence Foundation, p. 2.

42. Ibid.

43. Ibid.

44. Ibid., pp. 2-3.

45. Ibid., p. 3.

46. Ibid.

47. Ibid.

48. Ibid., p. 4.

49. Beliles and McDowell, *America's Providential History*, p. 108.

50. William McGuffey, *The Eclectic Fouth Reader*, Cincinnati: Truman and Smith, 1838, reprinted by Mott Media, Milford, MI, 1982, p. x.

Conclusion

1. John Quincy Adams, *An Oration Delivered before the Inhabitants of the Town of Newburyport on the Sixty-First Anniversary of the Declaration of Independence, July 4th, 1837*, Charles Whipple, Newburyport, 1837, pp. 5-6.

2. Cited in B.F. Morris, *Christian Life and Character of the Civil Institutions of the United States*, Philadelphia: George W. Childs, 1864, p. 239.

3. Benjamin Rush, *Essays, Literary, Moral and Philosophical*, Philadelphia: printed by Thomas and William Bradford, 1806, p. 113.

Appendix

1. Benjamin Weiss, *God in American History*, Pasadena, CA: Geddes Press, 1975, p. 13.

2. Skousen, *The Making of America*, p. 32.

3. Ibid.

4. *The Story of the Seal*, Merrimac, MA: Destiny Publishers, p. 19.

The Providence Foundation

The Providence Foundation is a Christian educational organization whose mission is to spread liberty, justice, and prosperity among the nations by instructing individuals in a Biblical worldview. Providence Foundation representatives and associates around the world provide education for general audiences, but primarily help churches, schools, and other organizations to train Christians in a comprehensive Biblical worldview and mobilize them to reform their society.

The Biblical worldview resources that are produced by the Providence Foundation especially emphasize historical examples from previous generations of how Christian statesmen and citizens who believed in "Divine Providence" applied Biblical principles that influenced their nation. Resources also stress the application of a Biblical worldview in families, schools, businesses, and political activities today.

Our goals and objectives include: 1) Education of general audiences in the principles of a Biblical and providential worldview in the U.S. and worldwide. 2) Comprehensive training of Christians in Biblical thinking and to mobilize them in reforming society. 3) Produce Biblical worldview resources.

Our long term goal is to restore to America's homes, churches, and schools the ideas that form the foundation of freedom as well as to infuse these same ideas into the fabric of all nations. The training we provide is with the goal of having individuals apply the principles they learn, the result being godly reform in all spheres of life.

About the Authors

Stephen McDowell, President of the Providence Foundation, has taught inspiring seminars throughout the United States as well as in Asia, South America, Australia, and Africa. He has trained thousands of people from 70 countries, consulted with numerous government officials, assisted in writing political documents and starting political parties, and helped establish classes on godly reformation in numerous churches. He has authored and co-authored several books and videos. After obtaining a B.S. in Physics and a M.S. in Geology, Stephen went on to work in the ministry. He pastored churches for six years before moving to Charlottesville to work with Mark Beliles in starting the Providence Foundation. He and his wife, Beth, have four children.

Mark Beliles has served in the ministry since 1977 and is presently the pastor of Grace Covenant Church in Charlottesville, Virginia. His concern for equipping pastors and Christians in applying biblical principles to all of life led him to help start the Providence Foundation in 1983. He presently serves as Chairman of the Board of Directors. He has authored and co-authored several books, has participated in training many Christian leaders for the ministry, has taught seminars on biblical reformation throughout the United States and in other countries, and has assisted in establishing churches in America and other nations. Mark and his wife, Nancy, have three children.

Providence Foundation Resources

Books

America's Providential History   (B01) $15.95

How the Lord guided our nation from the very beginning. Proof from history: our nation grew from Christian principles. How to bring them back into the mainstream.

Liberating the Nations   (B02) $12.95

God's plan, fundamental principles, essential foundations, and structures necessary to build Christian nations.

Defending the Declaration   (B04) $11.95

How the Bible and Christianity influenced the writing of the Declaration.

Watchmen on the Walls   (B06) $5.95

The role of pastors in equipping Christians to fulfill their civil duties.

In God We Trust   (B03) $13.95

A Christian tour guide for historic sites in Washington D.C., Philadelphia, Jamestown, Williamsburg, Richmond, Mt. Vernon, Charlottesville, and more.

Jefferson's Abridgement   (B05) $5.95

An abridgement of the Words of Jesus of Nazareth as compiled by Thomas Jefferson while President. With an introductory essay on Jefferson's religious beliefs.

In Search of Democracy   (B07) $4.95

Foundations, framework, and historical development of biblical government and law.

Independence, Drums of War, Vol. 1   (B08) $6.95

First in a series of historical novels for youth and young adults designed to teach in an enjoyable way the principles, events, and persons behind America's independence.

Videos/Game

The Story of America's Liberty   (VT01) $19.95

A 65-minute video that looks at the influence of Christianity in the beginning of America, examining principles and providential occurrences.

Dawn's Early Light   (VT02) $19.95

A 28-minute version of *The Story of America's Liberty* with up-dated statistics.

America: the Game   (GM1) $29.95

An exciting way to learn about the history of America and God's hand in it. Over 2000 questions.

Audios

In Search of Democracy	(ATS02)	$19.95
Four-tape series on biblical government and law.		
The Principle Approach to Education for Home or Church Schools	(ATS01)	$99.95
A biblical approach to teaching the academic subjects. Includes 24 tapes and a 160-page manual.		
America's Freedom: Founded on Faith	(AT14)	$4.95
No Cross, No Crown: Exemplified in the Life of William Penn	(AT1)	$4.95
Reforming the Nations — an Example from the Life of Noah Webster	(AT2)	$4.95
Teaching History from a Providential Perspective	(AT10)	$4.95
The Principle Approach	(AT9)	$4.95
God Governs in the Affairs of Men	(AT11)	$4.95
Biblical Economics	(AT7)	$4.95
Honest Money and Banking	(AT8)	$4.95
Biblical Government and Law	(AT5)	$4.95
Forming a Christian Union	(AT6)	$4.95
Women: Preservers & Propagators of Liberty as Teachers of the Human Race	(AT13)	$4.95
Fundamental Principles of Christian Nations	(AT3)	$4.95
Christ's Teaching on Public Affairs	(AT4)	$4.95
Biblical Principles of Business, Exemplified by Cyrus Hall McCormick	(AT15)	$4.95
We Hold These Truths — Governmental Principles of America's Founders	(AT12)	$4.95
The American Christian Revolution — Christianity: Foundation of America's Liberty	(AT16)	$4.95
Education and the Kingdom of God	(AT17)	$4.95

RESPONSE & ORDER FORM

I want to join you in spreading God's liberty, justice, and prosperity among the nations and restoring to America's homes, churches, and schools the ideas that form the foundation of freedom by becoming a:

☐ **SPECIAL SUPPORTER:** those who contribute any amount toward the ongoing ministry of the Providence Foundation receive the *Providential Perspective* and *Reformation Report*. Enclosed is my gift of: **$** [   ]

☐ **MEMBER:** those who contribute $100 or more per year receive our newsletters, a 30% discount on all our books, videos, and materials, plus discounts to our Summer Institute. I will send a regular gift of $_____ per month / quarter / year (circle one). Enclosed is my gift of: **$** [   ]

I wish to order the following items from your catalog:

Quan.	Title/Product code	Price	Total

Shipping & Handling:		Subtotal	
* US Mail: $3.00 minimum, 10% if over $30.		Sales tax (VA orders add 4.5%)	
* UPS: $5.00 minimum, 12% if over $50. (Game orders will be sent UPS. Allow 7-10 days longer for items sent via US Mail.)		Shipping	
		Member discount (30%)	
Total contribution and order: $		**TOTAL**	

Method of Payment: ___Check/Money Order ___VISA ___Mastercard ___Cash

Credit Card Number:_____ Exp. date: _____

Name:_____ Signature:_____

SHIP TO:

Name:_____

Address:_____

City:_____State:_____ Zip:_____

Phone: (_____)_____

Make checks payable to:
Providence Foundation
PO Box 6759
Charlottesville, VA 22906
Phone/Fax: 804-978-4535

Also, order by phone or at website:
www.providencefoundation.com